1066

and

The Battle of Hastings:

Preludes, Events and Postscripts

Detail from the 'Senlac' window of St. Mary's Church, Battle. This modern window designed by Michael Farrar Bell (1911–93) was installed in 1984. William's window to the left shows arms of Normandy and another based on the arms of St. Valery sur Somme. In Harold's window to the right, are displayed the modern arms of Battle town and the arms of Battle Abbey. William confronts Harold against backgrounds of multiple images depicting individual events from the Bayeux Tapestry.

Photos © Keith Foord

1066
and
The Battle of Hastings:
Preludes, Events and Postscripts

Keith Foord and

Neil Clephane-Cameron

PER BELLUM PATRIA

Battle and District Historical Society Research Group 2015

ISBN: 978-1-903099-02-5

First published in the UK in 2015
by the Battle and District Historical Society
c/o 16 Upper Lake, BATTLE, East Sussex TN33 0AN

Reprinted with minor corrections 2016
Reprinted with modifications to the first part of Chapter 16, 2018

Tel: 01424 775590 / 07836 522257
E-mail: neil@clephane-cameron.com
Contact: Neil Clephane-Cameron, Honorary Secretary
www.battlehistory,btck.co.uk

Typeset in Cambria by Helm Information
amandahelm@uwclub.net

Cover illustration from *The Bayeux Tapestry: The complete tapestry in full colour* by David M Wilson © 1985, Thames & Hudson, Ltd. London.

Printed and bound in Great Britain by
CPI Group (UK) Ltd, Croydon CR0 4YY

Contents

The Abbey Gatehouse in 1818

FOREWORD

The battle of 14th October 1066 was probably the most significant in English history. It was an essential element in determining the future course of British and Irish history and that of much of the Commonwealth and the United States. The abbey erected on the orders of William the Conqueror retains its commanding presence in the town and is a major attraction for visitors of all ages and all countries. Those of us who live in or pass through the town are reminded of the Battle of Hastings and its consequences every time that we pass down the High Street and see Battle Abbey gatehouse dominating the view. The monks planned and built almost the entire old town, a mile in length and centred on the ridge that King Harold tried unsuccessfully to defend. Much has changed since then but the land plots remain of monastic origin and the town retains many buildings from the monastic era, although often re-fronted.

The town of Battle would not have its name and even perhaps its existence if it were not for the meeting of two armies there in 1066. The Battle and District Historical Society's constitution has as the object of the Society '... to educate the public in the study of local history in Battle ... and the surrounding areas.' In fact, the Society's activities range more broadly to take in historical events anywhere which have affected or are affecting our area and its people. Nevertheless, the core of the Society's activities remains local history. The constitution goes on to say that, in furtherance of the Society's object, it shall have the power, among others, to arrange for the publication of matters of local historical interest.

It is therefore entirely right on every count that the Society should publish this book about the battle, its causes and those who took part in it, all the more so because the two authors are long-term residents of Battle and members of the Society: Keith Foord is its Vice-Chairman and Neil Clephane-Cameron has been its Secretary for some twenty years. They are also members of its Research Group which continues to place on the Society's website (http://battlehistory.btck.co.uk/Collectanea-OurVirtualLibrary) a large and ever-growing number of papers of historical interest of all periods affecting not only Battle itself but also the surrounding area.

This book is a significant addition to the many books written about the Battle of Hastings and its causes.

George Kiloh
Chairman, Battle and District Historical Society,
2018

King William bithought him alsoe
Of folke that was forlorne,
And slayn also thoruz him
In the bataile bi-forne.
And ther as the bataile was,
An Abbey he lete rere
Of Seint Martin, for the soules
That there slayn were.
And the Monks wel ynoug
FefFed without fayle,
That is called in Englonde
Abbey of Bataile.

Robert of Gloucester *c.*1260–*c.*1300

King William also thought to himself
of the folk who had become saddened
or had been killed because of him
in the previous battle.
And there on the battle site
he let be built an abbey of St Martin, for the souls
that were slain there.
And the monks were well funded without fail!
That abbey is called in England, Battle Abbey

INTRODUCTION AND ACKNOWLEDGEMENTS

I n this book we went back to basics, which include local geographic and cultural histories, and have put together a book of interlocking chapters that tell the full history of '1066' as accurately but briefly, and above all, as enjoyably as possible. Where alternative explanations or doubts arise we have dealt with these as logically and honestly as possible.

The local events around the 950th commemoration in 2016 of the Battle of Hastings, fought at Battle, involved Battle and District Historical Society (BDHS) in producing documentation, organising a commemorative lecture and giving advice. This was the trigger for this book, first published in 2015, which we titled *1066 and the Battle of Hastings: Preludes, Events and Postscripts.*

As we researched deeper, we realised that the preludes to the battle were not very well known and that many strands had accumulated for some thousands of years to create the circumstances that led to the Battle of Hastings. So we have covered the preludes on both sides of the English Channel in some depth, particularly the dynastic and coastal geographic histories – for these are easy to overlook and misunderstand, although critical to the 'How, Why and When?' We also found many confusing myths, fabrications and unproven or unprovable theories and some clear interpretive errors in the literature about the build up to and the events of the battle itself and some of these we challenge.

Great encouragement to produce a new book to commemorate the Battle of Hastings, fought on 14th October 1066, was forthcoming from the former chairmen of BDHS, Richard Moore and Hugh Arbuthnot CMG, also from the coordinator of the BDHS Research Group, George Kiloh, who is now chairman of BDHS and continues to support this work. Hugh and George in particular spent many hours reading our words, making very valuable and incisive suggestions and corrections to the texts. George was meticulous in spotting spelling mistakes, grammatical errors and challenging the odd theory.

The past Honorary President of BDHS from 1999–2016, Professor John Gillingham FBA, was also involved in what he called a 'critical editing' role, steering us away from dubious records and gently questioning some of our interpretations, all the while encouraging us onward. Such help is invaluable to local historians and he is warmly thanked.

Other assistance, including a postscript and encouragement was received from Adrian and Sarah Hall, of the BDHS Research Group, from Lynn and Kevin Cornwell of Hastings and Area Archaeological Group (HAARG) who double checked the archaeological data that we have presented, and from Amanda Helm of BDHS, who prepared this book for publication and each of its printings.

The work did not stop in 2016 as the Research Group of BDHS has been further motivated to produce a series of well researched articles, some based on this book and other publications by the authors, and also much new work ranging in length from two pages to 100 or more pages on a wide spectrum of historical events, people and developments with some relationship to Battle and District and where appropriate to wider eastern Sussex. These articles are published on the BDHS website, free for all to view and are also lodged with East Sussex Record Office at 'The Keep' in Brighton. Thus a wide up to date history of the district is slowly being collated.

Second Printing

Happily the first printing sold out which gave us the opportunity to make minor clarifications and corrections. We added some extra pages, including this small extension to the introdution and an enlargement of the timeline to four pages from two, making it easier to read. The changes are minor: not substantial enough to call this a revised or second edition

Since the first printing more detail and information has emerged from time to time. We thank those who have taken the trouble to comment so positively about the book and those who have constructively pointed out some minor problems. There is a modification of a diagram in Chapter 2, some minor corrections and additions particularly in Chapter 3 and a tiny change to the battlefield diagram of Chapter 13 (you are challenged to spot this!). We have also very minimally added to the extensive list of sources. Any remaining actual error of known fact, omission of a critical detail, or any inadvertent breach of copyright is still our mistake. Please tell us about these as we shall put things right in any future edition.

The 950th Anniversary year of the Battle of Hastings was celebrated in 2016. The year also saw the 1000th Anniversary of the crowning of king Cnut. This was an critical event in its own right because of the many constructive changes to the governance of England that occurred in his reign, and his and his second wife's influence on the English regnal succession, as you will discover in this book. It does not appear that this anniversary will have been much commemorated in spite of the fact that this resulted in a successful merging of Danish and Old English worlds in stark comparison to the Norman takeover of 1066.

2016 saw events around '1066 Country' including displays of a 'Battle Community Tapestry', which simulates surprisingly well the appearance of the Bayeux Tapestry and portrays eight scenes concerning the development of the town of Battle after 'the battle'; a specially commissioned people's opera, a partnership project involving Battle Festival, Glyndebourne Opera and 'Root 1066'; public displays including 'Concorde 1066'; 1066 themed lectures throughout the year by Battle and District Historical Society; English Heritage sponsored re-enactments of the battle on the battlefield; and further displays and talks at Battle Museum of Local History included the Alderney Tapestry, and a probable axe head from the battle site.

Wider afield a commemorative 50 pence coin was struck by the Royal Mint for the '950th' and the Royal Mail issued a commemorative sheet of stamps. And Battle's neighbours in Hastings, who had the 'pleasure' of hosting William's army for a few weeks, before they moved on to conquer the rest of England, commemorated under a banner of the 'Root 1066 International Festival of Contemporary Arts'.

Third Printing

This book has sold well and we are now into a third printing.

Since the first printing more detail and information has emerged from time to time. In this third printing we have made some small but important updates to Chapter 16, and have subsequently taken the opportunity to minimally add to the list of sources for this chapter. The book is otherwise unchanged from the second printing. The changes are still minor, not substantial enough to call this a revised or new edition.

We thank those who have taken the trouble to comment so positively about the book and those who have constructively pointed out minor problems, which we have been able to address in the subsequent printings.

Any remaining actual error of known fact, omission of a critical detail, or any inadvertent breach of copyright is still our mistake. Please tell us about these as we shall put things right in any future edition.

Keith Foord and Neil Clephane-Cameron, Battle 2018

Timeline
700–1070 AD

Viking, Norman,
English and Flemish
Events relevant to 1066

VIKING	NORMAN	Year	ENGLISH	FLEMISH
Viking raids on England begin		770	Viking raids begin	
Viking raids on Normandy begin	Viking raids begin	820		
Rouen razed	Rouen razed	841		
Huge Danish raids on England		870	Huge Danish raids	
		871	Alfred the Great begins reign	
		878	Great Viking army in England	
		884	Danelaw starts	
Siege of Paris		885–6		
Appledore (Kent) raid		892		
		899	End of Alfred's reign	
	Treaty of St Clair-sur-Epte. Rollo becomes Lord of Normandy	911		
		925		Arnulf of Flanders defines eastern boundary of Normandy
	Rollo hands Normandy over to son, William Longsword	927		
	Longsword killed by Arnulf of Flanders. Richard I duke of Normandy, aged c.10. King Louis IV of France controls Normandy during his minority	942		
	Richard I, aged 13, confirmed duke of Normandy	945		
		954	Danelaw ends	
		955	King Eadred finally restores Ango-Saxon laws across all England	
	Richard I marries Emma, sister of Hugh Capet	960		
	Pact of Gisors improves relationship with France	965		
		978	Aethelred II crowned	
	Richard I daughter Emma born, future queen of England	985		
Sweyn Forkbeard and Olaf Tryggvason lead attacks on London		994		
	Richard I dies, Richard II duke of Normandy	996		
	Vikings descent on Normandy 'accommodated'	1000		
		1001	Godwin Wulfnothson born	
	Emma marries king Aethelred II of England	1002	Aethelred II marries Emma of Normandy. St Brice's Day massacre	

VIKING	NORMAN	Year	ENGLISH	FLEMISH
Reprisal attacks by Forkbeard	Richard II marries Judith of Brittany	1003–1005	Danish attacks Edward the Confessor born at Islip between 1003/5	
Danes penetrate deeply into England led by Thurkill the Tall		1009	Danes invade	
Danes in SE England and E Anglia		1011	Danes harry all of SE England and East Anglia	
		1012	Thurkill becomes a mercenary for Aethelred	
Sweyn Forkbeard invades England	Emma and her children (Edward, Alfred, Godgifu) take refuge in Normandy. Followed by Aethelred	1013	Danish invasion led by Sweyn Forkbeard. Emma and children flee, followed by Aethelred	
Sweyn becomes king of England by conquest		1014	Sweyn becomes king of England by conquest	
Cnut Sweynson invades England	Edward precedes Aethelred in returning to England	1015	Aethelred briefly king again. Cnut Sweynson invades. Resistance by Edmund Ironside	
Cnut becomes king of England	Emma and children back in Normandy	1016	Aethelred II dies. Ironside, possibly with Edward, fights to a stalemate. He and Cnut briefly co-rule England but Ironside dies. Cnut crowned king of England. Children of Ironside sent to Sweden, then to Hungarian royal family	
	Judith dies, Richard II marries Papia	1017	Cnut marries Emma, widow of Aethelred	
Cnut becomes king of Denmark		1018	Great Meeting at Oxford. Cnut becomes king of Denmark. Thurkill regent of England.	
		1020	Cnut appoints Godwin Wulfnothson earl of Wessex	
		1022	Harold Godwinson born	
	Richard II dies, Richard III inherits	1026		
		1027	Cnut goes to Rome for coronation of emperor Conrad II	
Cnut becomes king of Norway. Hákon Ericson, then Sweyn oldest son of Cnut appointed regents of Norway	Richard III dies, brother Robert I inherits. Robert I starts affair with Herleve, son William born	1028	Cnut takes Norway from Olaf Haraldsson.	
	Relations with England deteriorate. Alençon annexed. Robert helps Henri I of France	1030	Relations with Normandy deteriorate	Eleanor, sister of Robert I of Normandy marries Baldwin IV
Magnus Olafson takes Norway		1034	Norway lost. Sweyn Knutson flees to Denmark then dies	
	Robert goes on pilgrimage to Jerusalem, dies at Nicaea on the way back. William becomes duke William II of Normandy, aged c.7	1035	Cnut's death	

VIKING	NORMAN	Year	ENGLISH	FLEMISH
	Possible foray by Edward to England repulsed. Alfred forays via Flanders	1036	Harold I Harefoot, son of Cnut by his first wife crowned. Alfred murdered in England	
	Archbishop Robert dies, followed by anarchy	1037	Emma flees to Flanders	Emma in exile in Flanders
		1039		Harthacnut visits Emma in Flanders
	Henri I of France supports William. Edward invited to join Harthacnut and Emma in England	1040	Harefoot dies, Harthacnut, son of Cnut and Emma, becomes king. Emma returns	Baldwin V supports William of Normandy
		1041	Harthacnut and Emma arrive at Sandwich	Harthacnut and Emma sail to Sandwich from Flanders
Magnus takes Denmark. Emma toys with the idea of supporting Magnus as king of England		1043	Harthacnut dies, Magnus inherits Denmark under a tontine arrangement. Edward the Confessor becomes king of England	
War in Denmark between Magnus and Sweyn II Estridsen, a cousin of the Godwinsons		1044	Harold Godwinson appointed earl of East Anglia. Help refused to Sweyn II in Denmark.	
		1045	Edward marries Edith, Godwin's daughter	
Magnus Olafson dies. His half-uncle Harald Hardrada is king of Norway. Sweyn II king of Denmark	Western areas of Normandy revolt led by Guy of Burgundy. Henri I of France and William defeat rebels at Val ès Dunes. 'Truce of God' established	1047	Sweyn Godwinson is banished	Sweyn Godwinson arrives in Flanders
Viking raids in England		1048	Viking raids	
		1050		Baldwin V at war with emperor Henry III. English navy blockade Channel to provide Henry with naval support
	William marries Matilda of Flanders. William makes possible visit to Edward in England. Problems in Maine.	1051	Tostig Godwinson marries Judith of Flanders. Robert Champart appointed archbishop of Canterbury. Godwin rebels and banished, youngest son Wulfnoth and Sweyn's son Hákon held hostage by Edward. Sweyn Godwinson dies on a pilgrimage to Jerusalem	Matilda of Flanders marries duke William of Normandy. Judith of Flanders marries Tostig Godwinson
		1052	Godwin makes visits to southern ports to obtain support, ships and sailors. Returns to England and is reinstated. Champart flees to Normandy, probably taking the hostages to William	Godwin makes sorties from Flanders to England

VIKING	NORMAN	Year	ENGLISH	FLEMISH
		1053	Godwin dies. Harold made earl of Wessex. Aelfgar appointed to East Anglia	
	Henri I of France starts to act against William as he is getting too strong. Battle of Mortemer won by William	1054		
		1055	Earl Siward of Northumbria dies. Tostig given Northumbria	
		1056		Harold Godwinson visits
	Battle of Varaville	1057	Earl Leofric of Mercia dies. Earldom passes to his son Aelfric, whose earldom of East Anglia goes to Gyrth Godwinson. Ralf of Hereford dies and his earldom split up. New earldom between Buckingham and Kent goes to Leofwine Godwinson. Edward Aetheling and his family return from Hungary. Edward Aetheling dies but his son Edgar is placed in the royal household	
	Henri I of France dies	1060		
		1062	Edwin, son of Aelfgar, inherits Mercia	
	William campaigns with and knights Harold. Maine and Vexin annexed	1064	Harold Godwinson visits Normandy	
Tostig Godwinson arrives in Norway via Flanders		1065	Northumbria revolts against Tostig. Banished and Morcar, brother of Edwin of Mercia given the earldom	Tostig Godwinson exiled to Flanders
Tostig persuades Harald Hardrada to invade England. Hardrada imagines himself an heir to Cnut. Tostig and Hardrada killed at Stamford Bridge.	Assemblies at Lillebonne, Bonneville-sur-Toques and Caen. Papal support sought and given for invasion of England. Ships assembled at Dives. Ships depart Dives on 13th September and arrive at St Valery-sur-Somme in a storm. Leave St Valery for Pevensey on 27/28th September. Joined by mercenaries from Flanders, France and Brittany	1066	Edward dies. Harold Godwinson crowned king Harold II. Tostig raids S & E coasts of England. Hardrada and Tostig invade the north-east. Battles of Fulford and then Stamford Bridge at which both killed. Battle of Hastings, at which Harold and his brothers Gyrth and Leofwine are killed. Final English submission at Berkhamsted. William crowned at Christmas	Mercenaries from Flanders join Tostig's raids on England and William's invasion of England
		1067	Ermenfrid's *Penitentiary* (1067/70)	
		1070	Battle Abbey construction started	

1

PROLOGUE

Keith Foord and Neil Clephane-Cameron

So much has been written about the Battle of Hastings that it is difficult to sort out fact from fiction and fantasy. The authors of these interlinked chapters live in Battle, East Sussex, and are amateur historians who are members of the Research Group of the Battle and District Historical Society. So it could be said that we have a special interest in the subject as its background forms part of our day–to–day lives.

950 years on from 1066 we wanted to put down our thoughts on how the Battle of Hastings came to be fought, and the main and clearer elements of the history behind the story, trying to focus as much as possible on how it affected the local area – not just Battle, but the whole area now called 1066 country, which corresponds to the geographic area of south-east Sussex centred on Battle town, and extends from beyond Pevensey to the west, beyond Rye to the east and northwards as far as what was the Andreadsweald, a huge dense forest that extended across northern Sussex, into south Surrey and into Kent as far as Ashford.

As 2016 approached, we aspired to write as accurate an overview as possible, but not (if we could avoid it) getting into the minutiae of history, and certainly not to produce a textbook. The deeper we looked, the more we realised was often overlooked and relatively unexplained outside of academic circles in the general telling of the tale. We have tried to include as many of these topics as possible, without getting overcomplicated, although where necessary we go into some detail.

The Battle of Hastings was not just a one-off event: a whole series of interlinked events gradually came together over the millennia to be focused on that one day in 1066. The nature of England and its foundations is discussed in this context with some detail of the genetic makeup of the English, and the effect of various migrations into the British Isles, including that of the Romans, Anglo-Saxons and Vikings on the culture of England. The discussion of this particularly focuses on the acculturation rather than displacement effects of the invasions. With respect to the Vikings we also examine their parallel role in the development of Normandy and in the Norman foundation myth.

There was a related event which had its 1000th anniversary in 2016, and is just as important to English history. This was the crowning of Cnut as king of England in 1016. Just like William he took the throne by conquest and made major changes to the governance of England.

Cnut married the widowed Emma of Normandy. Of vital importance was her influence as a princess of Normandy, daughter and sister of dukes of Normandy, and widow of king Aethelred II. She was the mother, by Aethelred, of king Edward the Confessor, who was childless by the time he died, which contributed to the later complications concerning the crown of England.

This led on to the next acts in the drama, which concerned the relationships of the Godwin family and of Emma to Cnut and his sons before Edward became king, and of Edward to the various members of the Godwin family once he became king. This period also covers the story of Harold Godwinson's rise, and the birth and life of duke William II of Normandy, who will forever be known in the English-speaking world as William the Conqueror. These lives – and chapters – inevitably overlap.

Another significant key to understanding what happened in south-east Sussex is to have a general appreciation of the geographic history of the area. We have given a whole illustrated chapter over to this, as it is so very important to the appreciation of potential invasion landing points and the complete story, also in comprehending that, in 1066, Hastings lay at the tip of a narrow- necked peninsula, the only way out of which on land was via the ridge at what is now Battle.

In addition, to set the scene, we present a general history of the south-east Sussex area, pulling together the strands of what has happened here – pre-Roman, Roman, Saxon and pre-Norman English. Admittedly some of this has to be conjectural, and this is clearly indicated in the text. We make no assertions about any of these items; they are laid out for the reader to decide for themselves what is likely, what is probable, what is possible, what is invention, and what is myth.

The final chapters cover some thoughts about the individuals, events and scenarios involved in the battle itself; the aftermath of the Battle of Hastings, up until William I's coronation; a consideration of the site of the battle, of the building of Battle Abbey; and finally some musings about what the Normans did for us. This book can go no further, but you are encouraged, if interested, to read elsewhere about the complex – and often dreadful – events involving both England and Normandy following the Norman Conquest which led to the full establishment of William I as overlord of England and Wales.

In our opinion the complete story of '1066' can never be known. We can only work with what we are left – the bare bones of the *Anglo-Saxon Chronicle*; the various written 'lives' and 'sagas' of the main characters; the post-Conquest writings mainly by Norman churchmen; the amazing Bayeux tapestry; old grants and charters; a comprehensive well-researched geomorphic and geographic history of our coastline, and an unfortunately extremely sparse archaeology.

Many great minds have poured over this data and made their own, sometimes vigorous, arguments and interpretations. Numbers of different theories about landing sites and battlefields have been proposed. But none of us can get into the minds of those who were directly involved and knew exactly what happened – between Edward the Confessor and the Godwins; between Harold Godwinson and William of Normandy; between Emma and her two husbands and their children; nor can we view the battle itself.

Dear reader, all the interpretations of 1016 and 1066 and the many years before and between these critical dates are yours. We have tried to help in a minimal way and have written this book to assist. There is, of course, some duplication because of the overlapping lives of the main characters and events. We have tried to ensure that although each story may be told from a different perspective, there is no contradiction between the chapters, and have tried to lay to rest some conjectures. We have omitted some less important events and more obscure issues, to keep each part short and, we hope, readable.

Any actual error of known fact, omission of a critical detail, or any inadvertent breach of copyright is our mistake. Please tell us about these as we shall put things right in any future edition. We give an extensive list of sources, so that you can go into more depth if your curiosity is aroused.

As Geography without History seemeth a carkasse without motion; so History without Geography wandreth as a vagrant without a certaine habitation.

John Smith, 1580–1631

2

HISTORICAL GEOGRAPHY OF THE 1066 COUNTRY COAST

Keith Foord

The coastline of south-east Sussex has changed dramatically over the millennia. The changes both before and since 1066 have been very large, to a point where it is difficult to comprehend the overall vistas of the cliffs and shallow harbours which made this area an attractive spot to land an invasion fleet 950 years ago; for Vikings to raid; for Roman ironmasters to export from; and before that, for ancient peoples to hunt and fish and live in.

If we were transported back to the time of the Conquest we might have wondered where we were as we gazed at more prominent headlands, sea inlets that no longer exist and, if we were viewing from Fairlight, a completely changed panorama over Rye Bay and Dungeness! So a look at the difference between the coastline today and that of 3000BCE, and some pictorial illustrations of the changes down the centuries in between may help set the scene and aid understanding of the environment of early man, the coastline and 1066 landing site(s) in south-east Sussex. This chapter is really a mini-atlas and a simple interpretation of many studies which have been carried out.

Williamson highlighted the coastal changes as long ago as 1931, but did not include any discussion of the major associated sand and shingle movements, nor of the effect of 'inning' of the marshy areas (reclaiming for farming). In these contexts, of particular note is the painstaking work reported by the Romney Marsh Research Trust (RMRT), most of which is available on-line. Their papers, particularly Eddison's, on this complex environment are invaluable, as they enable us to understand the historical geographic context of the eastern end of south-east Sussex's former coast, from Fairlight eastwards, particularly the changes which might have affected a safe invasion landing.

There is also much work published on the behaviour of the chalk coast from Beachy Head westwards. Perhaps a bit lacking in study is the littoral between Beachy and Fairlight, where the High Weald meets the sea. Here it is particularly obvious that the headlands that we see today, and the shallow eroded cliffs that lie slightly further back from the coast, were much more prominent 8000 years ago. Sea-levels were also much lower 8000 years ago and the climate colder.

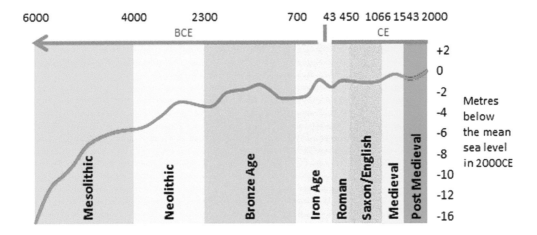

Sea-level change in English Channel since 6000BCE by historic period

Pevensey levels and the smaller Bulverhythe/Combe Haven levels were wide dry areas in the late mesolithic/early neolithic periods, but became prone to inundations as sea-levels rose. Pevensey became an embayed shallow open estuary, dotted with small islands. These islet areas can still be recognised today as their place names are suffixed 'ey' or 'eye'.

The history of Bulverhythe/Combe Haven appears more complicated as the recent archaeological work related to a new road across it has confirmed the earlier proposition of Smyth and Jennings that the margins of the valley became used by man from the neolithic period. There was also evidence of ironworking within its river catchment area, e.g. at Crowhurst during the Iron Age, followed by much heavier ironworking in Roman times. This activity was also associated with local cereal farming, but must have caused considerable tree loss as quantities of alluvium were washed into the valley floor, covering what had been freshwater marshland. After this, as there was increased river run-off which maintained the entrance to the sea, the sea encroached perhaps a little more and created salt-water marshland behind a small port at Bulverhythe.

Both Pevensey and Bulverhythe/Combe Haven also became subject to intermittent blocking by new shingle banks, and the mouths of the rivers draining them were sharply deviated eastwards by the shingle laid down by the inexorable eastward longshore drift. This gradually caused loss of port access.

In the lee of the former White Rock promontory at Hastings there also evolved a small harbour at the mouth of the Priory stream, now covered by the town centre of modern Hastings. The Bourne stream in the present Hastings Old Town valley was probably never big enough to have produced more than a tiny natural harbour, and later attempts to create a harbour in this area have all been beaten by the sea.

The chalk and sandstone/clay cliffs, both formed of remarkably soft rocks, have eroded in 'fits and starts' at average rates that mean that we may have lost somewhere between 300 and 800 metres (1000 to 2600 feet) of headlands from White Rock (Hastings), West Hill (Hastings) and East Hill/Ecclesbourne/Fairlight since 1066 alone. During certain periods such as the major storms of the 13th century the retreat was obviously significant enough to disrupt the lives of our forebears, and must have caused considerable distress and economic change.

Today we still see occasional massive rock falls and cliff retreats, particularly where the cliffs remain exposed to the sea. At Birling Gap, just west of Beachy Head, rock falls may cause retreats of as much as five metres in one year. In 2014 massive falls were seen from the sandstone cliffs just east of Hastings Old Town.

The Wealden sandstone cliff at Rock-a-Nore, Hastings, with the Fairlight cliffs beyond showing recent rock falls, vertical fissures and horizontal strata. © Keith Foord

There are huge shingle deposits on the floor of the English Channel, comprising flints released aeons ago from what was an overlying chalk anticline, the edges of which we see today as the white chalk cliffs of the south-east coast of England, mirrored on the northern French shore. Before 6000BCE these shingle deposits were in quite shallow waters, but between 6000BCE and 3000BCE there was a post-glacial period sea-level rise, in total of about 16 metres (53 feet) or of about 5 mm (0.2 inch)/year (see p. 6). Vast quantities of this shingle became subject to exposure to greater wave power than before, and started to be released. This massive shift of shingle eastwards appears to have been a 'one-off' movement on a grand scale over

A Google Earth view of extensive cliff slumps and falls at Beachy Head, between the lighthouse and Eastbourne. The fallen chalk blocks slowly break up, by mechanical wave action plus continuous wetting and drying all year, plus freezing and melting of water contained in rocks in winter; also limpet and mollusc secretions dissolve the chalk. The released hard flints gradually wash away eastwards with longshore drift.

A Google Earth view of the layered sandstone and clay cliffs at Fairlight in 2013. Two big cliff slumps can be seen, and the longshore drift eastwards of the displaced clay and sand is obvious. The clay and sand become re-deposited further along the coast.

3000 years after *c.* 6000BCE. Although the shingle is now slowly topped up by flints falling off the chalk cliffs to the west (see picture above), what has happened since *c.* 3000BCE has been the shifting around of the previously released shingle in a very complex way

There has been a much smaller overall sea-level rise in the last 5000 years of another approximately three to four metres (10–13 feet) at 0.7 mm (0.3 inch)/

year, but there has been a recent acceleration since the early 1990s to a rate of approximately 3 mm (0.1 inch) per year, or three metres (10 feet) every 1000 years. This 3 metre rise would be enough to flood low-lying areas not just in East Sussex and south Kent, but all low-lying parts of the world.

By Roman times, some 2000 years ago, some consolidation of the loose shingle had taken place, and some stable linear shingle beds had been laid down at Dungeness. The land to the east of these stable areas became of some agricultural use and early settlements arose. By 800CE even more stabilisation had occurred, and a large shingle bar (akin to Chesil Beach) which had been formed across Rye Bay remained intact. Behind this was trapped a large freshwater lagoon, with its outlet to the English Channel at its eastern end near Lympne in Kent The communities of Old Winchelsea and Broomhill were probably just being established on the bar as small fishing hamlets, and there was a direct connection between these settlements along the bar.

According to records in the 9th century, a burghal fort was established at or near Newenden, and a further burghal fort or, more probably, a fortified settlement at Hæstingaceastre (the pre-cursor of Hastings), but no definite evidence of the latter fortification has been seen for many centuries. Historical analysis suggests that it may well not have been at the location of the present Hastings Castle, and that the fort or fortified settlement may have stood somewhere between the White Rock and Bulverhythe and has been lost to the sea by cliff erosion. Its small port probably initially lay at Bulverhythe, behind which is the Combe Haven river valley, which was freshwater marshland only a few metres above sea-level, liable to seawater flooding at its seaward end. Later shingle partially blocked the river exit to the sea and diverted its opening eastwards blocking what remained of any port at Bulverhythe.

There was also for a short time an even smaller port in the narrow Priory valley, although the Priory stream was scarcely large enough to have created much more than a small hythe. The Bourne stream in the valley of the present Hastings Old Town is smaller still, and there could only have ever been a tiny hythe there.

The illustrations on the next pages show how things changed between 6000BCE and 1750CE.

The changes to 800CE and between then and the mid-12th century indicate an interesting situation concerning Old Winchelsea, and issues concerning access to the Rye Camber – the large stretch of water enclosed by the shingle banks. Eddison (RMRT) considers that Old Winchelsea could not have been of much significance as a harbour before the end of the 12th century, when it rapidly enlarged in both size and importance for a while, at that time being the preferred English port on the route from London to France.

Sadly, Old Winchelsea's demise was as quick as its rise. It was extensively damaged and flooded during the great storms of the 13th century, with a shingle bar breach in 1250, and was finally lost to the sea along with its shingle bank after 1287.

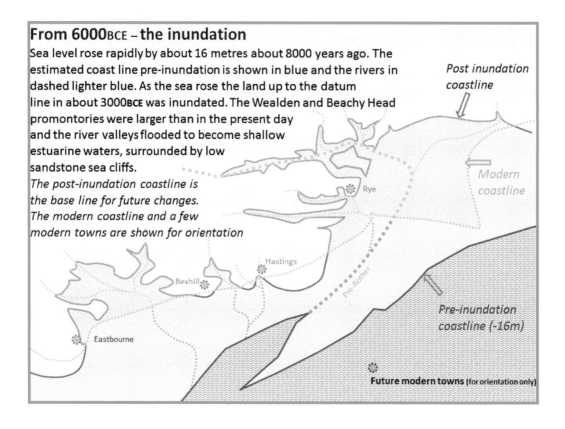

From 6000BCE – the inundation

Sea level rose rapidly by about 16 metres about 8000 years ago. The estimated coast line pre-inundation is shown in blue and the rivers in dashed lighter blue. As the sea rose the land up to the datum line in about 3000BCE was inundated. The Wealden and Beachy Head promontories were larger than in the present day and the river valleys flooded to become shallow estuarine waters, surrounded by low sandstone sea cliffs.

The post-inundation coastline is the base line for future changes. The modern coastline and a few modern towns are shown for orientation

Post inundation coastline

Modern coastline

Rye

Hastings

Bexhill

Pre-Rother

Eastbourne

Pre-inundation coastline (-16m)

Future modern towns (for orientation only)

In the following diagrams the key to describe landform changes is as follows:

Blue lines = coastline
Dashed brown lines = coastal erosion since previous diagram

Land form types

3000 BCE

Already the cliffs are receding, but the risen sea levels allowed the great
shingle banks of the English Channel to release vast quantities of shingle, which moved inshore
and north-eastwards by longshore drift. The shingle was deposited in the lee of the Fairlight
headland, forming a great shingle bar, akin to Chesil Beach, across
Rye bay with just habitable mud-flats to the east.
Rye Camber at that time was essentially a fresh
water lagoon with an outlet
near Hythe.

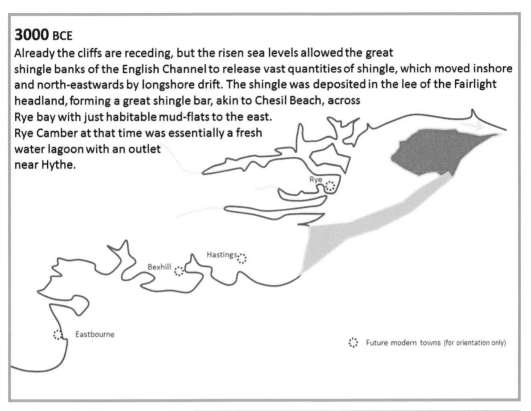

Roman times

Extent of headlands in 6000 BCE shown as dotted brown lines. The
headlands eroded erratically, but at average rates of 1 to 5 mm per year
depending on their structure. The shingle bar across the bay had become
a bit porous centrally, but linear stable shingle banks had formed in the
shallow seas of Dungeness and the land to the east
was more extensive and stabilising, with some in use.
Sea access to Bodiam/Brede
was still probably to the north
via the Roman port at
Lemanis (Lympne).

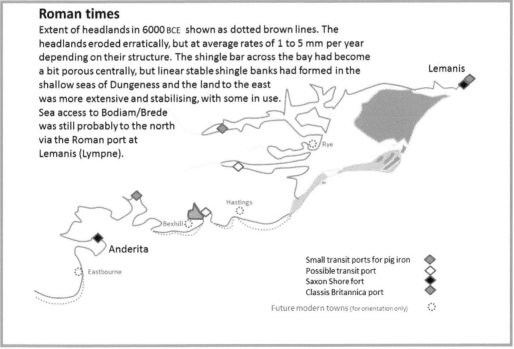

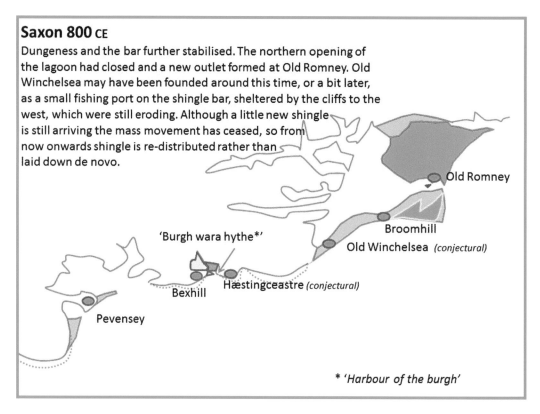

Saxon 800 CE

Dungeness and the bar further stabilised. The northern opening of the lagoon had closed and a new outlet formed at Old Romney. Old Winchelsea may have been founded around this time, or a bit later, as a small fishing port on the shingle bar, sheltered by the cliffs to the west, which were still eroding. Although a little new shingle is still arriving the mass movement has ceased, so from now onwards shingle is re-distributed rather than laid down de novo.

Old Romney

Broomhill

'Burgh wara hythe*'

Old Winchelsea *(conjectural)*

Hæstingceastre *(conjectural)*

Bexhill

Pevensey

* *'Harbour of the burgh'*

So in 1066 its developmental situation and harbour approaches would have been at some sort of intermediate stage between the situation around 800CE and the next of the 12th century (opposite). Broomhill too was partially lost in 1287.

Would this have affected William the Conqueror's choice of landing site? We can put ourselves in a ship with William and his steersmen. He faced a broad-mouthed shallow port at Pevensey, a small port at Bulverhythe, a much smaller one at the Priory Valley, and a possible entry through a small opening in the Rye Camber spit, which only allowed scouring from the small Tillingham and Brede rivers – as the Rother still exited the Rye Camber at Old Romney. The opening may or may not have allowed access to the Camber and its estuaries, perhaps just to a small port*. William had 700 to 1000 ships to land in a short number of hours to use the optimal rising flood tide to help 'float in' his fleet.

All of the harbours/ports were tidal with the large tidal range and tidal flows still seen today. William's ships had relatively poor manoeuvrability, and he would have had to choose which inlet to aim for, and enter on the rising tide, so that the tidal

* *Ordericus Vitalis reports that William returned from Dieppe to Old Winchelsea in December 1067, so, if correct,there must have been at least a small harbour there at that time unless for some reason they made a beach landing.*

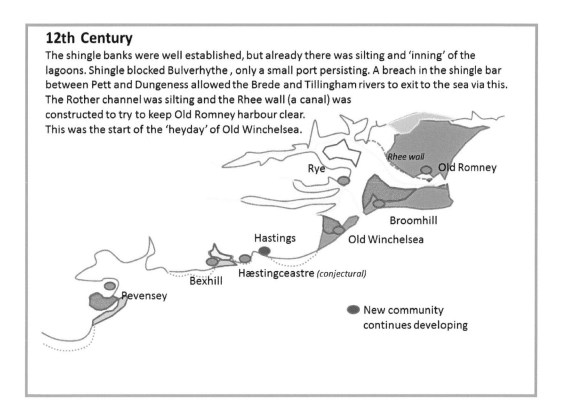

12th Century
The shingle banks were well established, but already there was silting and 'inning' of the lagoons. Shingle blocked Bulverhythe, only a small port persisting. A breach in the shingle bar between Pett and Dungeness allowed the Brede and Tillingham rivers to exit to the sea via this. The Rother channel was silting and the Rhee wall (a canal) was constructed to try to keep Old Romney harbour clear. This was the start of the 'heyday' of Old Winchelsea.

Rhee wall

Rye

Old Romney

Broomhill

Hastings

Old Winchelsea

Hæstingceastre *(conjectural)*

Bexhill

Pevensey

New community continues developing

inflow would help the ships make landfall. Given the circumstances, his safest point of landing was Pevensey, possibly with some ships entering Bulverhythe. To the east of these beyond Hastings, the massive cliffs would have prevented landings. Beyond these cliffs was the large shingle bar, but to be certain of getting into the Rye Camber, he would have had to go in by the Old Romney entrance**. He could have considered direct coastal landings and beaching, but this would have been less inviting as small but steep sandstone cliffs directly backed some of the beaches east of Pevensey (as still seen at Galley Hill, Bexhill and Bo-Peep, St Leonards today).

Although not of direct interest to this chapter, the further evolution of the coast is shown below. Loss of some protection from the Fairlight headland and shingle movement in the great storms of the 13th century destroyed Old Winchelsea's shingle bank and with it the town itself.

Then new shingle banks started to block Pevensey harbour. Already Pevensey was being extensively 'inned' to claim extra farmland, and Bulverhythe/Combe Haven had long ago become freshwater marshland, farmed at its edges, particularly

*** There is the story of the two ships which ended up at Old Romney, whose crews were killed by the townspeople, who in turn received severe punishment from William during his post-victory march from Hastings to Dover. Might they have been pathfinders or did they just get lost?*

on the ridges inland. Inning also progressed apace on the Romney marshes, and this gradually reduced the tidal scour on which Rye relied for its harbour. The old course of the Rother north of Oxney silted up, and the river ran south of the inland Isle. Even the little Priory stream port at Hastings was being blocked by shingle as the headlands had eroded further back and no longer protected it. The end of the Priory hythe came before the large rocks at White Rock were cleared, but when they were, the sea promptly reminded the citizens of Hastings that headlands could be useful, as floods then occurred in the Priory valley.

The final straw was the reclamation of the Brede valley. Rye was left with a not very big tidal river and a small port.

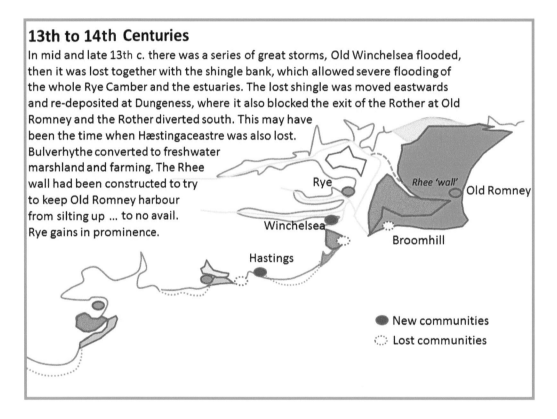

13th to 14th Centuries

In mid and late 13th c. there was a series of great storms, Old Winchelsea flooded, then it was lost together with the shingle bank, which allowed severe flooding of the whole Rye Camber and the estuaries. The lost shingle was moved eastwards and re-deposited at Dungeness, where it also blocked the exit of the Rother at Old Romney and the Rother diverted south. This may have been the time when Hæstingaceastre was also lost. Bulverhythe converted to freshwater marshland and farming. The Rhee wall had been constructed to try to keep Old Romney harbour from silting up … to no avail. Rye gains in prominence.

Rye

Rhee 'wall'

Old Romney

Winchelsea

Broomhill

Hastings

● New communities

⋯ Lost communities

What we see today between the still massive cliffs is an artificial coastline, with groyning and sea walls. Huge quantities of shingle are moved in a shingle merry-go-round by lorry, from the east to the west. Once tipped onto a western beach it gradually and inexorably moves eastwards again, keeping the beaches topped up with shingle. For example, 30,000 to 40,000 cubic metres of shingle a year are recycled to the west end of Pett Level beach.

The coastline today is still changing, although for now extensive groyning protects the coasts between the cliffs. A sea-wall was essential at Pett Level as erosion

1650 CE

Pevensey had been extensively 'inned' from 12th–13th c. onwards. New Winchelsea had been built on Iham hill and there was farming on 'inned' land, including land behind a new beach forming beyond Cliff End. The single outlet to the south for the Rye Camber rivers was narrowing as there was less water from the Camber to scour the entrance. Old Romney was no longer a port and Dungeness had become well established.
A big sand and shingle bar at Langley.

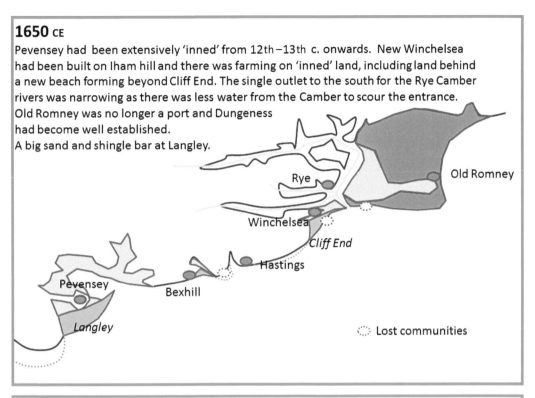

1750 CE

Pevensey completely 'inned' and Rother diverts south of the Isle of Oxney. Rye Camber significantly diminished in size.
Priory valley filling to become the 'America ground'.
Residual White Rock promontory physically removed in Early 19th c.

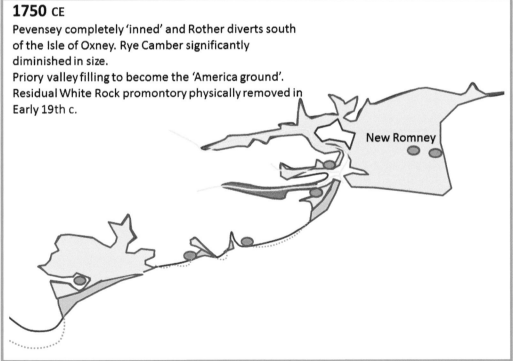

of the cliffs to the west exposed the beach, as history repeated itself. Unprotected sandstone and clay cliffs at Fairlight continue to slump, and there is the occasional spectacular cliff fall. The chalk cliffs are also mainly unprotected and Beachy Head gets slowly less prominent every year.

If there were no sea-walls at Bexhill and Hastings the sea would wash over the promenade areas. At Pett Level the sea would reclaim the low-lying land behind the wall. The pictures below illustrate the effects of groyning and longshore drift at Hastings. A photo taken from a balloon 110 years ago shows just how much shingle has been deposited since the aborted harbour arm was built. There is also a comparison from about 60 years ago when one of the co-authors of this book remembers the sea sometimes washing around the landward side of the old harbour arm at high tide.

To understand completely and visualise what happened in south-east Sussex 950 years ago, historians should take full account of the physical and geographic changes

The pictures above and below of the beach at Old Town, Hastings, illustrate the effect of groyning and longshore drift. In 1905 (from a balloon, above) the harbour arm was just finished. In just over 100 years the shingle piled up on the western side of the old harbour arm and the beach to its west has almost doubled in width.
The light blue dashed line superimposes the beach line as seen in 2015 on the 1905 image.

The Google Earth image from 2015 has a superimposed yellow dashed line showing the beach line in 1905 and a green dashed line for circa 1955. This accumulation was accelerated by recharging the Hastings beaches after re-groyning with huge quantities of dredged shingle from offshore in the late 1980s/early 1990s.

described above. The narratives, motivations, politics, theories and personalities taken alone, whilst obviously very important, are not enough.

Those theorising about the Conqueror's landing should also take into account the nature of William's ships, which were essentially Viking *langskips* (an open war boat, long and narrow with a very shallow draft, perhaps as little as 20cm) and *knörrs* (trading boats, broader beamed and with deeper drafts). Neither type of ship could sail very well into the wind, were relatively easily capsized if the wind was abeam (from the side), and steering was difficult as they had outboard steer-boards – not rudders. They used the tides much more than sailing boats do today – preferring to enter harbours on rising tides which helped them to float in on inflows and to leave them on falling tides which swept them into deeper water out at sea. This tactic of using the tides was exactly what William employed on leaving St. Valéry-sur-Somme and arriving off Pevensey (see Chapter 12). Because the ships had shallow drafts they could enter shallow harbours and sail or pole up rivers, but still needed space to tie up and unload. They could also be directly beached.

The large shallow harbour that attracted William disappeared centuries ago. William ended up on what was then a peninsula, whose neck was at Battle. He turned the peninsula into a fortress and a forward supply base, and ended up having to fight to gain his way out and, in due, course fully to conquer England.

Hastings is a town of large extent and many inhabitants, flourishing and handsome, having markets, work people and rich merchants'.

al-Idrisi, *Book of Roger*, 1154

3

EARLY SOUTH-EAST SUSSEX

Keith Foord

*With contributions from Adrian and Sarah Hall,
Kevin and Lynn Cornwell*

Nothing major happens in history on a whim, but each major event is the culmination of many smaller and not-so-small events that have happened before, to set the stage or to fire the ambition of men to migrate, loot, build, destroy or conquer. The invasion of England in 1066 by William II, duke of Normandy did not happen on a whim. Far from it, as the planning of the expedition and the acquiring, building, crewing and sailing of between 700 and 1000 ships, with soldiers, horses, stores, equipment and pre-fabricated defences, was a triumph of medieval military politics and logistics.

To understand why this momentous day for the history of the English-speaking world occurred at Hastings in October 1066 and to set it in its full historical context, it is necessary first to go back and examine just what occurred locally over a very long period of time. To do so, the present small town of Battle and its surrounding area of south-east Sussex need to be placed in many different contexts.

One of the first to consider is that in 1066 there was essentially nothing but forest, scrub and the odd wandering swineherd living on the site of the town of Battle that we know today. But it was at a crossroads of ancient tracks that led from Hastings to the north and towards Winchelsea to the east and Heathfield to the west. Another perspective is that the whole south-east Sussex area was relatively sparsely populated, and somehow a 'bit different' from the adjacent areas of south Kent and Sussex west of Pevensey.

As we saw in Chapter 2, a time traveller to East Sussex and Kent in the pre-Norman eras would notice that the coastline was markedly different. There has been much coastal erosion, shingle and sand deposition and loss of marshlands, both from natural causes, and the activities of man. 2000 years ago, the Romans were able to use several small local ports now kilometres inland to import goods and export the iron ingots produced locally across the Channel to Gaul. Winchelsea was briefly a major port in post-Conquest times, and the area around Rye and Dungeness would have been significantly different.

The pre-Roman period in eastern Sussex from the mesolithic period (*c.* 10,000 years ago) was characterised by scattered settlements in an unpromising environment of heathland and dense forest (the Andreadsweald forest was 30 miles deep and 120 miles long and stretched over the north of Sussex and into Kent). Isolated settlements might have shared common activities such as iron extraction, and the larger centres of population were probably based in what are now the Eastbourne and Hastings areas.

An estimate of the extent of the Andreadsweald in 250 and 1086

Based on the distribution of *Domesday* meadowlands from Derby and Campbell's *Domesday Geography of SE England* and conjectured Iron and Roman Age forest clearances for agriculture and for making charcoal for iron smelting.

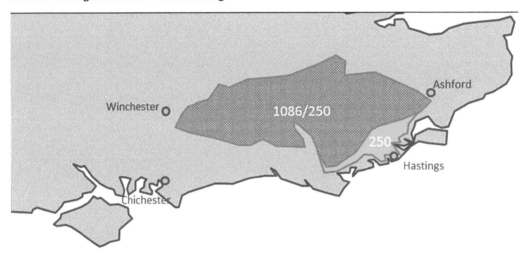

This map assumes that the Andreadsweald in 1086 occupied the inland area where virtually no meadowlands are recorded in *Domesday*. It may have extended virtually to the coast in the late Iron Age and Roman times, with the coastal zone being deforested at that time. Modern place names given for orientation.
© Battle and District Historical Society

The Historical Atlas of Sussex (Leslie and Short, 1999) tells a story showing the south-east Sussex area as largely devoid of settlements. But recent excavations associated with the Hastings–Bexhill link road suggest significant prehistoric and historic habitation, sometimes only temporary, around the Combe Haven valley. Thinking of England as a whole, the landscape altered in the period 2000BCE– 1500BCE as fields, trackways, boundaries and settlements became evident. So it is likely the countryside in the East Sussex area would have been noticeably altered by cultivation over a thousand years before the Romans arrived.

In addition, there is evidence of some Iron Age ironworking activity in the area, notably at Crowhurst Park but also at several nearby sites. Even small ironworking endeavours would have led to considerable deforestation as trees were cut down to make charcoal for furnaces, which cleared land for cultivation, mainly of cereals.

To the west of Battle on the South Downs, over 50 Iron Age sites have been found. Remains of cattle and sheep are mixed with iron ploughshares and sickles, suggesting mixed farming. There is evidence of weaving and shellfish would have supplemented the diet.

Towards the end of the Iron Age, around 75BCE, the Atrobates, one of the tribes of the Belgae (themselves derived from a mix of central and northern European peoples) moved into southern Britain. Then came the Regni and others followed by the Romans. Very likely the indigenous inhabitants of Sussex encountered several centuries later by the immigrating Saxons would have been from a wide gene pool.

Some scholars speculate that the Iron Age inhabitants of Sussex created the north–south droving roads, which were later used by the Saxons and, in due course, had an effect on the pattern of Sussex settlement. Later churches and villages might be sited, it has been suggested, where a drove road crossed a river. A known prehistoric ridge road leads from Fairlight through Ore along the ridge to Battle then via Netherfield to Heathfield, a cross-country route still used today. At Netherfield this track was joined by another which followed the ridge from Rye via Brede and Udimore.

THE COMING OF ROME

What interested the Romans about this remote end of eastern Sussex? It was virtually cut off – to the west by the extensive wide tidal flats of Pevensey and its surrounding marshes, to the north by the dense Wealden forest and to the east by the flooded estuarine waters of the Rye Camber and the tidal valleys of the rivers Rother, Brede and Tillingham. Their routes in were by road from the north-east and by sea from the south.

No known Roman road directly links south-east Sussex to the nearby late Roman shore fort at Pevensey (Anderita) which stands on what was a peninsula on the western shore of what was then the large tidal expanse of sea water and salt flats and marshes. Hastings Area Archaeological Research Group (HAARG) have found elements of a small Roman town at Kitchenham Farm, near Boreham Street, near to extensive Roman finds, tile kilns, old Roman saltpans, and a Roman period jetty at the head of Waller's Haven. This was probably a small Classis Britannica port or settlement pre-dating the fort at Pevensey.

It has been postulated by HAARG that there may have been a high-ground earthen trackway eastwards between this and Beauport Park and westwards to the

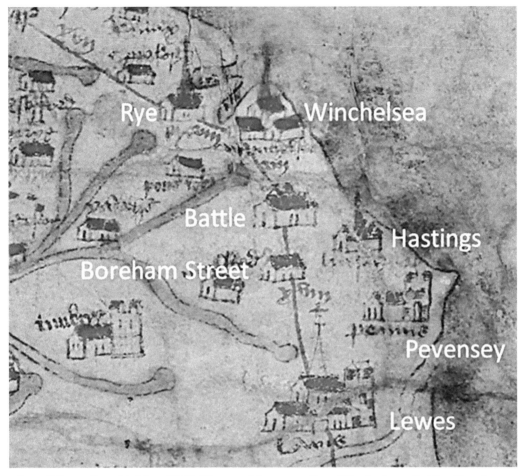

Detail from Gough's Map 1360. The road between Rye, Winchelsea, Battle, Boreham Street and Lewes. The orientation of the map is curious, with the English Channel to right. Modern place names overlaid. Reproduced by kind permission of the Bodleian Libraries, University of Oxford: MS. Gough Gen. Top. 16 (East Sussex) via 'Linguistic Geographies: The Gough Map of Great Britain and its Making, www.goughmap.org/

area north of Eastbourne. Interestingly a cross-country road along the south coast is shown on Gough's map of 1360 which links Rye, Winchelsea, Battle, Boreham Street (which is specifically depicted and named) and Lewes, with Pevensey lying off line to the south. Could this follow an old Roman line?

What spurred the building of a substantial Roman road from the north, and also harbours for the berthing of ships, was the presence of iron ore and wood – lots of both. The Romans may have heard about iron production in eastern Sussex and when they arrived in 43CE, they found an established local tradition of ironworking. Julius Caesar had first drawn Rome's attention to iron being produced in the coastal

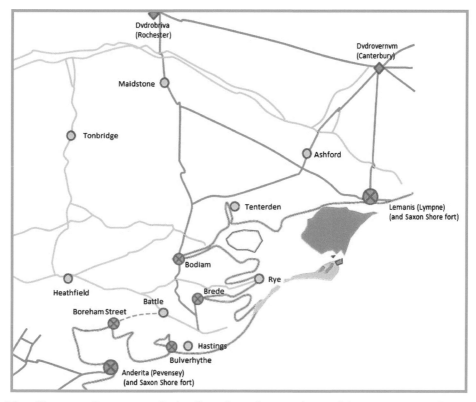

**After Margary: Roman roads (red) and track ways (green) in SE Sussex and S Kent.
The dashed line represents a possible high level Roman track way between Boreham
Street and Battle. The 400CE coast is shown in blue, small ports blue, larger ones pink.
The Saxon Shore forts and the small ports were not necessarily contemporaneous
(see text). Modern towns and place names are shown as small yellow circles for
orientation. (For coastal changes at Dungeness refer to Chapter 2)**
© Battle and District Historical Society

parts of Britain in 55/54BCE. The Romans' own surveyors would also have noticed
the rich orange-brown colour of many streams and drawn their own inferences. It
is interesting that there is also evidence of Roman trading with this area from well
before 43CE as HAARG member Alan Charman found Roman coins dating from 83–
31BCE at Ashburnham.

At the eastern extent of a new road corridor at Upper Wilting near Crowhurst,
occupation from the 1st century CE through to the late 2nd century CE has been
found, comprising a large ironworking site and an adjacent ditched enclosure.
The ironworking site included areas for preparing charcoal, roasting ore and then
smelting, with the remains of fourteen bloomery furnaces and hundreds of cubic
metres of overlying slag and cinder deposits.

Evidence for Romano-British settlement has also been found on the ridges of the Combe Haven valley. This suggests that the rural landscape of the Roman period around Bexhill and Hastings would have appeared quite settled. Once more, deforestation would have been obvious as the furnaces' hunger for charcoal would have been huge.

The ore was prepared before smelting by roasting it, breaking it and removing unwanted stone. The prepared ore was then smelted using a technique called 'bloomer smelting', where the particles of iron metal formed do not melt, but stick together to make a spongy 'bloom'.

The Beauport Park iron bloomery between Battle and Hastings was possibly run under military supervision by the Classis Britannica fleet. Its and other furnaces' peak activity was up until about 250CE, during and just after the Roman northern British campaigns and the construction of Hadrian's Wall. It may also have supplied the Roman legions in Gaul and the wider Roman Empire with iron for weapons as it has been estimated that this was the third largest iron bloomery in the whole Roman empire. The bathhouse for the ironworks was excavated by Gerald Brodribb in the 1970s, and was re-covered to preserve it, but was noted to be a 'Scheduled Ancient Monument at risk' in 2013. Beauport Park is one of the Romans' lasting industrial memorials and deserves better attention than to be buried under earth and covered with corrugated iron. It is apparently one of the most complete Roman buildings ever to have been discovered in Britain and never opened to the public. When excavated, the remains were found to contain cold, warm and hot rooms, plunge baths and changing rooms. There are also furnaces, underfloor heating chambers, flues in the walls which channelled heat around the building, and painted plaster which decorated the walls.

The local haematite iron ore from Petley, Sedlescombe, Icklesham, Beauport, Bynes Farm, Brede and Crowhurst Park, etc. was smelted with charcoal, and then the crude iron shipped out – northwards via a port run by the Classis Britannica at Bodiam, which sat at the upper end of a then navigable River Rother, or by a smaller port at Brede, just north of what appears to be a large iron-processing site, and to the south by a possible port at Bulverhythe. It is likely that the chosen route was down-hill to the nearest port which would have made transporting the heavy iron easier. Slightly to the west, further bloomeries produced iron which was exported via a small port at Boreham Street at the Waller's Haven headwater of the Pevensey harbour.

Margary traced the Roman road from Beauport on the edge of Hastings via Sedlescombe (where there is a side road to Brede) and Cripps Corner to Bodiam, where it continues north to near Sissinghurst, then divides, continuing north to Maidstone and eastwards to Tenterden, Ashford and Canterbury. At Sedlescombe there is a large road connecting to the ironworking site at Footlands Farm.

The Roman Empire in 300–400CE was in decline, but Roman interest in the Battle area had declined well before that. The iron-extracting industry moved north-westwards into the higher Weald, possibly as local ore deposits were becoming more difficult to find and the Hastings area had been denuded of timber. The Classis Britannica had withdrawn. This dating is evidenced by coin finds, the majority of coins in the area being dated between 69–193CE, with much reduced activity occurring after about 250CE. There were also increasing Saxon raids on the vulnerable coast. The Roman shore fort of Anderita was built *c.* 293CE in response to Saxon raiding. This was mainly a trading station, but also protected the Roman interests in the Vale of Sussex, between the South Downs and the Weald. In terms of their fortifications, Pevensey fort is a lasting Roman memorial.

With the departure of the Romans, the area suffered setbacks. The ironworking sites had been abandoned; the Roman navy had gone; natural decay set in and Saxon attacks increased. The ironworking industry collapsed, with only minimal and cruder ironworking in the later Anglo-Saxon period, with no true revival until medieval times.

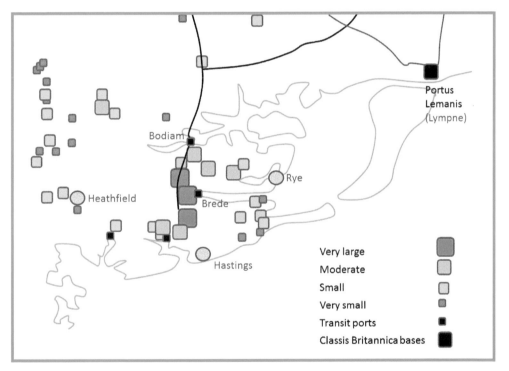

After Hodgkinson (2008): iron bloomery sites by slag volume. The very largest (red) and moderate sized (yellow) bloomeries together produced 88% of the Wealden iron. The green-coloured sites contributed 10% of the total, and the blue sites only 2%. Note the concentration of activity between Hastings and Bodiam, along the line of the Roman road, particularly around Brede. Sites not shown on this map, deeper in the Weald, although numerous were all only small or very small. The Roman period coastline is in blue, modern place names (for orientation only) in purple.
© Battle and District Historical Society

SAXONS AND JUTES

Jutes invaded Kent, and western Sussex was invaded, via somewhere near Selsey, by Saxons led by Ælle and his sons in about 477CE. Angles had focused their attentions on the east coast north of the Thames. Ælle may have indecisively fought the Romano-Britons at 'Mearcred's Burn' in 485. The site of this has never been confirmed but there has been some local speculation that this tussle may have been near Ashburnham, at a place which some have called 'Towncreep' in Creep Wood. Later he overwhelmed the garrison at Andredceaster – probably Pevensey – in 491. This was the absolute end of the 'Saxon Shore' defence policy begun under the Romans to keep out invaders. Nothing written remains from this period – the above stories are from retrospective writing down of oral history in the *Anglo-Saxon Chronicle* (A and E versions).

Ælle – assuming he existed – has been associated by some scholars with saucer brooch scroll designs found across much of southern England. If this were so, then his influence would have been substantial, But the earliest (fifth to seventh century) cemeteries and settlement sites in what would become the kingdom of the South Saxons are almost all restricted to the South Downs west of Eastbourne and on the Chichester coastal plain.

Saxon influence east of Pevensey appears to have been weak as on the eastern side of the estuary and marsh there were settlers that were known as the Hæstingas. Not very much is known of the Hæstingas, but it has been suggested that they may have been a separate people to the Saxons, possibly Jutes. Given the presence of Jutes in East Kent and the access routes described earlier, this might be correct. Chevallier suggested that there may have been some north Frankish influence on the Hæstingas, partially supported by Loyn who also suggested that Sussex as a whole was influenced by the same peoples. Some of the Saxon charters dating from the years of the kingdom of Sussex suggest the existence of two separate dynasties in Sussex. For example, the charters of king Northelm (or Nunna), who ruled Sussex in the late seventh and early eighth century, show a second king by the name of Watt (or Wattus). Otherwise little is known about the Hæstingas except that it was their habit to settle and farm the land. In the late Saxon era, Hæstingaceastre/Hastings developed into a thriving fishing port, later providing both men and ships to the English navy. So it seems we may owe south-east Sussex mainly to the Jutes, possibly with some Frankish influence.

The development of English kings and sub-kings was slow, and boundaries between 'territories' fluctuated, but finally the division of England into a 'Heptarchy' evolved. Through the fifth to ninth centuries the seven major kingdoms evolved, with some sub-kingdoms such as the Hæstingas, some short-lived, others persisting through to the eighth century. Some of these are shown on the map of southern England overleaf. The three largest kingdoms eventually exerted major influence in turn, without overwhelming the other two. That is the reason that Offa of Mercia became overlord of Kent and Hæstingas in the late 700s. After this, the house of

Wessex became the most powerful, and an embryonic English kingdom started to evolve after 871 although a definitive single English kingdom was not true reality until the mid-10th century and the reign of Eadred. This is illustrated in the table below.

The 'Heptarchy' – evolving through periods of supremacy to become England	Kingdom of Kent c.455	Kingdom of Sussex c.477	Kingdom of Mercia c.585	Kingdom of Essex c.527	Kingdom of East Anglia c.575	Kingdom of Wessex c.495	Kingdom of North-umbria c.547
	(Jutes)	(Saxons)	(Angles)	(Saxons)	(Angles)	(Saxons)	(Angles)
	Northumbrian supremacy						607–679
	Mercian supremacy						679–820
	Wessex supremacy						820–871
	Kings of England						after 871

The Saxons may also have left a legacy in the form of the Sussex dialects. In his 1957 book on the subject, the Rev. W D Parish says that many of the Sussex dialect words are Anglo-Saxon, e.g. addle = stupid, hurst (hyrst) = copse and drib (from dripen) = a small quantity. Saxon words are retained in some place names. We retain almost unchanged Saxon words for days of the week: Tuesday (tíwesdæg); Wednesday (wódnesdæg); Thursday (Þunresdæg [Þ=Th]) and Friday (frígedæg). Many such Germanic origin words persist in modern general English, although perhaps for legal, culinary, ecclesiastical and academic linguistics later influences of Latin and secular influences of Norman French were important.

More can be said about the legacy of the Saxons in England generally. Famous Anglo-Saxon literature included *Beowulf*. Religious houses in the Anglo-Saxon period produced beautiful manuscripts such as the *Grimbald Gospels* illustrated by Edwin Basan; *The Life of St Benedict*; and an early 11th-century map of the world which came into the possession of Battle Abbey in the twelfth century. The Alfred Jewel – a pointer for reading – symbolises the efforts made by that king in the areas of Christian worship, values and scholarship. Leaving Alfred aside, it is a matter of conjecture how far scholarship in the monasteries and at court developed because of, or in spite of, the Anglo-Saxons. Still less is it clear what, if any, impact Anglo-Saxon culture at that level had in the Sussex area. A further point of caution is that it should not be assumed the Normans who came after were incapable of outstanding scholarship and fine manuscript production: they were not.

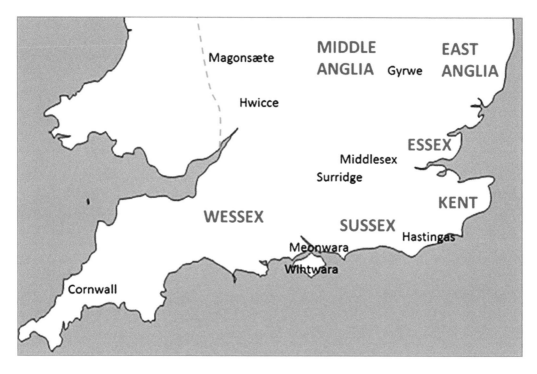

The major and some minor kingdoms of southern England to the end of the 8th century; Middle Anglia became southern Mercia.

The position of Christianity in the early Anglo-Saxon period is difficult to assess. According to the *Anglo-Saxon Chronicle*, in 681 the exiled St Wilfrid of Northumbria founded Selsey Abbey in western Sussex and remained there for a five-year ministry, but not without opposition from the polytheistic South Saxons. Wilfrid's biographer records that in 666 his ship ran aground on the Sussex coast and was attacked. By 681, however, Sussex had its first Christian ruler, Athelwealh. It was not until Alfred some two centuries later – an interlude mainly comprising inter-Saxon conflict, about which our knowledge is limited apart from of the wars between the Anglo-Saxon kingdoms – that Christianity was consistently promoted at the royal level. So how much did the English do to embed Christianity, and how far did they permit Christian reformers such as St Wilfrid to carry out their ministry? We also need to bear in mind the possible influences in the Anglo-Saxon period from three directions: from Burgundy – through orders of monks; from France and Italy, again through monastic orders; and from Northumbria (did for example Bede have an influence at the time in the south of England?) Is there any evidence the Saxons travelled from this area to those? If eastern Sussex had been influenced from any of these sources then presumably there would need to have been a pre-Norman religious node of influence in or near eastern Sussex, but where?

CHARTERS AND HASTINGS/HÆSTINGACEASTRE

Much of the administrative structure of the Norman state after 1066 was built on English foundations, for example the administrative units of the shire and hundred, with an accompanying structure of officials which was later to be instrumental in gathering the information for the *Domesday Book*. The English and Norman 'rape' division of Sussex may derive from the earliest times in terms of how the Saxon Shore was organised, according to the north–south divisions of the principal rivers.

A 12th-century source suggested that the Hæstingas were 'absorbed' by Offa of Mercia after the ascent of Mercian power; the chronicler Simeon of Durham records the defeat of the 'gens Hestingorum' by Offa of Mercia in 771. In 772 Offa established a minster church at Bexhill, with eight hides of land, serving the surrounding area and becoming a 'node of influence'. By 790, Offa controlled Hastings effectively enough to apparently grant land in Hastings and Pevensey to the Abbey of St Denis in Paris. These and later grants contain some phrases which have led to confusion about the geography of the port(s) of Hastings and Pevensey. This has led Tyson (2014) to suggest that a singular port called 'Hastinges and Pevenesel' might be the flooded Brede valley. Most experts consider these grants to be forgeries or modifications of pre-existing charters, but the abridged transcriptions containing the relevant words and notes about them are below (the **S** numbers are referenced to Sawyer – see sources).

S1186, pp. 549–550: AD 795. Berhtwald, dux, to the Abbey of St Denis; grant of land at Rotherfield, Hastings and Pevensey, Sussex Donatio Bertoaldi Ducis de Hastinges, et Pevenesel, *portubus** maris; et villa Radrefelda in Anglia ... **meæ possessionis portus, qui sunt in eadem vicinitate super mare, Hastingas et Pævenisel, cum salinis et omni integritate sua** .... * This is the ablative or dative plural of portus, here referring to both of the ports and his association with them.*

Berthold was a 'sub-regulus' with some devolved powers of grant.

Translation: (use of) my possession of the harbours, which are in the same area, beside the sea, Hastings and Pævenisel, together with salt-pans and all that belongs to them.

S133, pp. 550–551: AD 790 (Tamworth, Staffs., 12 April). Offa, king of Mercia, to the abbey of Saint-Denis; grant of privileges for land at London, and confirmation of land at Rotherfield, Hastings and Pevensey, Sussex. **Preterea donatum quod amicus noster et fidelis Berhtuald dux, et frater ejus Eadbald, de receptaculo suo Ridrefelda, quod est in pago qui vocatur Successa, super fluvium Saforda, et de portu** super mare Hastingas et Peuenisel ....**
*** This is the ablative singular of portus, which might suggest that Hastingas/Peuenisel is one port, but it could also refer to the fact that Hastingas is a singular port and there is a separate place called Peuenisel. Word order is often different in Latin from modern English.*
Translation: In addition, our friend and faithful Duke Berhtwald and his brother

Eadbald provided a place of refuge at their property Rotherfield, which is in the county called Sussex above the river Saford and the sea port of Hastings (,) and Pevensey.

S318, p. 551: AD 857 (London, Nov.). Æthelwulf, king of the English, to the Abbey of Saint-Denis (Paris); *confirmation of lands at Rotherfield, Hastings, Pevensey, Sussex; and at Lundenuuic (London)* Ubi cum inter cætera querimoniam pro injuria a nostris hominibus Colonis sancti Dionysii martyris qui sunt in diversis Britanniæ locis, et maxime in Ridrefelda, et in Hastingas, et in Pevenisel, in salinis quoque, et in Lundenuuic, miserabiliter illatam deplorasset.

S686, p. 552: AD. 960. King Edgar to the Abbey of Saint-Denis, Paris; *restoration of animals and property at Rotherfield, Hastings and Pevensey, Sussex:* ... conquestum est super domus nostræ prepusito Togred, quod in villa eorum Ridrefelda CCC oves, et L buves, et de salinis eurum C mensuras salis, et ab agriculis qui sunt in Hastengas et Pevenisel... *restoring to the abbey animals (300 sheep and 50 catttle), salt production and farms which had been appropriated by the reeve 'Togred' from the estates at Rotherfield, Hastings and Pevensey.*

It has been suggested by Tyson that Pevenisel is from Latin-derived Peue-insula and is the peninsula north of what was the Brede estuary, not the town of Pevensey. Professor Richard Coates of the University of the West of England has explained the rather curious *Pevenesel(il)* form of Pevensey: He says '*Pevenisel* is an artefact of the way the Normans processed some English names. It is not really understood why, but the final -l sprouts in several names (and alternates unstably with other consonants too) and should not be considered an integral part of this name. So Pevensey means 'Pefen's river' in Old English (OE) – and ēa does mean 'river', so some explanation of how it comes to apply to a peninsula would be required. Watts says that the final part might be for OE ēgel 'small island'. This is theoretically possible, but the word is not recorded, has no parallels in other Germanic languages, and the explanation ignores the other names that show final -l' (*personal communication to George Kiloh 2014*).

By 1190 Roger of Howden in his *portulan* (pilot notes) for English crusader ships going up or down the English Channel was noting that '*the port of la Crumbie* [the Crumbles], *below Bealcef* [Beachy Head], *is very unreliable as sometimes it is blocked by sand*'. He also mentions the '*town and castle of Hastinges, though there is no port there*'. He would have been observing with respect to the usefulness to the moderately large crusader ships. This does not therefore exclude a small fishing port, but by then shingle was starting to block Bulverhythe, and the Priory valley port must always have been small. The struggle to maintain a port at Hastings was probably the reason that Rye and Winchelsea became 'members' of the Cinque port of Hastings in 1191, when together they provided five times more ships than their 'parent'.

Today the translation from the Latin of Roger of Howden's words still causes speculation; with one 2012 translation (Spence's in Hughes' paper on Howden's description of the English coast) describing the ports of Winchelsea and Pevensey being clearly separated each side of Hastings. A second 2014 translation by Tyson leads to her interesting conjecture that a port of 'Hastinges and Pevensel' was in the Brede valley, and based on an hypothesis that also involves the words in the Charter to St Denis (S133), ends up concluding that the long established consensus that the 1066 landing was focused on Pevensey is incorrect.

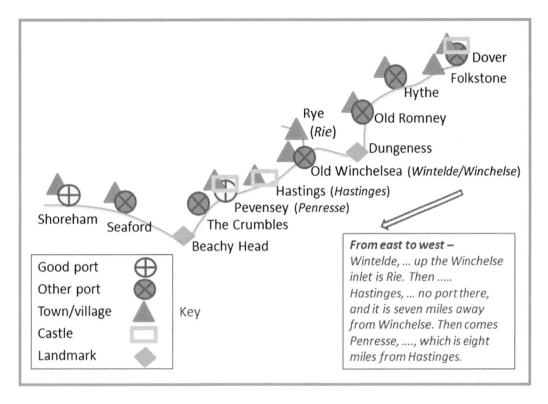

Named places from the 1190 *De Viis Maris* by Roger de Howden. Extract of English translation by Spence in Hughes (2012). Plotted on the modern coastline.
© Battle and District Historical Society

The precise words in this debate are (following a description of Winchelsea and Rye) *'Deinde est Hastinges villa et castellum, sed non est ibi portus, que distat a Winchelse vii milaria'*. One translation of the underlined words is *'but (Hastings) does not have a port, it is 7 miles distant at Winchelsea'*, the other *'but (Hastings) does not have a port, and it is 7 miles away from Winchelsea'.* The critical choice is deciding whether the last phrase refers to 'Hastinges' or 'portus': Latin grammar and word order does vary from modern English and the use of *'que'* referring back to Hastinges villa (f.) instead of 'qui' which would refer to portus (m.) suggest the latter translation is more correct (Gillingham, *personal communication*). The theory becomes even more suspect when the geo-history of the Rye bay area is reviewed (see Chapter 2).

Mercian over-lordship of south-east Sussex was ended when the Mercians were defeated in 825, by King Egbert of Wessex, at the Battle of Ellandun. Egbert went on to annex the territories of Essex, Kent, Surrey and Sussex, suggesting that by this time the Hæstingas had been subsumed into Sussex. But it seems that the Hæstingas retained a local identity until the 11th century as the *Anglo-Saxon Chronicle* records for 1011 that Vikings overran 'all Kent, Sussex, Surrey and Hæstingas', indicating the area was still to a degree considered a separate entity to its neighbours 240 years after Offa's conquest.

EARLY HASTINGS AND THE SITE OF THE BURGH

During the reign of Athelstan, a royal mint was granted in Hastings in 928. This, combined with the fact that Hæstingaceastre was a burgh established at the end of the reign of Alfred, gave Hastings status and some of its inhabitants were burgesses. The place name Hæstingaceastre is found in the *Anglo-Saxon Chronicle* (D) entry for 1050, and the same name is also used once in the Bayeux Tapestry. This may be an alternative name for Hastings related to the old Alfredian 'burghal hidage' fort or township, for which there is sadly an absence of any known archaeological remains.

Burghal forts were established in the late 9th century as English defences against Viking raids, and were part of the Alfredian strategy to recover all of England from the Danes, with the coastal forts designed to deter further Viking raids. The burgh of Hæstingaceastre had the income and support of the people of 500 hides (94sq.miles/243sq.km) of productive land attached to it. The wall length of all the burghal forts correlated well with the supporting hidage and for Hæstingaceastre is estimated to have been about 625m (2060ft). If it was square, each wall would have been about 160m long and the contained area about 2.5Ha (6 acres). If the southern boundary was a cliff face it may have been larger. Often the OE 'ceastre' meant not a just castle or fort, but a town enclosed by an earthen wall topped with timber or sometimes of stone, and Hæstingaceastre appears to mean the walled or stockaded town of Hastings.

The burghal fort may have been on the site of the Norman stone castle that is still a prominent feature of the Hastings skyline. But it has been hypothesised that this Anglo-Saxon burgh was actually a fortified township, akin to Wareham or Wallingford, somewhere to the west of the present centre of Hastings. In support of this, the name Bulverhythe derives from OE *Burhwara hyð* (the harbour of the people of the burgh), and this lies at the west of modern Hastings and St Leonards. There is a record of a charter for a parcel of land in the parish of St Michael which was west of the Priory valley, dated approximately 1280, granting land north of a road leading from Hastings market place towards Battle, from which we can infer that the market place was also west of the Priory valley (Gardiner). The first mention of a market at Hastings was in 900CE, i.e. well before the move to the Bourne valley. There was also a place name *Esthethe* (East Hythe) in the Bourne valley, with properties on each side of the stream (Gardiner). This suggests that a name differential was being made between places in 'new' Hastings in the more eastern Bourne valley (East Hythe?) and those that had developed in the more western Priory valley adjacent to the even more western 'old' Hastings/Haestingaceastre.

Churches called St Michael, St Margaret, St Peter and St Leonard – all existed west of the Priory valley from before 1291 when a return was made to the pope. This return also included St Andrew sub Castro on the east side of the Priory valley, and St Clement and All Saints in the Bourne 'new Hastings' valley.

The earliest records were of St Margaret in 1205 when Simon de Waltham was appointed priest; of St Michael in *c.* 1195 when its advowson ws given by Roger of Crotteslege to the newly formed Priory of Hastings; and of St Peter 1240 when its advowson was transferred from Combwell Priory near Ticehurst to Hastings Priory.

In 1294 the hospital of St Mary Magdalen was gifted land of over 5 acres (2 Ha) between what is now Warrior Square and Bohemia Road. At least part of this still existed as a wall of an old barn when drawn in 1815, and the sketches show 12thc. Norman features. it was partially excavated in 1862, when the mayor reported that *'the centre of the building was found full of bones'.*

In 1340 there is a record from the canons of the collegiate church of St Mary in the Castle that respite from payments was given to St Michael, St Peter and St Margaret because their buildings and those of their parishioners had been burnt by the French in the previous year. St Clement had to be rebuilt in 1286 as it 'had been broken and destroyed by the force of the sea' and again in 1377 after French raids. Similarly, All Saints was also rebuilt in the early 1400s. Both of these churches still stand in Hastings Old Town. But St Michael was the town 'saint' before the 14th century and appeared on early town seals.

The important part of all the above conjecture, as far as 1066 is concerned, is that the fortifications that William established were likely, but not certainly, to have been on top of the burghal fortifications of Haestingaceastre, which may have used the cliffs as part of its protection.

After 1066, Hastings briefly continued to thrive as a port, to the extent that it appears between Shoreham and Dover on the world map made by the Arabic geographer al-Idrisi for king Roger II of Sicily (a Norman outpost) compiled in 1153/1154CE. In its descriptive text, Hastings is described as *'a town of large extent and many inhabitants, flourishing and handsome, having markets, work people and rich merchants'.* In 1155 king Henry II granted a royal charter to the Cinque Ports, as long as they provided 57 ships for 15 days each year. Hastings was still a major provider of ships at that time, but only just, as by 1191 the struggle to maintain a good port at Hastings led to Rye and Winchelsea becoming 'limbs' of Hastings, and as noted above they provided five times more ships than their 'parent'.

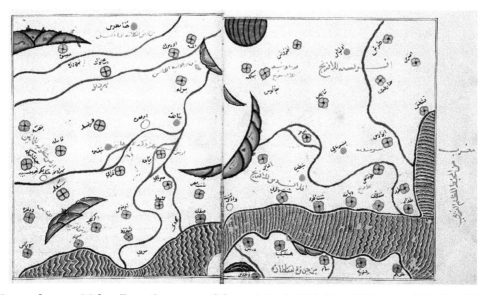

Pages from a 16th c. Egyptian copy of the original al-Idrisi 1154 map of the English Channel. Continental France and the French coast are to the top of the image, the SE coast of England at the bottom. Hastings is arrowed, with Dover to its left and Shoreham then Southampton to its right.
MS. Pococke 375 fol. 281b-282a   The Bodleian Libraries, University of Oxford.

Hastings Priory of the Holy Trinity was established in the reign of Richard I (1189–1199). This was sited just above where Hastings Post Office is on Cambridge Road. Sometime later, 192 acres (78 Ha) of land were transferred to it from St Michael's parish. This land was all on the west side of the Priory valley, and some of it would have been a typical water meadow so beloved of monastic institutions. The sea encroached until the priory was in danger of being swept away, and in 1413 Sir John Pelham gave them a site at Warbleton, and king Henry IV licensed them to remove. A small farm persisted on the residual Priory land for many years and is still shown on the OS map from the 1873 survey. St Andrew sub Castro on the eastern side of the Priory valley was also first mentioned in the return of 1291, and again in 1372. Probably plundered by the French, and also threatened by sea flooding, St Andrew sub Castro fell into disuse by 1440, although there is evidence that some ruins were still visible in 1610, and the graveyard was still in use after that time. A new church dedicated to St Andrew was built in 1869 and served as the parish church for the western side of the Priory valley until it was demolished. A supermarket now occupies its site.

Old drawings of the White Rock and the hill behind it (Cuckoo Hill) on which St Michael stood are also informative. Views from the east show rock faces which today are mainly unnoticed. The main reason for their obscuration was the railway. Huge quantities of stone came from the tunnels carved through the sandstone between St Leonards Warrior Square and Hastings stations and the Ore tunnels, only some of which could be used to make embankments on the west side of the Priory valley; the remainder was spread out to reduce the inclines of Cambridge and Havelock Roads. This will explain the height changes in Priory Street and the steps down from Cambridge Road to Claremont. A reminder of the height of the rock can be seen on the north side of Cambridge road approaching White Rock Gardens.

St Michael's parish and the Holy Trinity land was still marked on the Boundary Commission map of 1832, and St Michael's ruins were discovered when building Prospect Place. During the construction of an electricity sub-station in 1970 in St Michael's Place bones from 22 to 35 bodies were found in a single grave. Hastings museum believed that they came from the original graveyard of St Michael's Church and had been re-buried after the cutting of a new road in 1834.

St Margaret's stood on top of the small cliff behind 50 Eversfield Place behind which its ruins were found and its name is preserved in St Margaret's Road. Its parish was the same as the newer St Mary Magdalene.

St Leonard's was in the area of Norman Road, west of London Road, nowhere near the present St Leonard's church. St Leonard was valued at £4.13.4d in 1291 and in 1334 belonged to the abbey of St Katherine of Rouen. Old St Leonard's graveyard was disturbed when building the former Methodist Church there.

The modern St Peter's church is at Bohemia, nowhere near the presumed location of the 1240 St Peter's which has disappeared, the suspicion being that, as its name suggests, it might have been the 'fishermen's and sailors' church, it would have stood nearest the sea, and went over a cliff.

This cluster of four chapels west of Priory valley is not insignificant, and does suggest that they were serving a community of reasonable size. Of these only St Leonard is mentioned after 1372, although a parson for St Michael is named in 1404. The Bishop of Chichester, in 1440, reported that *the parishes of St Andrew's, St Leonard's, St Michael's, and St Margaret's, had so suffered from the depredations of the sea in the last 100 years, that they had no longer any churches*. He could also have mentioned the unwelcome attentions of the French! There was no mention of St Peter's at all.

We have some tantalising glimpses of possibilities in old books. In 1873 some embankment lines were described 'near the present Cornwallis Gardens and north of White Rock Villa', which stood at the top of the steps to White Rock Gardens. Dawson in his 1909 book says *'Dr Bruce informs us that some extensive entrenchments were still to be seen in the vicinity of the railway station at Hastings'* and then *'such traces of earth-works in the existing meadows behind White Rock are extremely indistinct and of doubtful origin'.* But see the extract from the OS map of 1873 below.

The extensive White Rock Gardens area was acquired by Hastings Council in 1902 and re-landscaped completely after 1920. Any archaeological evidence in this area, if it ever existed, may well have been completely destroyed at that time. Additionally, just as two-thirds of Hastings Castle has disappeared under the waves since it was

Gun emplacement on White Rock (from the west before 1834). Both images from *Hastings of Bygone Days and the Present* by Henry Cousins (1920).

White Rock (left) and the old bridge over the Priory Stream (from the east) in the early 19th century. Note the roads in front of White Rock and through the natural gap between the White Rock and Cuckoo Hill and the road 'carved' through the hill to the north. The rock faces would have been approximately 20m high.

built on the West Hill, other structures between White Rock and Bulverhythe may, sadly, also be under the sea, or already under a housing development. No definite fort embankments can be seen, even on the earliest maps of Sussex/Hastings which date from the 1500s which suggest that, if they existed, their major features may have disappeared by then. Earthworks associated with burghal forts are very obvious in some other places. Nothing was noted on the early 1806 Ordnance Survey 2 miles to the inch map of this area, but a well and some embankments were shown near the site of St Margaret on the 6 inch to 1 mile OS map surveyed in 1873, published before substantial landscaping.

The great storms of the 13th century, the continued erosion by the sea, shingle movements, inundations of the Priory valley and predations by the French through to the 15th century could have hidden a lot of local history. The losses clearly finalised

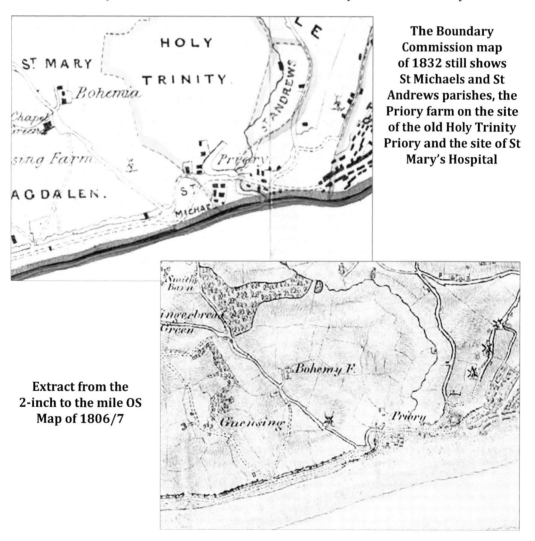

The Boundary Commission map of 1832 still shows St Michaels and St Andrews parishes, the Priory farm on the site of the old Holy Trinity Priory and the site of St Mary's Hospital

Extract from the 2-inch to the mile OS Map of 1806/7

a wholesale move eastwards into the Bourne valley starting with the small 'Hastings' of *Domesday*, as the areas described above appear to have depopulated well before 1440, perhaps by the mid-14th century in the wake of the French raids, the Black Death and incessant erosion.

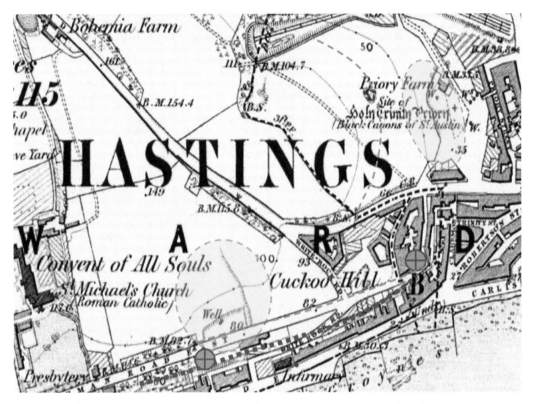

Extract from the 1873 6-inch to the mile OS map. There are embankments shown in the areas shaded blue. The 1873 cliff line is shown in dashed purple and the 25m contour line in dashed red. The sites of the old churches of St Margaret (left) and St Michael (right) are the green circles.

The maps opposite show possible coastal changes between 1291 and 1450 (with dotted outlines of damaged/lost buildings). A possible township would have enclosed St Michael's, St Margaret's and St Peter's plus a market place (grey square). The site (triangle) mentioned by Gardiner is north of the market. Severe cliff erosion may have caused loss of St Peters and the market place and two-thirds of the Norman castle on West Hill, also exposing other churches and the Priory to sea damage.
Light buff shows the 25m contour, the darker buff the 70m contour. Thick lines show possible cliff positions from approx. 1291 and after 1450. Some similarities exist with Cole's map of 1291(drawn in 1844), and Gardiner's (1999) who both clearly followed the same logic.
Both maps © Battle and District Historical Society

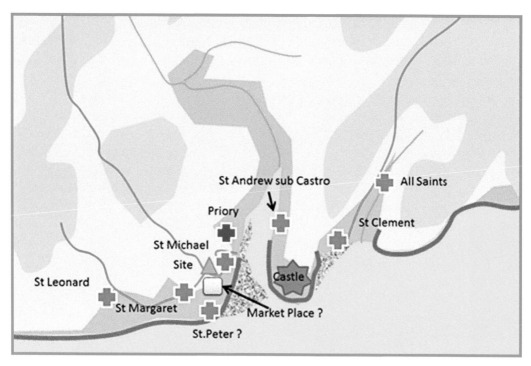

↑ 1291 ↑   ↓ 1450 ↓

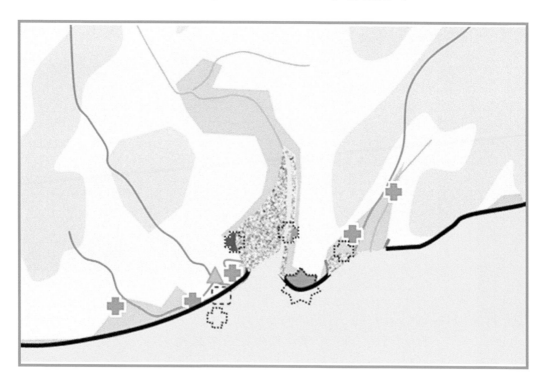

HASTINGS AND AREA BEFORE 1066

The non-entry for Hastings within the Baldslow hundred in the *Domesday Book* causes some consternation. This was not a unique situation in *Domesday*. There are a number of similar blank spaces at the start of other counties in *Domesday*, and blank spaces for Winchester and London. Where these spaces contain entries, such as for Dover in Kent, the first entry is a borough. It has been conjectured that in virtually every county there were boroughs, requiring different treatment to the standard *Domesday* recording. These were either never finally recorded, or were too big for the space left for them, or they were recorded separately and the recordings have been lost. The recording of a 'new', but obviously small, Hastings in the adjacent hundred of Guestling within the manor of Rameslie is probably our first hint that all was not well with 'old' Hastings on a hill to the west, that would have clearly been in the different hundred of Baldslow, and that a 'new' Hastings was developing in the shelter of the small Bourne valley.

Places in the Baldslow hundred, now subsumed into Hastings and St Leonards, are named in *Domesday*, such as Filsham, Hollington, 'Cortesly' and Bulverhythe. It should be noted that Filsham was a very large manor with 15 hides (1800 acres/730Ha) of productive land, and was formerly held directly by king Edward himself. Post conquest, about half this manor was directly held by the count of Eu and the rest held from him by 11 others. Filsham would appear to have supported over 100 households, and there were another 70+ families in adjacent manors, which might suggest a population of nearly 1000 in the area of the present day Hastings borough.

20 burgesses are recorded paying rent for three virgates (90 acres/36Ha) of land directly held by the Count of Eu at Bollington, which was in the area of Pebsham/Worsham, on the other side of Bulverhythe. Most of the rest of Bollington belonged to the abbey of Tréport. Were these the town burgesses of Hæstingaceastre, paying rents for nearby land?

Bexhill/Bollington between them had a recorded population of about 150 families; say 700 people; Ninfield plus Hooe had about 100 households, say 500 people. Battle pre-1066 was in the adjacent hundred of Hailesaltede (later Netherfield) with no recorded population, but there were a few dwellers in the area, at Uckham (4 households), Mountfield (11), Whatlington (9), Catsfield (13) and Ashburnham (24). Taking into account other nearby small manors and some undercounting by *Domesday* agents the whole population of the Hastings/Bexhill/Battle area at that time may have been approximately 3000.

We know that in 1086 other areas around Hastings such as Wilting and Crowhurst were still waste or recovering after the predations of 1066, also that the *'castellaria de Hastinges'* – castelry of Hastings (its direct jurisdiction) was given to the count of Eu in 1069. The castelry of Hastings must have been most of the Rape,

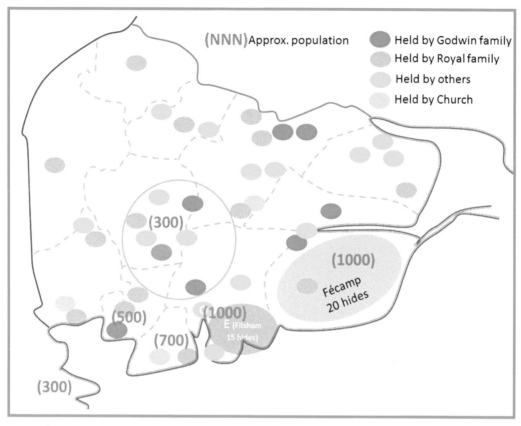

Land ownership and estimated populations in South-East Sussex pre-Conquest, by Domesday manors. Dashed lines – hundreds, the solid circular line shows the post-Conquest banlieu of Battle Abbey. Very small holdings not shown.
© Battle and District Historical Society

minus some defined holdings – for example the banlieu (estate) of Battle Abbey and also the lands held by Fécamp and Tréport abbeys. The castelry must have initially included Bexhill hundred as bishop Alric (of Selsey [pre-cursor to Chichester]) held Bexhill both before and after 1066 until 'the gift', after which 'Osbern' held it from Eu. This land was returned to the bishop of Chichester by king Henry II in 1148. The later subsidy rolls of 1296, 1327 and 1332 for both Baldslow and Guestling hundreds are unhelpful as by then Hastings was in the Cinque Ports Confederation, and the members of that set their own taxes, of which records have been lost.

It has been strongly argued that William's original pre-fabricated wooden castle at Hastings would have been somewhere nearer Bexhill, rather than on what is the present site of the stone castle of Hastings on the West Hill. The latter site in its elevated position may not have been suitable for immediate defence of the landings. The wooden castle could have been erected on the site of the old burghal enclosure, which would fit with the pictorial description on the Bayeux Tapestry and the words of the *Carmen de Hastingæ Proelio*.

The other local burgh was at Eorpeburnham, which has not been clearly identified, but is believed to have been at Castle Toll near Newenden on the Kentish border. Interestingly, king Alfred himself held an estate near this at Beckley. This burgh took the form of an 8Ha (20 acre) enclosure on a low peninsula which was defended primarily by the marshland of the former River Rother on three sides and by a broad bank and ditch on the southern side. Partial excavation of this southern ditch in 1971 showed that it was not completed in its intended form but was reduced in scale and remained unfinished. There is a strong possibility that this is the unfinished Eorpeburnham of the Burghal Hidage, mentioned in the *Anglo-Saxon Chronicle* for 892 CE as having been an incomplete fort attacked by the Danes, whose fleet of 250 ships made landfall at Appledore.

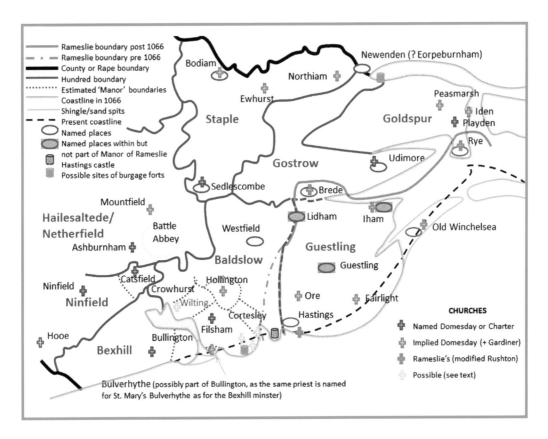

11th century places, churches and hundreds named in the text. Part of this is 'logical deduction' based on *Domesday* and other information. Boundaries of manors and the possible site of the Hastings burghal fort are particularly conjectural.

© Battle and District Historical Society

To the west, the medieval borough of Pevensey originated as a quite late Anglo-Saxon settlement and, by the mid-11th century, Pevensey was established as a significant borough. It had grown quickly as there was no significant population there around 800CE. Pevensey is referred to by name in a charter of 947, but the name is simply used to locate a saltpan. In 1054CE, a saltpan and 12 houses formed part of a local grant to the abbey of Fécamp. More significantly, *Domesday* records that Pevensey was a pre-Conquest town with 52 burgesses, with tolls to the value of 20s and port dues of 35s. When the count of Mortain was given Pevensey in about 1069CE there were only 27 burgesses, but by 1086CE there had been a rapid expansion to 110 burgesses and it was regarded as a large town.

As in the Roman period, late Saxon development must have been influenced by the shallow harbour at Pevensey which developed into a port in the late 10th and 11th centuries. Examples of significant use of the port at Pevensey include earl Godwin's arrival from Sandwich with a fleet of 42 ships in 1049 and again arriving in 1052 from Bruges, whilst he was exiled, when he augmented his fleet by taking ships from Pevensey.

ARCHÆOLOGY

Some evidence about south-east Sussex in pre-Norman times can be gleaned from archaeological evidence and we can briefly look at these before moving on to the major issues in the final period before 1066.

Bexhill to Hastings Link Road sites

In 2013/15 extensive findings were made by Oxford Archaeology (assisted by HAARG) in the Combe Haven area during road construction. There is extensive evidence of prehistoric and historic period settlements. Very large numbers of flint scatters were identified, from the mesolithic period, but it is not yet known whether these imply hunting, base camps, processing camps, or just casual stops. From the neolithic period a possible causeway and a gapped ring ditch have been found, and dating from the Bronze Age 'burnt mounds', comprising burnt stones on the wetland edges. The latter are associated with other artefacts, and each mound with a square pit and a round pit, channels and post holes. Dating from the early Roman period (*c.* 150CE), in a different area, is a large bloomery (iron works) with many furnaces and a huge bank of slag. There were also, at other sites, pits with the imprint of wattle and daub linings, containing traces of charcoal and charred cereal grain. It is tempting to think of these as for storage and hence as part of settlements but we cannot yet be sure. From the Roman period, Samian and Rhenish pottery fragments were unearthed.

There was also a 76mm high small Saxon pot. Whether the original items belonged to travellers or settlers, we do not yet know. Finally Upper Wilting has been confirmed as a Saxon manor of the 7th–8th century.

The area has obviously been found to be rich in very early periods and Roman period finds and there is also clear evidence of Romano-British farming. What has not been found are any metal artefacts dating from before 1840, nor anything associated with 1066. Analysis of all the materials and sites found will clearly take many years. Unconfirmed features proposed by, and scattered finds of Austin and other amateur archaeologists, whilst seeking to confirm alternative interpretations about the Norman landings, may actually be related to the above professional archaeological findings.

Eastbourne

Eastbourne also has archaeological finds mixing different eras. Recent excavations have revealed some 150 skeletons, of which eleven have been analysed. With one exception they date from the fifth to early eighth centuries. One had fine Saxon grave goods; others had beads; some had bone deformities or stress arising from hard manual labour. Remarkably one had survived an amputation of the left hand, suggesting an organised settlement. Some of Eastbourne's burials have a Christian alignment; others do not. Some might have been Saxons, others from the European tribes which preceded them as invaders. A reminder of the international nature of the Roman Empire is provided by recent Eastbourne excavations, in which was found the first-century skeleton of a young woman, born in the area but with her ethnic origins from sub-Saharan Africa.

What do the local hoards tell us?

Hoards have been found at Ashburnham, Sedlescombe, Ore, Mountfield, Hastings, St Leonards and Burwash. All were deliberate burials. The *Sedlescombe Hoard*, found in 1876, comprised some 2000 silver coins from the reign of Edward the Confessor (1041–1066), notably from the Hastings and Romney mints but from many other mints around the country, a reminder of the extent of exchequer infrastructure established by the Saxons. Scholars surmise that this hoard might have been intended to pay Saxon soldiers after the battle of Hastings; or it might have been buried by a merchant who hoped to retrieve it later. The latter interpretation would remind us of the richness of England in the late Saxon period, a factor not lost on William.

At Mountfield in 1863 a Bronze Age torc, chain and rings were found after a plough went through an old wooden box. The remains dated to the period 1400–1100BCE are in the British Museum today – only some of the originals were recovered after they had been sold off at the time. In the absence of other evidence or corroborating context, it is difficult to draw inferences about Sussex at the time, but this hoard may have been associated with a burial.

The so-called *High Weald Hoard* featured on temporary loan to the Battle Museum of Local History in 2013. It was discovered in the Burwash area in 2006 by a metal detectorist. It comprised several thousand coins, some silver, all from the second half of the third century, as demonstrated by the Roman emperors' heads. We can only speculate what happened. At this period in Sussex's history, there was relative stability before the invasions of the Jutes/Saxons, so sudden collapse of social order does not seem to be a reason for the burial. Another hoard of 50–60 Roman coins was found together with five or six broken pots whilst digging foundations for a house on the west side of Warrior Square, St Leonards.

Larger Roman sites

Bodiam: An extensive Romano-British settlement, lay adjacent to the River Rother where it is crossed by the Roman road. The site has yielded quantities of 1st to mid-3rd century pottery, glassware, coins and tile, scattered over a fairly wide area. In particular CLBR stamped tiles have been found and it is thought that there was a Classis Britannica river port here.

Brede (Chitcombe): This very large site yielded large quantities of pottery ranging from late 1st century to early 3rd. Remains of masonry can still be seen on the ground surface today, together with numerous tile fragments, indicating the presence of a substantial building. As seen on the Roman bloomery sites map, large workings have been found on several sites around Brede and this building was probably associated with this. There may have been a small river port here but this is not proven.

Sedlescombe (Footlands): This is another large ironworking site, believed worked before Roman times, but then greatly expanded to be the third largest production site in the eastern Weald. Huge quantities of slag were removed from this site for roadmaking in the 1800s. The site was linked both north and south to Margary's Roman road route by gently inclined slag paved roads 6 to 7.5 metres wide.

Sedlescombe (Oaklands Park): This is a smaller site almost adjacent to the old main Roman road

Others: There are also very many smaller Roman sites in south-east Sussex and individual Roman coins have been found scattered all over the area. There is an excellent listing of these in the monographs of the Romney Marsh Research Trust (RMRT).

WHY DID WILLIAM LAND HERE?

The most famous use of the landing places of south-east Sussex was the arrival of the fleet of William, duke of Normandy on the morning of 28th or 29th September 1066, after an overnight crossing from St Valéry. It may not have been the first-choice landing place, but the area was well known in Normandy thanks to the ownership of lands in south-east Sussex by the abbey of Fécamp. So William's choice of landing site in 1066 was Pevensey and when William returned to Normandy in March 1067, for the first time since his invasion, he did so, symbolically, from Pevensey.

Today Pevensey is clearly not a port or tidal estuary, but in 1066 it was a clear choice once the two issues which confuse interpretations of what happened in the area in 1066 are understood. These are the status of the manor of Rameslie in the *Domesday Book*, and the coastal changes.

First, the manor of Rameslie had been given by king Cnut, at queen Emma's request, to the abbey of Fécamp in Normandy, which gave the manor both political and strategic importance, as its geography would have been well known in Normandy. 'Rameslie'/'Rammesleagh' presents us with the conundrum of the words used both in pre-Conquest royal grants and in *Domesday*.

In grants Rameslie is described as an estate. It is described as a manor, not a town in *Domesday*. It should therefore best be accepted as the name of the manor or estate alone, with no need to search for a 'lost town'. As we have seen above, the early pre-Conquest charters issued by Saxon or Mercian kings in favour of French abbeys still offer problems of interpretation for the student of local history. Offa and his successors may have given local lands to St Denis of Paris. But the most important abbey involved was the Norman Abbey of Fécamp, a favoured foundation of the Norman dukes, which was given land by Cnut. The extensive holding of Rameslie which included Rye, Old Winchelsea and at least part of present day Hastings, five churches and a hundred saltpans, was a grant first planned by Æthelred II, but not actually made until Cnut's reign.

The link was queen Emma, second wife both of Æthelred and then of Cnut. Emma was the daughter of Richard I, duke of Normandy, and she was the sister of Richard II, William the Conqueror's grandfather. Æthelred had been deposed by Cnut's father Sweyn in 1013, but Sweyn soon died, and Æthelred came back but died himself in 1016. Cnut, son of Sweyn, then fought Æthelred's son, Edmund Ironside, for the throne of England. When he finally achieved this, he married Emma, who already had two sons by Æthelred: Edward and Alfred (Alfred murdered it is believed on the orders of Harefoot by earl Godwin's men; Edward to become king Edward the Confessor) and a daughter Godgifu/Goda, who had all been sent for their own safety to grow up in Normandy.

A charter of Cnut in 1017 grants to Fécamp an estate at *'Rammesleagh'* with its harbour, *'as promised by Æthelred'*. A second charter (of 1032) confirmed by

Harthacnut adds an estate at Brede and ⅔ of the tithes of Winchelsea. The latter may not be genuine, but there is no doubt that the church at Brede was started by Fécamp.

Domesday says *Fécamp holds of the king three manors, Rameslie, Steyning, and Bury*, all in Sussex. This was 'ding-dong' ownership as Steyning had been usurped from Fécamp by the Godwin family prior to 1066. Earl Godwin had also seized some of Pevensey from the abbey of Saint-Denis in 1042. Abbot John of Fécamp petitioned in 1054 for the return of Steyning and was fobbed off with the return of a saltpan and 12 houses at Pevensey, and some farmland at Eastbourne and Langley, all very probably the former property of St Denis. But even this gift might have had future consequences as Fécamp gained extra knowledge of the Sussex coast. There is no evidence to suggest that the Godwins also usurped Rameslie as has been claimed.

The stolen lands were restored in due course to Fécamp by William, who took some of Hastings (to add to the castelry?) in exchange for which he gave the monks Bury in western Sussex, which had previously belonged to countess Goda, Edward's sister. The large Rameslie manor, which included 20 hides (2400acres, just under 1000Ha) of productive land, was mainly in Guestling Hundred and also included Rye (in Goldspur hundred) and Brede (in Gostrow hundred), but excluded Guestling, Udimore, Iham (including what is now 'new' Winchelsea) and part of Lidham. It also originally extended to include some of Hastings west of the Priory valley. *Domesday* in 1086 only records the Old Town area of present Hastings: *The Abbot of Fécamp holds Rameslie from the King, and held it from King Edward. Then it answered for 20 hides now for 17 ½ hides (2100 acres/850 Ha) … 5 churches which pay 64s, 100 salt houses at £8 15s … In this manor is a new borough; 64 Burgesses pay* £8 less 2s. *Value of the whole manor before 1066 £34 now the Abbot's lordship £50, the men's 44s.* So the estate had gained in value since 1066, but had lost 300 productive acres (120Ha). When Hastings Castle was built, Fécamp lost the area to 'the castelry', granted to the Count of Eu, so these 300 acres must have included the West Hill of Hastings, where the castle remains stand, and both sides of the Priory valley and the small port, which area is now the town centre of modern Hastings. It is noted that Filsham, a large manor in Baldslow hundred, was held directly by King Edward before the Conquest with 15 hides (1800acres, 700Ha). Was Filsham the manor containing Hæstingaceastre? It was the property of the king TRE (TRE =the time of king Edward).

The harbour of Rameslie manor must have been the small one at Old Winchelsea, and the new borough with 64 burgesses must have been Rye, which later had a mint, but is not specifically mentioned by name (just the 'new borough'). It cannot have been 'new' Hastings as this only had four burgesses, and the other burgesses of Hastings had interests at Bullington, near Bexhill. Rye's Anglo-Saxon name was *Atter ie* ['on the island'], later shortened to Rie. As the *Domesday Book* did not change English place names, it's just an oddity that the 'new borough' is not named. Rameslie was clearly a valuable estate, with a developing port (Old Winchelsea) on the Channel coast and 100 saltpans, more than the rest of Sussex put together. It is interesting that the later Manor of Brede covered much of the same area, minus Winchelsea and Rye, which had been removed from the ownership of Fécamp by king Henry III in 1248. There is an interesting discussion about this in the *Victoria History of the County of Sussex* Vol.9 (1937).

As well as the issues surrounding 'Rameslie', the coast has changed significantly as described in Chapter 2, with huge changes occurring between the 13th and 15th centuries. Longshore drift of shingle, and erosion of the local clay and sandstone headlands, of Galley Hill, Bo-peep, White Rock, West Hill and the massive cliffs beyond Old Town Hastings to Pett Level and many great storms changed the coast line dramatically.

The openings of the shallow harbours became fully or partially blocked by shingle drift and various estimates are that the cliffs have eroded between 300 to 800 metres (1000–2600 feet) since 1066, or as much as one kilometre (just over half a mile) of headlands since Roman times. In addition, the White Rock outcrop was physically removed in 1834/5, as was a lower hill below Hastings Castle called the 'Gun garden'. Because of this, whole coastal communities such as large chunks of the manor of Rameslie, and defensive features such as the burgh of Haestingaceastre (if it existed), may have been lost.

The small shallow port west of Pevensey shore fort known as the Crumbles was lost to shingle drift, and secondary to the same drift, the previously good entrance to Pevensey harbour was impeded. Similarly there was probable partial blocking of the entrance of the old small port at Bulverhythe adding to Hastings' struggle to fulfil its duties as a Cinque Port. Later inning (reclamation of the edges of marshland) for farming would lead to marked loss of water volume, and thus power, of the tidal scours which had kept the residual shallow harbours of Pevensey, Winchelsea and Rye navigable, and they gradually silted up with the results that can be seen today.

The best recorded loss is of Old Winchelsea (formerly known as OE *Wines cesel ie = Protector shingle isle* and ME *Gwent-chesel-ey = Shingle Isle on the level*, both good descriptions) which stood on a large shingle and sand spit extending eastwards from Cliff End at Pett Level and positioned at an inlet of the huge Rother Camber which led to the Brede, Tillingham and Rother estuaries and smaller inland ports.

The thirteenth century was a time of recurrent great storms in the English Channel. Old Winchelsea, on its shingle bank and gradually losing the protection of the eroding Fairlight cliffs, was under siege by the sea. In 1236 Old Winchelsea was inundated. On 1 October 1250, the town was almost destroyed, and again on 14 January 1252. It was finally destroyed by the great storm of 4 February 1287. Old Winchelsea was wiped from the map, the Rother outlet at Old Romney was blocked and the River Rother changed course to have its new outlet at Rye, which would in due time allow Rye to become the local predominant port.

Looking at the evidence provided by the RMRT it is possible that the only safe way to access the Brede estuary in 1066 would have been via the Rother outlet at Old

Romney. It is not clear if there was any breach at that time in the large shingle bar on which Old Winchelsea stood and that extended from Cliff End at Pett Level towards Broomhill on the far side of what is now Rye Bay. A breach at that time could only have been sustained by the small tidal scour from the Brede and Tillingham rivers, which are both much smaller than the Rother which was still exiting at Old Romney.

If Ordericus Vitalis correctly records the return of William from Dieppe *'with a south wind'* in December 1067 *'to a harbour called Winchelsea'* there may have been a small port at Old Winchelsea in 1067. But even in 1191 when the breach, if persisting, would have been wider, Howden does not describe Winchelsea as a 'good' port and says that that Rye was *'up the Winchelse inlet'* – which would have meant following the small Brede/Tillingham channels. This suggests that Winchelsea's heyday was indeed short, as Eddison concludes in her RMRT Monograph *Catastrophic Changes: A Multidisciplinary Study of the Evolution of the Barrier Beaches of Rye Bay.*

Even the first settlers ... left different genetic traces on the east and west coasts of Britain. That difference was merely added to by subsequent migrations across the North Sea.'

Stephen Oppenheimer,
The Origins of the British, 2006

4

FOUNDATIONS OF ENGLAND

Keith Foord

T he English and the Normans fought a bloody and decisive battle in East Sussex in 1066. Thousands of men were slaughtered during a daylong conflict during one fine day in October. One leader had everything to lose. The other had nowhere to retreat to except into the sea. So it was definitely a case of winner takes all. The battle was fought between king Harold Godwinson of England and duke William of Normandy, with an intensity and ferocity that was generated by unfulfilled perceived promises, oath-breaking and deceptions. It was a battle that was to lead to English landholding and influence being significantly reduced and replaced by a Norman-French system of lordship and vassalage, representing the two sides of a bond of mutual loyalty and service, plus payments of cash or labour that reflected the lord's continued rights over property. The result, that we can appreciate today, was the redefinition of a mainly Anglo-Saxon culture that had begun long before king Alfred, had had significant Viking (mainly Danish) influences, and had become England, but would become changed by king William after his Conquest. This process is called 'acculturation'.

The period 1000BCE–1BCE is historically a controversial time. There was dramatic cultural change in Europe, dominated by the emergence of the Roman Empire. In Britannia (basically England and Wales) it was a period of profound social and economic change, which saw the end of the prehistoric cycle of the neolithic and Bronze Ages and entry into the Iron Age.

Traditionally we have thought of the original pre-Roman Iron Age 'native' culture of Britannia as having 'Celtic' homogeneity, which was first disrupted by the Romans, then Angles, Saxons and Jutes (the 'Anglo-Saxons'), then Danes and Norwegians (the 'Vikings'), and then in 1066 by the Norman-French – themselves of mixed Viking and Frankish descent.

In the island which they named Britannia the Romans found a mosaic of many named tribes (see Map 1). The languages spoken by these tribes mostly had some resemblances to those believed spoken in ancient continental south-west Gaul, but the languages of south-east Britain may have been more akin to Belgic, a west-

Germanic language. So the tribes of Britannia, although they had 'Celtic' traits, should not be called collectively 'Celts' – a name which as far as Britain is concerned was an invention of the 18th century.

THE BRITISH/IRISH BASELINE

The forebears of these tribes were late palaeolithic/early mesolithic individuals or families who had moved northwards after the Last Glacial Maximum, approximately 15,000 years ago. These tiny groups still contribute over 50% to the modern gene pool. After 4000BCE they mixed with later neolithic migrants, mostly originally from central Gaul with others from Belgica and Germania (northern France & northern Germany). These neolithic groups were still small but were more genetically varied, and added another 20–25% to the modern gene pools of all north-west Europe. Nearly all these peoples had crossed the land bridge before Britain had become isolated from mainland Europe, although there were also some later migrations around the coasts. The situation was much the same in Ireland and Scotland except that there had been more, even later, maritime migration from south-west France and northern Iberia into Ireland, with some secondary migration of these peoples, which the Romans called Scotti, from Scotia in northern Ireland to south-west Scotland, plus to a lesser extent into north-west and south-west Wales – both at about the same time as the Anglo-Saxon migrations into England. There was also a little early maritime migration from Norway into Orkney, Shetland and north-east Scotland.

THE (MAINLY) ENGLISH BASELINE

In this chapter, the focus is mainly on the development of England, but has to include some neighbouring events. Echoes of some pre-Roman tribal gene structures may still be represented today by surprisingly localised, but internally homogeneous, genetic clusters, each with its own unique spectrum of genes, within the south-west, north-east, north-west and the Welsh borders of England, and also in west and north Wales (Map 1).

In pre-Roman Sussex and Kent were to be found the Cantiaci and Regni peoples. Any tribal genetic variation in these areas, as in a large area of England, may now be hidden by a higher proportion of incoming similar and/or new genes brought in by the larger proportion of migrants from the east settling in these areas rather than further west. So now much of England is represented by one big homogeneous genetic zone (yellow on Map 1) – although this large zone does have differences from the smaller clusters.

For thousands of years people have been moving into and out of England,

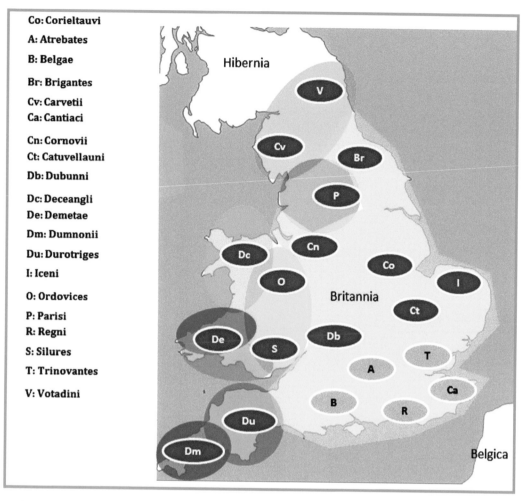

Co: Corieltauvi
A: Atrebates
B: Belgae
Br: Brigantes
Cv: Carvetii
Ca: Cantiaci
Cn: Cornovii
Ct: Catuvellauni
Db: Dubunni
Dc: Deceangli
De: Demetae
Dm: Dumnonii
Du: Durotriges
I: Iceni
O: Ordovices
P: Parisi
R: Regni
S: Silures
T: Trinovantes
V: Votadini

Map 1: The pre-Roman mainly 'Celtic trait' tribes of England and Wales in the first century CE and zones of genetic homogeneity in circa 1885.
© Battle and District Historical Society

The approximate locations of the major tribes which may have spoken 'Celtic trait' languages are in dark grey; possibly Belgic speaking tribes are in light grey. Areas of distinct but internally homogeneous genetic clusters are superimposed in various colours showing some concordance with single or two tribe areas.

Tribal distributions are mainly after Tacitus' and Ptolemy's writings on Britain. Genetic clusters are simplified from Leslie et al. (2015) who analysed genes from individuals having all four grandparents born in rural areas within 80 km (50 miles) of each other – giving the genetic patterns of their grandparents in circa 1885 before the major population movements of the 20th and 21st centuries.

sometimes in large migrations, but there has always been the baseline underlying genetic continuity of the earliest populations as described above. Overall, of the modern gene pool, this is 80% in Wales and Cornwall/Devon, and 68% in England (other than Cornwall/Devon). It has been estimated that after the neolithic period no one migration event (pre-Roman, Roman, Anglo-Saxon, Viking or Norman-French) contributed much more than another 5% and certainly less than 10% to the modern gene pool.

Although the genetic changes since the start of the Common Era were smaller than those of neolithic and prior eras, there have been huge shifts of culture, social structure, language and identity in the last two millennia. This fits with modern archaeological and historical studies which suggest that the picture of hordes of invaders physically displacing and ethnically cleansing their predecessors is quite wrong.

CULTURAL AND SOCIAL CHANGE

By 300CE, almost everyone in 'Britannia' was, in civil terms, 'Roman', even though the overwhelming majority were still of indigenous descent, and still mostly speaking pre-Roman native dialects. As there was now an entity called Britannia, we can call the people collectively 'Romano-Britons', and can examine the genetic, cultural and social effects on them of the next migrations, particularly those of Anglo-Saxons (from *c.* 400CE) and then Vikings from the east (from *c.* 700CE), plus the much smaller immigrations of Scotti into west Wales, Cumbria and north-west England at about the same time, plus later changes. The 'migration' maps below actually chart cultural changes, rather than mass displacements of natives – the 'acculturation'. Where the new immigrants did not physically spread, the culture of the pre-existing peoples and their localised genetic homogeneity persisted. Within the new Anglo-Saxon 'kingdoms' of what would become England, the local populations of Romano-Britons and the new immigrant Angles, Saxons and Jutes integrated and intermarried. The Anglo-Saxons became dominant socially and culturally and the developing 'Germanic' language came almost entirely from the north German plains (see Map 2).

The new evolving language was poorly compatible with the Gaulish non-Germanic 'Celtic trait' native languages, but better compatible with the west-Germanic 'Belgic trait' tongues. This may explain the paucity of 'Celtic trait' words in the language that would develop to become Old English, although numbers of 'Celtic trait' words persist in names of rivers and names of larger geographic features. Place names were passed on rather than changed.

Then when the Vikings arrived and settled the same thing happened (Map 3). Most of the established population, now of mixed Romano-Briton/Angle origin, with a developing 'west-Germanic' culture stayed where they were and took the changes

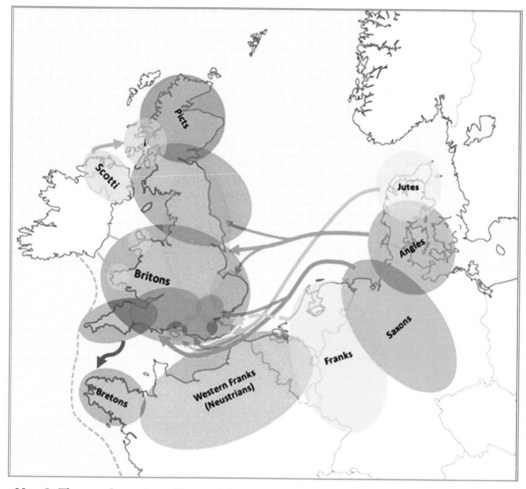

Map 2: The acculturation effects of the 'Anglo-Saxon' migrations. A possible Frankish influence on Kent and East Sussex is shown as a green dashed arrow. The influence of the Scotti on the western fringes is in yellow, with late coastal migration to Ireland from SW France as a dashed line. Note also some probable concurrent reverse coastal migrations of Romano-Britons to Brittany. © Battle and District Historical Society

in their stride. A Danish 'north-Germanic' culture and social structure started to influence these areas, and was strong enough to create the zone called the Danelaw, and new Old Norse (ON) 'north-Germanic' words entered Old English. Old Norse 'borrowings' in modern English are often commonly used words in modern English, including many with the first letters 'sc/sk' and 'th' and words for animals, birds, natural features and nautical terms. A possible major contribution of ON was to change pronouns and shift English away from an ending-based grammar, to a modern language relying more on particles and word order to carry the grammar. The north-Germanic ON language interacting with the very similar west-Germanic OE during the 7th–9th centuries had the effect of 'rubbing off' most of the many OE case endings, as the Danes could often understand the OE stem word without translation and could ignore the English grammatical endings. Soon the word endings and the genders which were a source of confusion disappeared. The west-German verb-final constructions were also lost in favour of north-German word order. English appears much closer to modern Scandinavian languages than modern German in terms of grammar.

Genetically the new incomers introduced another 5% or so of new, mainly 'Danish', genes which were mainly distributed in north-eastern, eastern and central England. The Saxon and Jutish south was strong enough at first to resist the Danish influence. Curiously, the modern genetic pattern is similar in south-eastern and south-central England where the Viking cultural influence was lower. It is postulated that the Jutes may have introduced 'Danish' genes earlier, during the Anglo-Saxon migrations and/or there was a later contribution of such genes from the Norman-

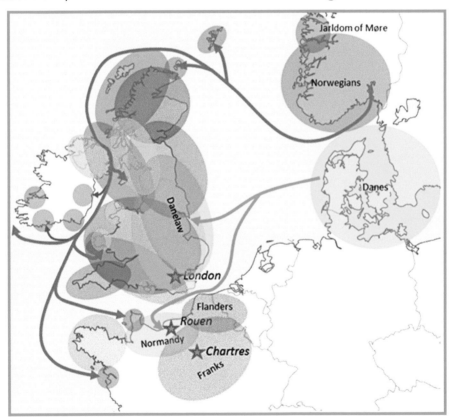

Map 3: The acculturation effects of the 'Viking' migrations. This map includes the effects on northern France which are important to the future of England. The large Frankish kingdom was simultaneously changing and fragmenting.
© Battle and District Historical Society

French who were partly of Danish origin. This may have fortuitously re-balanced southern England (except Cornwall/Devon) to match the 'Danelaw' genetic mix.

The European ancestry groups from which come the average modern white English person living in the yellow zone of Map 1 is descended are in approximate terms: northern France (36%), north Germany (26%), Denmark (11%), south-west/ central France (9%), and Belgium–Netherlands (9%) Norway–Sweden (8%) and Iberia (1%), but the constituent genes of these groups had originally come from even further away. Generally north German and Norwegian/Swedish influences are lower and SW French influences higher in SW England; French influences are lower and Scandinavian and north-German influences higher in west Yorkshire and to its west; and in the north of England northern and south-west/central French influences are lower and Norwegian and Swedish influences higher (but not as much as one might think). For much fuller details see Leslie *et al.*

The zones of degrees of genetic variance might have remained preserved in the west, which had been less genetically affected by the Anglo-Saxon and Viking ingressions, but in time they did not dodge the cultural and social changes of those migrations.

Whilst the Normans would introduce even smaller genetic change, the cultural, social and language changes would be significant and following the Norman conquest, middle English (late 12th to late 15th centuries), then modern English would develop.

THINKING OF ENGLAND

'England' probably started to think of itself as such by about 900CE, but this was not cemented until the mid-10th century. Then, after Cnut's invasion and coronation in 1016, and the rapprochement of Danes and English, the two halves of England fully melded into the English who fought at Hastings, although cultural differences were still apparent, and some even persist to the present day. Let us now have a look at some high level overviews reviewing the physical elements of the Anglo-Saxon and Viking immigrations.

ANGLO-SAXONS

Following the departure of the Romans in the very early 5th century, Picts from Scotland, Scotti via south-west Scotland, and Jutes and Angles from across the North Sea began raiding into England. Some Saxons may have settled in Wessex before the Romans left, but later more came into western Sussex, Essex and Wessex, and the Jutes ('Kentings') moved into Kent, the Isle of Wight and south Hampshire, and probably also the Hæstingas area. These are shown schematically by the arrows in Map 2.

The native Romano-Britons are believed to have at first recruited north-Germanic mercenaries to settle in eastern parts of England to help them defend their lands, but the mercenaries liked what they found rather too much, and Angles started to immigrate and settle in increasing numbers into East Anglia, Lincolnshire and Northumbria. As the migrant population and their offspring increased in number from the mid-6th century they changed the culture of the areas they inhabited, as discussed above. This cultural expansion was not without some physical resistance from the Romano-Britons, and numbers of battles are recorded such as at Mount Badon, Chester, Old Sarum, Barbury Hill and Dyrham.

Saxons were a tribe that came from a wide area in what is now northern Germany. These people are mentioned in the *Geographia* by Ptolemy which was written about 150CE, and there are further Roman comments that mention the Saxons as being thieves and pirates. Clearly they were a thorn in the flesh of the Roman administration of Britain. The Angles came from the region of southern Denmark where it meets Germany. The Jutes are the least well known, but are believed to have come from Jutland in northern Denmark, although there are also those who argue that they were of Frankish origin from the middle Rhine zone, and Frankish influence has been found in Kent. The Venerable Bede, a monk in the monastery of Jarrow in Northumbria, raised the concept of the 'English' people in 732, when he wrote his *History of the*

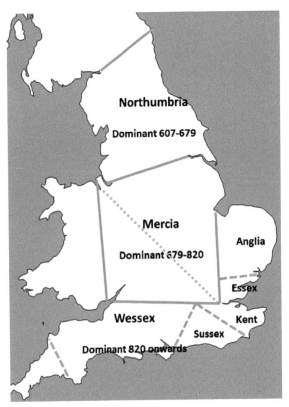

Map 4: The Anglo-Saxon kingdoms, their dominance, and the future division of the Danelaw (dashed green line)

English Church and People. He referred to those who lived in lowland Britain, whether Saxons, Jutes or Angles, as English. However the concept did not become widespread until about 900CE.

In 450–590 England gradually became divided into seven major Anglo-Saxon 'kingdoms' – the 'heptarchy ' of Northumbria, Mercia, Wessex (the three largest) and Sussex, Kent, Essex and East Anglia (Map 4), but smaller kingdoms or sub-kingdoms, such as Hæstingas(south-east Sussex), Wihtwara(Isle of Wight) and Surridge(Surrey) existed.

Initially Northumbria was the most powerful, then in time Mercia and then Wessex, with the house of Wessex slowly transforming to become kings of England.

VIKINGS

The Anglo-Saxons in turn were threatened from the 8th century onwards by 'Vikings' from Scandinavia. From sometime in the 700s, Vikings exploded out of Scandinavia in their sleek ships, extending their forays to Russia, the western Mediterranean, Ireland, Scotland, England, the Western and Northern Isles, the shores of North-western Europe, Iceland, Greenland, Labrador and Newfoundland (Map 5). It has been considered that this was due to overpopulation, but it seems it was actually mainly driven more by greed and the desire to have better farmland. They were also traders and were happy to just trade, but when they found neighbours who were weak they exploited this knowledge. If they met significant opposition they would normally look elsewhere for easier pickings. They were an interesting combination of merchants, settlers and pirates. When they attacked militarily they had one objective – to increase their wealth.

Via rivers and portages (moving ships overland between river systems) they extended south to the Caspian and Black Seas and reached Constantinople (Istanbul). They may even have reached as far as Virginia on the eastern seaboard of America. Certainly they reached Newfoundland, Labrador and the mouth of the St Lawrence river and 'Vinland' – which is thought to have been somewhere in New England, which was as far north as wild grapes could have been found.

The influence of the intrusion of Vikings, mostly Danes, into English social and political life in the 9th to 11th centuries was profound, both directly and indirectly. Other chapters show this in some more detail. Let us say here that without this deep influence on both England and France, the events of 1066 would not have happened as they did, although we cannot presume that an invasion from the other side of the English Channel, or once more from across the North Sea, would never have happened sometime in the 11th century.

The Gokstad ship at the Viking Ship Museum in Oslo, Norway 'Gokstadskipet1' by Karamell. Licensed under CC BY-SA 2.5 via Wikimedia Commons

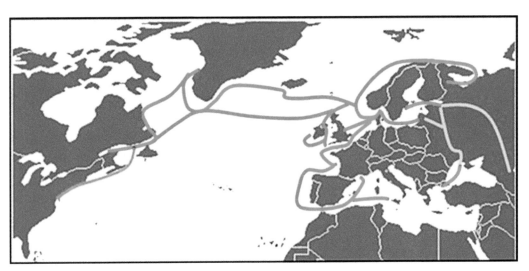

Map 5: The extent of Viking exploration. Red lines represent voyages, blue lines possible voyages and yellow lines portages to various rivers such as the Danube.
© Battle and District Historical Society

Viking raids on the British and Irish Isles began late in the 8th century. Danes invaded and settled in eastern and north-eastern areas of what would become England and Norwegians moved into the Western and Northern Isles, Isle of Man, North Scotland, parts of Ireland and north-west England, superimposing their cultures on the local populations. The Anglo-Saxons of the south and south-west in Mercia and Wessex held them off (Map 3), but in 870–871 a huge force of Danes invaded and gradually extended their influence. This 'Great Army' even briefly dominated all the English kingdoms for a few months in 878, after which Alfred the Great gradually pushed them back, so that between 884–954 rule in England was shared between Anglo-Saxon law and the Danelaw (divided NW to SE generally following the alignment of Watling Street – the great Roman road from London to Anglesey (Maps 3 and 4). Although Alfred was recognised as the king of all the English not under Danish rule Viking raids continued. There was one particularly large raid of 250 ships landing not far away from Battle at Appledore, Kent, in 892.

It took no fewer than four more English kings – Edward (901–924), Athelstan (924–939), Edmund (939–946) and finally Eadred (946–955) to remove the Viking threat, and restore Anglo-Saxon rule across the whole of England. Even then elements of Danish law persisted in Northumbria, Anglia and the East Midlands for another couple of hundred years, and the Vikings did not really go away, as many had settled, put down roots and intermarried with the local population.

The relief from Viking attacks only lasted 26 years. Initially king Æthelred II tried to pay them to go away, and even married Emma, daughter of duke Richard I of Normandy, in the hope that the Normans would help to see them off (to no avail). After paying the Vikings several times he foolishly ordered a massacre of those who stayed. Unfortunately one of those caught up in this ethnic cleansing was the sister of the Danish king, Sweyn. Sweyn took revenge and attacked England aggressively, eventually forcing Æthelred II to flee to Normandy in 1014.

VIKINGS BECOME PERMANENT

Sweyn became king of England by conquest, but died suddenly just five weeks later. Æthelred II was called back, but he, in turn, soon died in early 1016. After many battles all over England in 1015–16, one of Æthelred's sons by his first wife, Edmund (Ironside) briefly co-reigned with Sweyn's son Cnut during 1016, but Edmund died (probably murdered) in November. Cnut ruled England from 1016–1035, and divided his English kingdom into four powerful earldoms: Northumbria, Mercia, Wessex and East Anglia. Later he also became king of both Denmark and Norway, so he had a North Sea empire. He initially ruled Wessex directly, but placed regents in the other earldoms as well as in both Norway and Denmark. Later he appointed Godwin, a thegn from Sussex, to be earl of Wessex (Chapter 10). The fuller stories about Cnut, his sons by his first and second wives, and his second wife Emma are explored in more detail in Chapters 7 and 8, but before proceeding to discuss the early Norman dukes in the next chapter, it is necessary to explain a little more here.

On Cnut's death in 1035 his kingdoms were nominally split between two sons that he had sired by two wives. Harthacnut got Denmark plus Wessex, and Harold (Harefoot) got Mercia, Anglia and Northumbria. Harthacnut was pinned down defending Denmark against the Norwegians and their aggressive new young king Magnus. So Harold I (Harefoot) actually ruled England including Wessex where he was regent for a couple of years. He then ruled all England in his own right until he too died just two years later.

Meanwhile Harefoot had banished Emma, his stepmother, who had tried to preserve Wessex for Harthacnut, and whom he believed was plotting against him. She went to Flanders as Normandy was in some turmoil at the time (see Chapter 11). When Harold I died, Harthacnut was asked to become king and he, Emma and later his half-brother Edward returned to England.

Harthacnut only survived two years, and Edward (later to be called 'the Confessor') became king, restoring the West-Saxon (or Alfred's) line. Edward had spent many years in exile in Normandy, his brother Alfred had been murdered by Harold Harefoot's men, aided and abetted by earl Godwin, and he trusted Normans rather more than Godwin and his sons. Edward the Confessor's reign soon witnessed his Norman advisors achieving power and influence at Court. He remained deeply suspicious of the powerful, able and ruthless Godwin family, but he tried to contain them inside the ruling circle and even married earl Godwin's daughter, Edith.

Edward died childless just after New Year 1066. His closest related potential heir had been his half-nephew Edward Ætheling, (a grandson of Æthelred II by Aelgifu, and son of Edmund Ironside), who had lived nearly forgotten in Hungary but had been persuaded to come to England at Edward's request. Unfortunately he died soon after arriving in England, but left an underage potential family heir, Edgar, his half-great nephew.

Besides the young Edgar Ætheling, there were three other contestants for the throne of England. The first, duke William of Normandy, was a first cousin once removed to Edward via Edward's mother, Emma, who was William's great-aunt. The second, Harold Godwinson, was brother-in-law to Edward. Some have tried to prove that he had descent from Æthelred I, king of Wessex, a brother of Alfred the Great – but there is no record of any such claim in 1066 and the lineage seems improbable. The last, Harald Hardrada, believed himself to be Cnut's heir.

5

ROLLO, NORMANDY AND ITS DUKES

Keith Foord

So what about the Normans? How did the Vikings who settled in Normandy become Normans, and just what was Duke William's family background?

EARLY VIKING ATTACKS ON FRANCE

The early attacks by Vikings on what is now France, then Neustria – part of the kingdom of the Franks – started just after the attacks on Wessex (Map 3, Chapter 4), but Charlemagne and then his successor Louis the Pious had set up reasonably successful defences on the coast and on the large rivers, such as the Seine. These held the Vikings at bay at first, but from 840 domestic unrest set in amongst the Franks and defences weakened. The Vikings kept probing and sailed up the Somme, Seine, Loire and Garonne, just as they had the Thames, the Frome, the Humber and its tributaries, and the rivers that emptied in to the Wash.

In 841 Rouen on the Seine was razed, and in 843–4 Vikings overwintered on the Isle of Noirmoutier, near the mouth of the Loire. In 845 the Danes penetrated via the Seine to Paris, and then Charles the Bald, king of West Francia, paid them off. As always they returned time and time again, and in 858–862 a 'great army' stayed in the lower Seine area.

They gave France a break between 867–878 whilst they were preoccupied in England, but they returned and, as in England, they plundered deeper into the land. Then they resorted to the extraction of 'danegeld' which Charles the Bald paid no less than six times, with the amounts escalating. In 885–6 they made a massive raid on Paris, it is said with 700 longships and 40,000 men, and they besieged the city for eleven months. This time the Emperor, Charles the Fat paid them off, to the disgust of Count Odo who had commanded the Paris garrison.

Finally they obtained land, first in small pockets (for example the Norwegians established a zone around the Loire estuary, which they held for 18 years or so), but these were mostly temporary, apart from Normandy, which we shall look at below.

ROLLO (HRÓLFR/ROLF/ROU) THE VIKING:
born *c.* 846, held NORMANDY 911–*c.* 927

The story of Rollo (the Latin version of his name) is obscured in history, but has been described, saga-like, by Dudo, canon of the church of St Quentin. Unfortunately, Christiansen, a very good historian and the translator of Dudo into English, wrote: '*Dudo is not a reliable source for the early history of the Normans; nor did he know of any; nor do we*'. This is not a promising start for a history, but Norwegian and Icelandic historians, using Scandinavian sagas, have identified a Viking called Rollo as being Ganger Hrólfr (*Hrólfr, the Walker*), a son of Ragnvald Eysteinsson, Jarl of Møre (Map 3, Chapter 4) in western Norway, born in about 846. The *Heimskringla*, which should be treated with care as it was based on oral traditions, says: '*Earl Ragnvald was King Harald's dearest friend, and the king had the greatest regard for him. He was married to Hild, a daughter of Rolf Nefia, and their sons were Rolf and Thorer. ... One summer, he (Rolf) ... on a Viking's expedition to the coast of Viken (a district in southern Norway), landed there and made a cattle raid. As King Harald happened, just at that time, to be in Viken, he heard of it, and was in a great rage; for he had forbid, by the greatest punishment, the plundering within the bounds of the country. The king assembled a Thing, and had Rolf declared an outlaw over all Norway. Rolf Ganger went afterwards over sea to the west to the Hebrides and the Isle of Man; and at last farther west to Valland (the west coast of France), where he plundered and subdued for himself a great earldom, which he peopled with Northmen, from which that land is called Normandy. ... From Rolf Ganger are descended the earls of Rouen, who have long reckoned themselves of kin to the chiefs in Norway, and hold them in such respect that they always were the greatest friends of the Northmen; and every Northman found a friendly country in Normandy, if he required it.'*

The 12th century manuscripts of the *Anglo-Saxon Chronicle* pick up the sagas and for 876 say: '*This year Rollo penetrated Normandy with his army; and he reigned fifty winters*'. Behind this phrase is another possible story. He may have been the leader of a small settlement around the mouth of the Seine from 876, but in 885 Rollo was said to have been a lieutenant under another Dane called Siegfried at the siege of Paris. He stayed on in 886 when Siegfried went away having received 700 pounds weight of silver as 'danegeld'. Rollo became permanently based in the lower Seine, and then in Rouen. Perhaps he decided that he had had enough adventuring. What seems to have differentiated Rollo from other Viking leaders was that he led the reconstruction of Rouen which had been left in ruins.

To make Rollo stop raiding into France, King Charles the Simple of France had initially recruited him as a mercenary to fight the Burgundians, but in 911 the Vikings under Rollo again launched an attack on Paris before laying siege to Chartres. The bishop of Chartres made an appeal for help and on 20 July 911, at the Battle of Chartres, Frankish forces defeated Rollo. Even so, Rollo had clearly more than rattled the French, and king Charles by the 'Treaty' of St Clair-sur-Epte granted him the lordship, as his vassal, of the area around the lower Seine. In area this was made up of the modern French departments of Seine-Maritime, Eure, Calvados and part of Orne, bounded by the rivers Bresle and Epte to the east, the Avre to the south and Risle to the west. This created a situation rather like the Danelaw in England (see Map 3, Chapter 4).

One condition of this deal was that he should not allow further Vikings to penetrate through Normandy up the Seine to raid the developing kingdom of France. This turned out to be a mainly successful policy as far as France was concerned, but Vikings still opportunistically used the area as a base from which to attack the south coast of England. Remember ... *'and every Northman found a friendly country in Normandy, if he required it.'* No doubt they also paid to Rollo a share of the English 'danegeld' they had extracted for the privilege. This was the start of a 150-year long period during which Viking lordship evolved, the Viking and local Frankish populations assimilated, and the language gradually became a Norman-French dialect of Old French.

When Charles was deposed by king Robert I in 922, Rollo must have undoubtedly considered any oath he may have made to the king of the Western Franks null and void, and started to expand his lands – as always, Viking fashion. Negotiations ended with Rollo gaining Le Mans and Bayeux, and then he seized the Bessin in 924, and became established as far east as Eu by 925. By 933 Norman overlordship had been extended to be comparable with the boundaries of the ancient Roman province of Lugdunensis Secunda and the ecclesiastical see, containing the cities of Rouen, Bayeux, Avranches, Evreux, Sées, Lisieux and Coutances.

Two spouses are reported for Rollo, but there is no good evidence for either. Poppa may have been William Longsword's mother, but his mother is more likely to have been some unknown Hebridean, Manx or Danish-English woman as he was born in about 893 'overseas' – which could have been in England, the Isle of Man or the Western Isles. Rollo's second marriage is even more contentious – to the three- to four-year-old Gisela, daughter of Charles III of France. As with all information from this period it is very unreliable and cannot be confirmed.

WILLIAM LONGSWORD, COUNT OF ROUEN r. *c.* 927–942

Rollo passed his lordship to his son William Longsword some time before he died between 928–933. If the sagas about him are in any way accurate, Rollo may have died aged about 85, which was a great age for his time. William swore fealty to king Rudolf/Ralph of West Frankia (r. 923–936), who confirmed him as ruler over Rollo's lands sometime around 927.

William's only son Richard, with a woman called Sprota, was born at Fécamp in 933. Two years later he married Luitgarde, daughter of Herbert II of Vermandois and

Count of Meaux, who at the time was the local dominant ruler, but he had no further children.

William Longsword was more favourably disposed than Rollo towards the Church. For example he re-founded the abbey of Jumièges, and there was some Christian resurgence.

By 925 count Arnulf of Flanders used his forces to re-define the northern border of Normandy at the River Bresle, just south of the Somme estuary, which was presumably under pressure from the Normans. In 939 William reinstated the Count of Montreuil, an area Arnulf had tried to annex. Clearly relations on this border were not good, and William was assassinated while meeting with Arnulf on Saturday 17 December 942, on an island in the River Somme at Picquigny, west of Amiens.

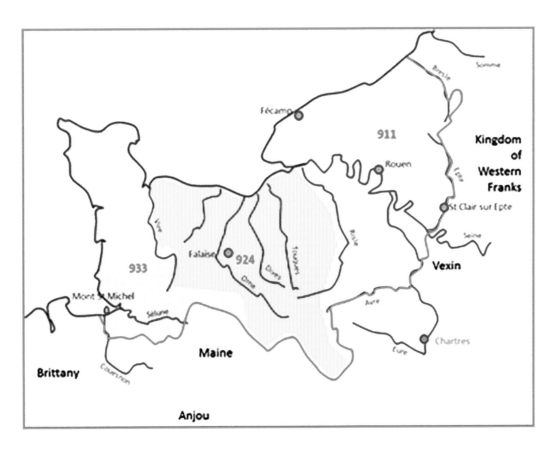

The Viking expansion into Upper and Lower Normandy 911–933.
© Battle and District Historical Society

RICHARD I OF NORMANDY r. 942–996

The province saw warfare between rival Viking groups during the early years of count Richard I, who was only nine or ten when he inherited. There was also some particularly unwelcome interest from a Viking called Harald, based on the Cotentin peninsula, and other 'pagans'. The French king, Louis IV, decided to take control of Normandy as overlord, and he and Hugh the Great, son of king Robert I of West Frankia, fought the pagans. After this Richard was put into the care of the count of Ponthieu. After many confusions, arguments and conflicts between various pagans, interlopers and invaders, too numerous and complex to be recorded here, Richard was confirmed in his position in 945, when he was still only 13, but difficulties continued internally with newly arriving opportunistic Vikings, as well as from Franks on the land borders.

In about 960 he married Emma, sister of Hugh Capet who was to become the first Capetian king of the Franks. Later Richard I aided the accession of Hugh Capet, his brother-in-law, to the Frankish throne in 987, and four years later Normandy fought once more on Hugh's behalf. When Emma died Richard I took a new wife, Gunnor. This was a turning point in stabilising Normandy as a dukedom. Gunnor was from one of the powerful newly arrived Viking parties. The partnership was of political significance, binding the settled and new groups together, with the marriage terms including the full recognition of Richard by the newly arrived groups, and conversion of pagan Vikings to Christianity.

Richard would continue to restore Christianity slowly. In spite of some aggression from France and others in 961–962, between 961–963 he restored the abbey of Saint Ouen in Rouen, and the abbey of Mont-Saint-Michel was formally re-established in 966. Gradually, after about 965 and the Pact of Gisors, he developed closer relations with France, and was increasingly subject to its strong Christian influence.

Normandy, having been significantly influenced by roving Vikings, presumably had at first adopted sociological and legal rules of behaviour from Scandinavia. Now there was also Frankish influence and a developing dukedom. Richard I had a long rule and, in his time, relationships in society started to change with fundamentals of lordship by some people over others started to evolve, moving Normandy further away from its Viking roots.

In a stable dukedom the duke and the counts were dependent for their successes and their very survival on others. These others may have been given or leased land from the duke and counts, but at the same time would look to them socially for advancement. In this context land might be held from one lord, but the tenant could either look to that lord or another for socio-political support within a personal relationship with mutual, not one-way, duties. The duty of a lord was to protect his people, militarily and with good laws, to grant privileges, to take back lands and tenancies no longer required, and to provide guardianship of and if necessary protect underage (normally taken at the time as under 15) inheritors from their own relatives, with respect to their inheritances and possible marriages. In return, the landholder or tenant might provide some military, community, farming and legal duties. With consent, a tenancy could even be exchanged from one lord to another. David Carpenter has put this in a nutshell: '*No ambitious lord could afford to be stuck with dud tenants, and no ambitious tenant could afford to be stuck with a dud lord.*' This was quite different from what has formerly been looked at as rigid feudal duties; it was a mutual dependency in which it would be an unwise lord indeed who overplayed his hand and alienated those on whose cooperation he ultimately depended.

Gunnor, second wife of Richard I, confirms a 12th-century charter of the abbey of Mont-Saint-Michel. From the archive of the abbey,

Pre-1066 English and Norman social structures were similar, but there were some differences because of the time and place in which each group had settled. The English system was older and had been influenced by its long complex history. The Norman system described above could be regarded as only a few generations old, was influenced by Frankish 'Germanic' practice and was still firmly entrenched in a complex set of family ties and loyalties.

In due course the Norman developments, later hardened under William from one of mutuality in which the lords were 'faithful men' to one of 'dominance', would be translated to England after 1066. This was surprisingly easy as pre-Norman England had become the most 'organised' territory in western Europe. Also there was the massive change in land ownership as William's entourage were rewarded with land as English landholders were largely displaced. The new landholders would have been familiar with the Norman approach. It was a bulk substitution of the English variant system in which there were also ties of two-way personal loyalty and reward, but English kings had bypassed the issue of lordship by imposing duties directly based on land ownership.

Richard I ruled for over 50 years, an exceptionally long period for the time, dying in 996. Even then Normandy was not yet totally free of Scandinavian influences, and clearly the Rouen area was a safe haven for Vikings who went off raiding elsewhere, notably England. On their return they would have traded their booty in Rouen, and a share of the danegeld raised in England would have entered the local economy. Remember *'every Northman found a friendly country in Normandy, if he required it.'* No wonder Aethelred II of England would in 991 sign a treaty (in vain) to try to kerb Viking raiding from Normandy, with the same lack of curtailment even after marrying Richard I's daughter, Emma, in 1002. This marriage would eventually become the root of William's claim to the English throne in 1066. It would also create a safe haven in Normandy for Emma and her sons by Aethelred II in the future, and even briefly for Aethelred himself. But it did not deter the Vikings.

RICHARD II OF NORMANDY r. 996–1026

Richard II, Emma's brother, became duke in 996 and reigned for 30 years until 1026. It is considered that it was during his rule that Normandy developed into a much more formidable and political entity and the continuity of one long rule after another must have also contributed significantly to stability. The political and administrative structure hardened with a comital structure developed with counts connected to the ducal dynasty. The first count, sometime between 1006 and 1011, was Rodolf of Ivry, a half-brother of Richard I by Sprota. Other sons of Richard I became counts, including archbishop Robert of Rouen, who also became count of Evreux. There were also 'viscounts', who in English terms were the 'sheriffs' of counties, responsible to the ducal authorities for local administration, rather than being deputies to the counts.

Around 1003, Richard married Judith, daughter of Conan, count of Rennes, which would have allied Normandy and Brittany. She gave him three sons, Richard, Robert and William, and three daughters: Alice who married Renauld I of Burgundy, Eleanor who married Baldwin IV of Flanders, and Matilda who became a nun and died aged 18–20. When Judith died in 1017, Richard II took a second wife Papia, with whom he had Mauger, who later became archbishop of Rouen, and William, who became count of Arques. The Flanders connection would have later relevance.

In 1014, the Normans had a border war with Blois and again Viking mercenaries appeared, this time positively recruited by Richard II to help the struggle. They included Olaf Haraldsson, a future King of Norway, whom we shall see again later.

RICHARD III OF NORMANDY r. 1026–1028

In August 1026 Richard III became duke. He was soon betrothed to Adela, probably a daughter of king Robert of France. However, his brother Robert almost immediately rebelled against him. Robert had been made count of Hiémois by his father. This was an area which lay centrally in Normandy and included Falaise and Sées. Richard had retained the castle of Falaise within Robert's domain, so Robert seized it. Richard then surrounded Robert, and won, but civil war had been sparked and a degree of anarchy with inter-baronial private wars started.

Richard suddenly died at Rouen in 1028. It was rumoured that he died from poisoning, but nothing was ever proved. Another brother, William, had become a monk at the abbey of Fécamp and had died in 1025, so was out of the reckoning. Nicholas, a young illegitimate heir of Richard, entered a monastery and later became abbot of Saint Ouen in 1034. He is recorded in 1066 as contributing ships and knights towards the invasion of England. Richard's illegitimate daughter Alix became vicomtesse of the Bessin. The affianced Adela in due course married Baldwin V of Flanders. Robert had cleared the possible competition.

ROBERT I OF NORMANDY r. 1028–1035

So Robert, soon to be father of William the Conqueror, became duke of Normandy in 1028. It was about this time that he became enamoured of Herlève by whom he had two children, William and Adeliza. Herlève was then married off to Herluin, viscount of Conteville, and they produced two boys, half-brothers to William – Odo, to be bishop of Bayeux and later an English earl, and Robert, to be count of Mortain.

There is no other Norman record of Robert and matrimony, or other liaisons or children. But it is possible that he may have married king Cnut of England's sister Margaret/Esthrith, but then rapidly repudiated or divorced her. Both Adam of Bremen and Rodulfus Glaber (an 11th century French historian in his *Historiarum Libri Quinque*) separately (but in a somewhat confused way) write of a marriage of a sister of Cnut to a duke of Normandy. If this event did occur it may not have endeared Robert to Cnut, and vice versa.

Short records of charters and gifts in 1030 and 1033 have been found witnessed by Robert's cousins, Edward and Alfred, the English princes in exile. A charter to Fécamp from sometime between 1032 and 1035 is curiously signed 'Edwardi regis'. Godgifu, Robert's female English cousin, was to marry Drogo of Mantes, an ally of Robert I, and to have sons, Walter, Fulk and Ralf (who would in the future become earl of 'Hereford', an area much larger than Herefordshire is today).

Robert had observed Cnut's rise to power in England and also in Denmark and Norway, and would have been concerned about his powerful neighbour. He was also very aware of his cousins' potential claim to the English throne. A non-confirmable story exists that Robert planned an expedition against England, but that the fleet that he sent was blown off course by a storm and landed in Brittany, where they took part in an action against count Alan III of Brittany.

Robert had a short reign, during which Alençon was taken into the duchy in about 1030. He also significantly helped Henri of France after his accession to the French throne in 1031. Before that, in a dispute with Brittany, Robert sacked Dol and then repulsed a revenge attack on Avranches. In 1033, Alan of Brittany and Robert were reconciled by Robert, the archbishop of Rouen, and conveniently uncle of both. Also in 1033, the king of France, Henri I, was ousted by his stepmother, Constance, who installed her own son, Robert, as king. Henri fled to Fécamp to seek the help of duke Robert, who dutifully helped Henri regain his throne, and received the territory of the Vexin as a reward.

Robert must have somehow considered that all was fairly stable in Normandy, or simply felt that the state of his own soul mattered more, as William of Malmesbury records that he went on pilgrimage to Jerusalem in 1035. The magnates of Normandy tried to dissuade him from going, but he was adamant. The date of Robert's departure can be estimated from his charter dated 13 January 1035 in which he announced his forthcoming departure for Jerusalem. Robert left the duchy under the command of his uncle, archbishop Robert of Rouen. Before leaving, he had gathered the nobles at Fécamp, and asked them to swear loyalty to William as his successor. King Henri of France also gave his assent to this plan and it is believed that William visited Henri to pay homage.

Writing around 1060, William of Jumièges records that in his final illness king Cnut sent envoys to Robert, offering to restore half of the kingdom of England to the sons of Æthelred to establish peace for his lifetime. Clearly nothing came of this, if it truly occurred, as both Cnut and Robert of Normandy died in 1035. Robert I died in Nicaea on 2 or 3 July 1035 during his return from Jerusalem. He was buried '*in basilica sanctæ Mariæ ... intra mœnia Nicenæ civitatis*'. His son became duke William II.

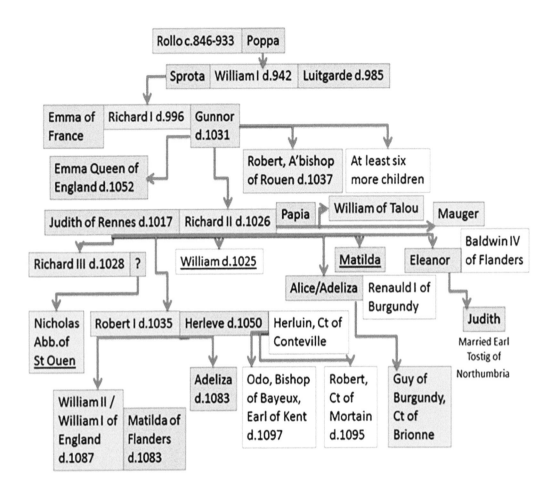

Basic family tree from Rollo to William II of Normandy. Counts/Dukes in purple, potential claimants to dukedom in blue, wives/daughters in pink

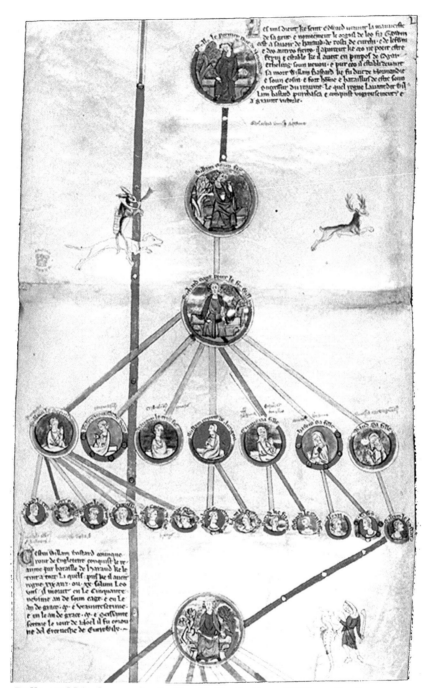

Rollo and his descendants. Top Rollo, bottom William the Conqueror
British Library Royal 14 B V Membrane 4 and 5 https://www.bl.uk/catalogues/
illuminatedmanuscripts/ILLUMIN.ASP?Size=mid&IllID=34131

... and every Northman found a friendly country in Normandy, if he required it.

The *Heimskringla,* Saga of Olaf Haraldson

Never accept what can be gained by giving in.

William the Conqueror

6

WILLIAM II and NORMANDY:
1028–1041

Keith Foord

Willliam 'the Bastard' was born at Falaise in 1027, 1028 or 1029 – there is no birth record, and calculation of his birth date varies according to various recorded life events, e.g. his recorded age at the departure of his father to Jerusalem and the record in *De Obitu Willelmi* which states that in September 1087 he was 59.

There was no formal marriage of duke Robert to Herlève, William's mother, and possibly the daughter of a tanner, so William was illegitimate. This was of less concern in Normandy with its Viking heritage than in most realms of Europe. For example the illegitimate sons of duke Richard I, Godfrey and William, became counts but it did mean that William's father had not taken advantage of a formal noble marriage, which might have conferred some feudal advantage and obligation on both parties. It is probable that William had a full sister by Robert and Herlève, Adelaide/Adeliza.

Robert's liaison with Herlève only lasted about two years, and after that she was married to Herluin, viscount of Conteville, with whom she had two more boys, half-brothers to William: Odo who was to become bishop of Bayeux then earl of Kent, and Robert to be count of Mortain. Herlève died in about 1050. She had two brothers Osbern and Walter, and William's uncle, Walter, is later recorded as having been a 'watcher' of the young duke, on at least one occasion saving him by hiding him amongst the poor.

There is no further Norman record of Robert having more liaisons or marriages, or of any more children. There are some comments from outside Normandy of a possible marriage to a sister of king Cnut of England, which if it occurred did not last long (see Chapter 8). There is also a surprising paucity of information about William's early childhood. We do hear, however, that duke Richard III's young illegitimate son Nicholas was promptly sent into the care of the abbey of Fécamp, then moved on to St Ouen in Rouen where he eventually became abbot. Robert I had reigned as duke from 1027 following the sudden suspicious death of Richard III. But the circumstances of Robert's accession had lit a fuse of discord and local wars sprang up between neighbours, many of the dispossessed leaving the Duchy, some ending up in Sicily where the Normans founded a kingdom. The ecclesiastical bodies also complained bitterly about being robbed of valuables and lands. Robert I was involved in the mayhem, and in 1028, Robert, archbishop of Rouen and Robert I's uncle, was besieged at Evreux by his nephew. The archbishop was forced into exile, promptly placing Normandy under an interdict.

Part of Falaise castle

Robert also found himself at war with Alan III of Brittany, who was his cousin. Normandy was slipping into anarchy, but this was avoided thanks to the intervention of the above archbishop Robert in 1030. This Robert, brother of Richard II, was a powerful man, not only archbishop of Rouen but also count of Evreux. Robert I recalled his uncle Robert from exile, the interdict was lifted, and the duchy stabilised. The archbishop called his nephews Robert and Alan together at Mont-Saint-Michel, and the Breton war ended in a truce, with Alan becoming an ally on Normandy's western flank.

From 1031 until his death in 1037 archbishop Robert was a keystone of stability and, thanks to this, a core group of Norman magnates formed supportive of Robert I. This group included Osbern, brother-in-law of Duke Richard I, and Gilbert of Brionne. Duke Robert also made an alliance with Baldwin IV of Flanders which protected Normandy from the east.

Then, suddenly, late in 1034, Robert I made the decision to go on pilgrimage to Jerusalem. Archbishop Robert and the other magnates tried to dissuade him, to no avail. At the end of their meeting the duke brought out William and persuaded them to recognise him as the heir and to swear oaths of loyalty to him. The 'consent' of king Henri of France was given to recognise William as heir, and it may be that William was sent to Henri to do homage.

Robert I did not return, dying at Nicaea at the beginning of July 1035. William became duke William II of Normandy at about the age of seven. His guardians were the supporters of his father. The particular support of archbishop Robert was critical at this point as he could have claimed the dukedom for himself, given his lineage, but was now elderly. Nicholas, son of Richard III, who also had a claim was happy to stay in his monastery. Other potential contenders were Mauger and William, sons of Richard II by Papia, and Guy of Burgundy, grandson of Richard II, through his mother Adeliza, but no immediate claim was made by any of these.

At this time we also hear a bit more about the English princes exiled in Normandy. They had many Norman uncles and first cousins through their mother, and must have moved from court to court, receiving favours but also gathering debts. They would have been in receipt of regular news from England and would have known that Cnut had also died in 1035, and that eventually Harold Harefoot had taken the throne of England. Harefoot dispossessed his Norman stepmother Emma, and she is supposed to have sent a letter asking for assistance to her sons in Normandy, but there is also a story that Harold Harefoot forged this letter.

Around 1035/36 there is another Norman story (written after the Conquest and not well corroborated from English sources) that Edward with about 40 Norman boats landed at Southampton. His party took some booty, but was promptly repulsed, and sent packing back to Normandy. Soon afterwards, in 1036, Alfred Ætheling presumably with indirect support from the ducal court, made a probe via Flanders into England. His party was promptly seized on arrival by earl Godwin, who is said to have handed Alfred over to Harefoot's men, who blinded him and left him to die with the monks of Ely. In the future this matter would come into play when his brother, Edward Ætheling, became king of England and had dealings with the Godwin family.

Back in Normandy things remained under control with justice being dispensed by a court of magnates until the beginning of 1037, when archbishop Robert died. Once more the duchy's chief feudal families felt the need to safeguard or enlarge their holdings by the sword. More private wars occurred, but somehow there seemed to be an underlying wish to retain some sort of residual ducal authority. For several years control over William was in chaos. Count Alan III died suddenly in 1039–40, and Gilbert who followed him was assassinated on the order of one of the sons of archbishop Robert. A steward was killed in William's bedchamber and his uncle Walter, brother of Herlève, took to sleeping in the room, frequently taking him into hiding for safety. So the period of 1037 onwards was a dark one for Normandy. Most of the records available are monastic and paint particularly black pictures, for the private wars were bloody indeed. Fortunately, sometime after 1040, king Henri of France took some measures to support William, in co-operation with members of the ducal family. Baldwin V of Flanders who was married to king Henri's sister Adèle also gave some backing, possibly with a view to marrying his young daughter Matilda strategically to William, and thus protecting his western flank, as he was in dispute with the German king.

In 1041 Edward Ætheling was invited by his half-brother Harthacnut who had become king of England in 1040 on Harefoot's death, and his mother Emma, now Queen Dowager, to join the English royal family in England. He went, which must have taken some courage, and a year later became king Edward the Confessor, being crowned on Easter Day 1043. Now Normandy had a real friend in England and the future scene was being set.

7

EMMA: NORMAN PRINCESS, TWICE QUEEN OF ENGLAND, QUEEN DOWAGER

Keith Foord

William would have had no blood claim at all to the throne of England but for Emma, princess of Normandy and daughter of duke Richard I. She has a slightly complicated life story as not only was she great-aunt to William the Conqueror, but wife to two kings of England and mother of two more.

She was the second wife of Æthelred II and mother of Edward the Confessor by him. After Æthelred's death and the invasion of England by Cnut, she once again became queen of England by marrying Cnut. Following Cnut's death she became queen dowager, but had a difficult time as Harold I (Harefoot), presumed son of Cnut by his first wife Ælgiva, became king, but it was fortunate for Emma that he did not live long, and soon she had influence again. Her son by Cnut, Harthacnut, briefly reigned after Harold I, before Edward her son by Ælthelred II became king after Harthacnut's premature death, as the Witan looked back to Saxon kings after the Viking interlude.

But, as you may guess, there is rather more to her story than the bare bones above, and she forms a critical link in many ways to the story of the Norman Conquest of 1066, although she died in 1052. Emma was born in about 985. At this time England was under constant threat of Viking raids and Rouen in Normandy was one of the Viking bases from which they launched their raids. Æthelred tried to suppress these raids by establishing a treaty with the Normans in 991, which was not very successful. In 1002 he agreed to marry Emma, sister of the new duke of Normandy, Richard II, partly with the same aim, but the deal placed the relationship between England and Normandy onto a more settled plane as there appeared to have been little formal relationship between them before this. The *Anglo-Saxon Chronicle* (E version) for 1002 says *'And in the same spring, the Lady, Richard's daughter, came here to the land'*. Emma took the Saxon name Ælfgifu for official occasions and to sign documents, which confuses rather than helps us as Æthelred's first wife was Ælfgifu of York and her future husband Cnut's concubine was Ælfgifu of Northampton. The marriage unfortunately still failed to stop the Vikings using Normandy as a raiding base.

We know little of Emma's relationship with Æthelred, but historic rumour is that Emma had little regard for him, and that this had translated into little regard for their first-born, Edward. She bore Æthelred three children, Edward, Alfred and Godgifu/Goda. This chapter is not about Æthelred, but his mistranslated nickname appears to have been warranted, and may even be misleading, as he was not just 'Unready'. He made many mistakes and appointed ineffective and inconstant individuals, including a notorious double-dealer called Eadric Streona, to key posts. The nickname that has been mistranslated was 'Unræd = bad counsel', perhaps even more appropriate than 'Unready'. His arbitrariness and sometime cruelty also generated mistrust and disloyalty. William of Malmesbury says, *'The career of his life is said to have been cruel in the beginning, wretched in the middle, and disgraceful in the end.'* Because of the complexity of the occurrences it is impossible here to describe the full history, and the next few paragraphs are very much a superficial overview of the difficult and convoluted events that occurred due to 'Un-readiness' towards the end of Æthelred's reign, which led to the crowning of Cnut.

Vikings had been a threat to England for centuries and it had taken the period from Alfred's reign though to the reign of Eadred (946–955) to remove the Viking threat and restore English law across the whole of England, but this relief from Viking interest only lasted 26 years. Initially, king Æthelred II, who took the throne in 978, paid them off with large amounts of danegeld. A massive attack on London occurred in 994 led by Sweyn and a rival Olaf Tryggvason, but they were beaten off and returned to harrying, with the coast of Sussex one of their targets. Æthelred paid them off again with £16,000. But although they initially went away for the three years 997–999, they returned to ravage the coasts of Wessex almost at will. In 1000 they descended on Normandy and appear to have been 'accommodated' rather than repulsed, so in 1001 they created havoc in Wessex again until they were paid £24,000.

Æthelred had married Emma in 1002 in the vain hope that her Norman relatives would help to restrain the Vikings. But neither paying them to go away nor marrying Emma had worked, so later in 1002 he ordered a massacre of those Vikings who had stayed in England. These included the sister of the Danish king, Sweyn (Forkbeard). This was guaranteed to attract massive reprisals. Indeed, Sweyn unsurprisingly took great exception to this event and started to attack England aggressively in 1003–1005. Paying the Viking army off yet again with £36,000 in 1007 did not succeed, and by 1009 they were back again, and penetrated deep into England. A strong English fleet had been assembled off Sandwich, but 80 ships were soon lost and at least 20 defected. Æthelred *'went home'*. He paid yet another £48,000 in 1012. By 1013 Sweyn invaded with serious intent. After briefly landing at Sandwich he sailed north to the Humber Estuary and landed his army at Gainsborough on the River Trent. This was a massive display of force and all the threatened districts submitted and gave hostages as he marched south. Briefly repulsed from London they went west, but soon returned, and London too capitulated. The growing difficulties meant that Emma fled for Normandy with her children in 1013, and eventually Æthelred was also forced to flee to join them, when *'all the nation regarded him (Sweyn) as full king'*.

Sweyn had become king of England by conquest; however he died suddenly just 5 weeks later *'ending his days at Candlemas'* (3 November 1014). The Danes elected

Left: Queen Emma and her sons being received by Duke Richard II of Normandy. Right: King Sweyn being pierced by St. Edmund, a fictitious murder, for which there is no record as Sweyn probably died of natural causes. From *Life of Edward the Confessor*, Reproduced by the kind permission of the Syndics of Cambridge University Library.

Sweyn's son, Cnut, king but in an about face *'all the councillors of England, ecclesiastical and lay took council and determined that Æthelred should be sent for, declaring that no lord was dearer to them than their natural lord "if only he would govern them more justly than before".'* Clearly the Danish hold had somehow rapidly weakened and Æthelred was called back and somewhat out of character rapidly attacked and drove off Cnut. Emma returned. Apart from this surprisingly acute episode of direct action he appeared to have learnt nothing. In the summer of 1015 Cnut returned and proceeded to march through England. *'[Cnut] came into Sandwich, and straightway sailed around Kent to Wessex, until he came to the mouth of the Frome, and harried in Dorset and Wiltshire and Somerset'*. By the winter of 1015–16 Wessex had submitted and Cnut marched north-east through Warwickshire to eastern Mercia. Emma and the children were back in Normandy.

Compromising events led to Æthelred's oldest surviving son by his first wife (although he was possibly illegitimate according to Malmesbury), Edmund (Ironside) taking things into his own hands. This was with great difficulty due to yet more internal treachery, particularly a defection by Eadric Streona, earl of Mercia and son-in-law of the king. Then Ælthelred died on 23 April 1016. This left a confused power vacuum with conflicts in many parts of England, but eventually Edmund, after the Battle of Otford, somehow managed to drive the Vikings into Kent and onto the Isle of Sheppey. After this the slippery Eadric Streona defected back to Edmund's side. Finally there was an evenly matched battle at Assandun in Essex in October 1016 which Cnut just won, but afterwards a sort of brief co-ruling arrangement was made with Edmund. Edmund died suspiciously on 30 November 1016, and Cnut became king of all England. This was followed by high level culling and numbers of high-ranking Saxons were executed in 1017, including the duplicitous Eadric Streona and later Eadwig, the only surviving stepson of Emma. Suddenly her son Edward, by Æthelred, became rather more important.

Cnut had won a country that was politically volatile but administratively had a surprisingly stable government. He went on to weigh the pros and cons of making a political marriage. He was already married 'in the Danish way' to Ælfgifu of Northampton, whom he was prepared to 'put aside'. William of Malmesbury offers the best explanation of the deal he then made to marry Æthelred's widow, Emma. There would be some placation of the English and reconciliation with Normandy. He would also hope to minimise any ambitious thoughts that Richard of Normandy might have for his nephews Edward and Alfred to eventually seek their birthright. He would hope to give him more nephews, who would have precedence over his stepsons Edward and Alfred, and maybe over his own sons by Ælfgifu of Northampton.

So a deal was done. Cnut *'had her fetched'* in 1017. Not long afterwards, probably *c.* 1018 (but before 1023) Harthacnut (Hörthaknútr) was born. Edward and Alfred prudently stayed in Normandy to be brought up in the ducal Norman household. Emma then had a daughter Gunnhildr, who was married at a young age to the future Emperor, Henry III of Germany in 1036.

Emma's life, particularly concerning the period whilst she was Cnut's queen, is described in a comprehensive text, the *Encomium Emmae Reginae*, a mid-11th century manuscript. At first she did not seem as important as queen as she had been with Ælthelred, but by 1020 was taking a more active role in the signing of royal grants and charters. She signed the grants to the Norman abbey of Fécamp, a favoured foundation of the Norman dukes, which was given land by charter of Cnut in 1017, soon after their marriage (indeed it may have been part of the marriage agreement), granting to Fécamp an estate at 'Rammesleagh' with its harbour, 'as promised by Ælthelred'. A possible second charter (of 1032) confirmed by Harthacnut (S982) and also signed by Emma adds an estate at Brede and two thirds of the tithes of Winchelsea.

Emma and Cnut present a gilded cross to New Minster, Winchester in 1031.

British Library Stowe 944 f. 6
King Cnut and Queen Emma
http://www.bl.uk/catalogues/
illuminatedmanuscripts/
ILLUMINBig.
ASP?size=big&IllID=47907

Cnut's reign gave England a rare period of peace. He divided England into four earldoms, Wessex, East Anglia, Mercia and Northumbria, to which he would add Denmark and later Norway. He initially ruled Wessex himself, but placed earls in the other three English earldoms and sent Harthacnut as a child 'half-king' to rule Denmark with the assistance of a regent. Men of ability gradually replaced the initial earls and Godwin took the role of earl of Wessex in 1020.

Cnut died on 12 November 1035 and Emma was briefly 'alone in England', staying in Winchester. The Witan refused to nominate Harthacnut, Edward or Alfred and instead eventually opted for Harold Harefoot, one of the sons of Cnut by Ælfgifu, although there were doubts about his paternity. Cnut's other son Sweyn (also rumoured to be of dubious parentage) had been sent to Norway with Ælfgifu, but he had died in Denmark in 1034. England's magnates favoured the idea of installing Harold Harefoot temporarily as regent or joint monarch, as Harthacnut had had to stay in Denmark, but initially baulked at crowning him, although this did occur eventually.

According to the *Encomium Emmae Reginae* (which may be biased), at first Æthelnoth the archbishop of Canterbury, refused to crown Harold Harefoot, before he had been approved by the Witan. Despite the opposition of Godwin, the earl of Wessex, and dowager queen Emma who made repeated attempts to unseat him, he eventually became *de facto* king. He initially shared the rule of Wessex with Emma, who acted as regent for Harthacnut, who remained in Denmark defending that country. Harold Harefoot did not respect the regency of Wessex, nor his stepmother, and promptly removed the most valuable state treasures, including presumably the

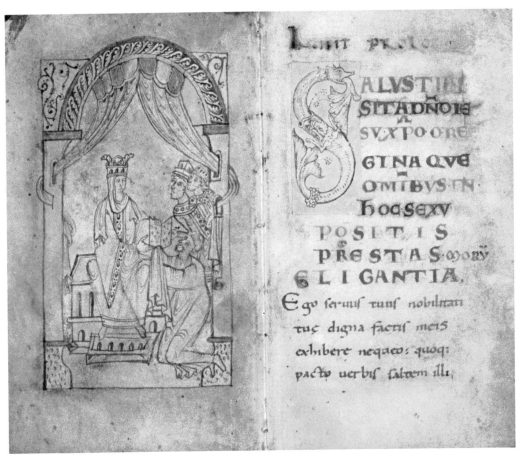

Emma is pictured here receiving the *Encomium Emmae Reginae*, from its scribe, with her sons Harthacnut and Edward in the background.
British Library   MS Add. 33241 f. lv, frontispiece   ©The British Library Board

coronation regalia, from Winchester.

Harefoot was clearly aware that Edward and Alfred, Emma's sons by Ælthelred, also menaced his hold on England. When Alfred tried to visit her at Winchester in 1036, in response to a supposedly forged letter by Harefoot, he is said to have been tricked by Earl Godwin into being taken to Guildford and handed over to Harold Harefoot's men, who seized and blinded him, then left him with the monks of Ely to care for him until he died of the wounds. Harefoot finally usurped his half-brother Harthacnut, who was pinned down defending Denmark, and ruled England alone.

Emma fled or was exiled to Flanders in 1037, taking refuge with count Baldwin V. She did not go to Normandy as there was considerable unrest there (see Chapter 6). However, she did summon Edward to visit her. Edward had obviously been well educated in Norman politics, and was well aware of the situation in England and also of his half-brother Harthacnut's better position. He prudently declined to act. Emma then sent a message to Harthacnut who came to visit her in Flanders in 1039. Whilst he was there they heard that Harold Harefoot had died on 17 March 1040 at the age of 24, and that the English Witan were inviting Harthacnut to become king.

Harthacnut and Edward were half-brothers; their mother was Emma. Harthacnut, we are told, knew that he was ailing. He is said to have invited Edward to join himself and Emma soon after the return to England, and may have involved Edward in a royal role for the two years before his death

Earl Godwin, who always had an eye on his own future, was instrumental after the death of Harthacnut in getting the pro-Norman Edward fully accepted by the English Witan as king of England instead of Magnus of Norway. Godwin, although implicated in the murder of Edward's younger brother Alfred, now supported Edward against his mother, now Emma the queen dowager. She, for her own reasons, flirted with the idea of supporting Magnus, which of course did not endear her to Edward. Godwin also supported Edward in promoting abbot Siward for the post of archbishop of Canterbury.

Emma ended her years as queen dowager. The difficult and equivocal relationship between herself and Edward was clearly deeply felt by Edward, and it came back to haunt her. Following his coronation in 1043, Edward ordered all her treasures to be seized (again) and bishop Stigand her personal advisor was dismissed from his bishopric. She continued to live in Winchester until her death in 1052.

Her contribution to the Conquest of 1066 was to give William a family link to the throne of England. Also indirectly she had produced the first 'Norman' king. Edward the Confessor was born at Islip c. 1003–1005, but spent all his formative years growing up and being educated from 1013 in the Norman court, only returning to England 27 years later in 1040. He may have known his younger first first-cousin-once-removed William the Bastard well, and indeed have preferred him as his heir to Harold Godwinson, son of a man who helped kill his brother – the only family member he had ever really known.

And in the same spring, the Lady, Richard's daughter, came here to the land.

Anglo-Saxon Chronicle (E version), 1002

Cnut: the most effective king in Anglo-Saxon history.

Norman F Cantor,
The Civilisation of the Middle Ages, 1995

8

CNUT, CANUTE, KNÚTR:
KING OF ENGLAND, DENMARK,
NORWAY AND PARTS OF SWEDEN

Keith Foord

When we think about Cnut, as he is called in this book, what immediately springs to mind is the seemingly fatuous episode when he tried to stop the tide coming in at Bosham (or wherever). Much like Æthelred II's modern nickname 'the Unready' (actually *Unræd* (ill-counselled), it is a '1066 and All That' like myth propagated for centuries. No doubt we shall return to this at the end of this chapter, but here starts the serious stuff.

Cnut was born *c.* 990, but Cnut's (Knútr Sweynson's) story is prefaced by that of his father Sweyn Forkbeard (Sweyn Haraldsson), king of Denmark, and his growing ambition to take England from Æthelred II.

Æthelred II had paid off the Vikings many times, who had constantly plagued England for two centuries. He gave them much danegeld, with the price escalating on each occasion. The difficulty was that, over the course of such a period, many Danes had long settled in England, mainly in the area of the Danelaw, and having put down their roots they were not about to leave. In 1001 Æthelred thought that he could pay them off to go away completely, giving them what at that time was the enormous sum of £24,000.

Æthelred did not gain his nickname of *Unræd* for nothing, as neither he nor his advisors had learnt anything about the Danes, who would either keep coming back for more or were not actually in a position to leave, having put down roots, settled and married. In 1002 he was even more ill-advised as in reaction to being informed: *'it was told the king, that they would beshrew him of his life, and afterwards all his council, and then have his kingdom without any resistance,'* he issued a royal charter dated 13 November 1002, and *'ordered slain all the Danish men who were in England.'* The order led to what is known as the St Brice's Day Massacre, which led to many people of Danish origin being killed south of the Danelaw line, but was less effective north of it.

According to later sources, Forkbeard was enraged by the death of his sister, whom William of Malmesbury names Gunhilda, plus her husband and their child in this massacre. The story goes that they and other fleeing Danes had sought sanctuary in St Frideswide's minster in Oxford and the local populace burnt it down with the Danes inside (it is now the site of Christ Church Cathedral). The event has long been obscured by misinformation, but two burials recently unearthed at Oxford and near Weymouth (Loe) suggest mass executions of peoples of Viking origin, carbon dated 970–1025, which brackets 1002. Could they be the first archaeological evidence of the massacre?

Clearly Sweyn was more than a little upset by these events, and proceeded to bring an army to England in 1003, landing at Sandwich then raiding into Wessex and East Anglia. In 1004 Æthelred issued a charter to St Frideswide making restitution, but the wording makes it clear that he had no remorse: *'it will be well known that a decree was sent out by me with the counsel of my leading men and magnates, to the effect that all the Danes who had sprung up in this island, sprouting like weeds amongst the wheat, were to be destroyed by a most just extermination.'* Sweyn was still in England at this time, no doubt being very unpleasant and making much mayhem, but a severe famine in 1005 caused him to retreat to Denmark. It was not to be the end of Sweyn's interest in England. Another visit in 1006 was bought off in early 1007 by danegeld of £36,000, and for the next two years Sweyn 'forgot' his vendetta and England had no attacks.

In 1008, Æthelred, in an unusual and very expensive spate of organisation, placed a levy on every community in England (possibly excluding Northumbria) – one warship for every 300 hides (56sq. miles, 146sq. km), plus one coat of mail and a helmet from every 8 hides (1.5sq. miles, 4sq. km) – and created a new fleet of warships, based on Sandwich. This huge imposition on the people of England was squandered. Æthelred's leadership was so poor that, in 1009 after Beothric, the brother of earl Eadric of Mercia, had accused Wulfnoth, father of earl Godwin, of some misdemeanour, Wulfnoth induced 20 of the ships to desert. Beothric then took another 80 ships to chase Wulfnoth, but ran into a great storm and lost all the ships either at sea or cast ashore. The remains may have been either burnt or recovered by Wulfnoth. What remained of the fleet was sent back to London.

With no fleet of note left to stop them, the Danes were soon back in August 1009, led by Thurkill the Tall and his brother Hemming. In 1011–1012 they harried all of south-east England and East Anglia as far as Huntingdon and Northampton, and the specifically mentioned Hastings area *(... and Suð Seaxe and Hæstinga)*. They were bought off, yet again, this time with £48,000. In 1012 the archbishop of Canterbury was killed by a mob of Vikings, an incident which is supposed to have made their leader Thurkill the Tall become a mercenary for Æthelred. The period was summed up by Stenton who wrote: *'The history of England in the next generation was really determined between 1009 and 1012 ... the ignominious collapse of the English defence caused a loss of morale which was irreparable.'* Æthelred the Unræd must have wished that he had been better advised in 1002.

He would wish that still more in 1013 as king Sweyn came in force with 300 ships. He first arrived at Sandwich, then sailed up the east coast to the Humber, and travelled up the River Trent to Gainsborough. He rapidly gained in turn the submission of all of Northumbria, then Lincolnshire and the East Midlands, then all the Danelaw. Then he struck south to Oxford and Winchester before turning to London. Queen Emma and her children were sent to her brother in Normandy, but Æthelred stayed with Thurkill by his side.

Right: Queen Emma and her children on horseback with an attendant (abbot of Peterborough) fleeing from Sweyn (on horseback, left). Far left: Prisoners being thrown into goal. Lower Centre: Peasants being maltreated and robbed.

From *Life of Edward the Confessor.* Reproduced by the kind permission of the Syndics of Cambridge University Library

Sweyn could not take London, so initially retreated to Bath. He was in control of all except London, and he was proclaimed king of England by conquest, after which London submitted. Æthelred had by now joined his fleet, and after landing at the Isle of Wight also fled to Normandy at Christmas.

Clearly England was in disarray after the previous years' predations by Sweyn, the famine and floods. Most places submitted to him, and only London held out. There took place in London the only significant battle, but it too submitted once Wessex

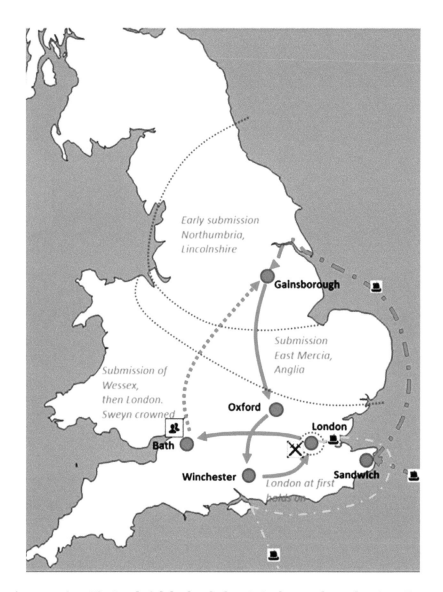

Sweyn's campaign. Via Sandwich he landed at Gainsborough on the river Trent. The Danelaw areas promptly submitted as did Oxford and Winchester when he marched south. London held out and there was a battle. Sweyn moved to Bath and Wessex, and then London submitted. Æthelred fled to Normandy via the Isle of Wight (dashed yellow lines). © Battle and District Historical Society

submitted at Bath. Sweyn was then accepted as king and he returned to Gainsborough.

Sweyn's reign was a short and probably not very sweet five weeks. He died on Candlemas, 2 February 1014 at Gainsborough. The Vikings immediately chose his son, Cnut, as king. The Witan, or what remained of them, had other ideas, and advised that king Æthelred should be sent for – as long as he would govern more justly than he did before. It is not at all clear how, if Sweyn had held England strongly, this could occur. The record on this is surprisingly blank, but clearly a bunch of Saxons were able to say 'No' to a Viking army, which may have been in some disarray or really quite small (the *Encomium Emmae Reginae* says that *'the number of his followers was insufficient'),* and had taken themselves off to Gainsborough to celebrate, thinking the English so malleable that they could be safely left to run the country, which they did.

Æthelred did not reappear immediately himself, but sent his son Edward from Normandy to check things out. Full friendship was declared all round and the Witan bravely declared *'every Danish king outlawed from England forever.'* Æthelred returned in the spring, bringing with him some mercenary Vikings under the leadership of Olaf Haraldsson, and queen Emma followed sometime later. Cnut was still in Gainsborough, where an English army caught up with him probably just after Easter. Cnut escaped with his fleet, taking his hostages, but the poor people of Lindsey who had had to support him were cruelly raided, burned and killed.

Cnut sailed to Sandwich where he cold-bloodedly mutilated his hostages, and then the fleet moved to Greenwich where Æthelred, still *Unræd,* paid them £21,000 to go away. The people of England then had to cope in September 1014 with a huge sea flood, possibly a tsunami from the description.

1015 was not a year of full friendship. There was a great assembly of English and Danes at Oxford, where the odious Eadric Streona, son-in-law of Æthelred and Earl of Mercia since 1007, impeached the leading thegns of the northern Danelaw, Sigeferth and Morcar, and had them murdered. The king was complicit and seized their property, and ordered the widow of Sigeferth to be sent to Malmesbury. The situation became more complicated when the king's son, Edmund (Ironside), rescued the widow, married her, and then took over the property of both thegns.

In the summer of 1015 Cnut, having obtained the support of his brother, Harald II of Denmark, and having been reunited with Thurkill, returned with 160 ships and proceeded to march through England. *'[Cnut] came into Sandwich, and straightway sailed around Kent to Wessex, until he came to the mouth of the Frome, and harried in Dorset and Wiltshire and Somerset.'* Eadric Streona and Edmund had briefly combined against him, but by the winter of 1015 the slippery Streona was with Cnut, and the weakened Wessex had submitted.

In very early 1016 Cnut marched into Mercia, plundering as he went and ravaged Warwickshire. Edmund Ironside, briefly with Ælthelred, attempted to muster an army to resist the invasion, but his efforts were not successful. Canute's forces continued unhindered into Northumbria and ravaged again. In response, Edmund and earl Uhtred of Northumbria ravaged the lands of the turncoat earl Eadric around Cheshire, Staffordshire and Shropshire. Earl Uhtred went back to Northumbria and submitted to Cnut, but was subsequently murdered and was replaced with Eric of Hlàthir.

Then Æthelred died on 23 April 1016. Cnut turned south again and threatened and eventually gained London, with part of his army going west to Somerset. There followed inconclusive battles with Edmund Ironside at Penselwood in Somerset and Sherstone in Wiltshire. Then Ironside began to make progress. He wheeled around the north of London and defeated Cnut at the Battle of Brentford. He then strategically retreated to reinforce, following which he chased the retreating Cnut across Surrey into Kent, and engaged him again at the Battle of Otford, forcing him to retreat to Sheppey. Eadric Streona defected back to Edmund at this time.

Cnut's ships were still available, and eventually they crossed the Thames estuary and landed in Essex, promptly harassing the county and the south-eastern counties of Mercia. Finally there was the evenly matched Battle of Assandun in Essex (at Ashingdon?) in October 1016 which Cnut just won, aided by Eadric Streona changing sides again at the last minute.

Edmund retreated to Gloucestershire, somewhere near the Forest of Dean. It is not clear if there was a final battle here, but he and Cnut finally made an accord. A sort of brief co-ruling arrangement was made between Cnut and Edmund, with Edmund ruling Wessex and Cnut the rest of England. Edmund died suspiciously on 30 November 1016 (Malmesbury later implicated Eadric in his murder), and so Cnut became king of all England. This was followed by a high-level culling and numbers of high-ranking Saxons were executed in 1017, including the duplicitous Eadric Streona. Eadwig Ætheling, the only surviving stepson of Emma (son of Ælgifu and Æthelstan), had been banished but was also executed after foolishly returning to the south-west. Edward and Edmund, the very young sons of Edmund Ironside, were said to have been sent to the 'king of the Swedes' to be killed, but he took pity and they ended up with the Hungarian royal family.

From 1016 Cnut ruled all England as king by conquest, this time permanently. He was about 26 years of age. Detailed comparisons with William in 1066 are difficult to make as the Norman record is far superior, although biased. Both took over a country that had a better administration than monarch, but Cnut did not have to deal with widespread native rebellions, the potential leaders of which had either died or he had ruthlessly had executed. No one wanted further fighting. He was crowned in London by archbishop Lyfing in 1017.

The only potential challengers were Edward and Alfred who were still young and now in exile in Normandy, and soon Cnut strategically married their mother Emma, widow of Æthelred, of whom more, and her attempts to protect (or rather use) her children from her first marriage, can be read in Chapter 7. Cnut also had a relationship with another woman, Ælfgifu of Northampton, daughter of earl Ælfhelm of Northumbria who had died in 1006 and been succeeded by Uhtred of Bamburgh who was killed in 1016. It is unclear when this liaison started, but he had two sons by her, Sweyn and Harold (Harefoot), before his marriage to Emma, and continued the liaison afterwards, which complicated things later.

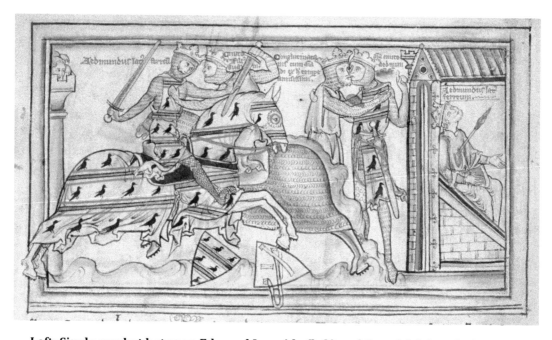

Left: Single combat between Edmund Ironside (left) and Cnut (right) at the battle of Assandun. Right of Centre: The rapprochement between Cnut and Ironside. Right: Ironside seated and pierced with a lance – referring to his later death of unknown cause.

From *Life of Edward the Confessor*. Reproduced by the kind permission of the Syndics of Cambridge University Library

In early 1017 he divided England into four parts, Wessex, Mercia, East Anglia and Northumbria. He ruled Wessex directly, but Mercia went to Eadric Streona, East Anglia to Thurkill, and Northumbria remained with Eric of Hlàthir. Streona only lasted until Christmas day when he was either strangled or beheaded. A re-organisation in 1018 saw military rule diminished, and two earldoms created out of Wessex, with probably Æthelweard to the west and Godwin Wulfnothson (previously thegn of Sussex, and Harold Godwinson's father) to the east (Hampshire, Berkshire, Surrey and of course Sussex), and the split of Mercia into two earldoms – one centred on Herefordshire and the other on Worcestershire.

A huge *heregeld* (army payment) of £72,000 was raised from the poor people of England, plus £11,000 from London, to pay off most of the force Cnut had brought from Denmark, but he kept a 'navy' of 40 ships, which represented a force of perhaps 3200 men. It has been suggested that at this time Cnut had created a force of 'royal guards', comprised of both paid 'mercenaries' and landholders, which formed an hierarchical guild. These *solidarii* or *stipendiarii* would be the housecarls, with guild

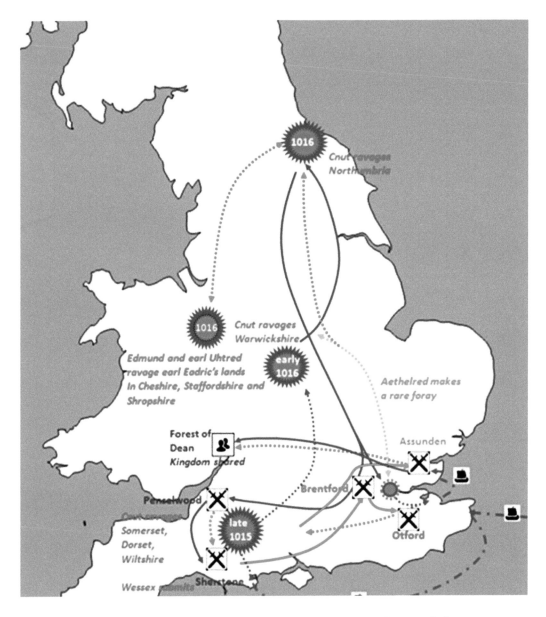

Cnut's campaign (blue lines, text=battles won), with Edmund Ironside 's responses (red). Re-positioning army movements in dotted lines, plus Æthelred's foray (yellow). Inconclusive outcome encounters in green. © Battle and District Historical Society

members of varying status from the king and earls down. It had jurisdiction over its members, with powers of banishment, outlawry (*niðing*) and death in extreme cases, and met as a gemot of housecarls. It was a mainly military organisation, but also had revenue collecting duties. In addition it was not based just around the royal court, but quartered throughout the kingdom with the earls and thegns. From time to time on special occasions they would eat with the king. They formed a powerful nationwide defensive core and would remain in existence through to the death of Harold in 1066. It must have been due to the presence of such a body that even the most powerful in the kingdom would have to obey its judgements. In Scandinavia similar corps would survive for another two or three centuries.

Later in 1018 there was a great meeting at Oxford. People of Danish and English heritage were declared equals, there would be one Christian god, and the observance of Edgar's laws – the ecclesiastical and secular parts of a single code established after the final suppression of the Danelaw. The folios of this code, held by the British Library, written in the early eleventh century, have a clear connection with Worcester and bishop Wulfstan (1002–1016). In return for this maintenance of continuity Cnut expressly required obedience and loyalty, and pledged the defence of the kingdom.

Harald II of Denmark died childless in 1018 and the *Anglo-Saxon Chronicle* reports that Cnut went to Denmark to claim the Danish throne, leaving Thurkill as regent in England. Cnut was accompanied by Godwin amongst others. Cnut finally returned to England in 1020 having had to undertake some military actions in Denmark, including against the Swedes, when Godwin made such an impression on Cnut that the king 'gave him' his brother-in-law Ulf's sister Gytha as a wife.

In 1020 another great meeting was held at Cirencester, following which earl Æthelweard was outlawed, apparently for having caused some subversion whilst Cnut was away. Also this year Cnut went to Ashingdon where he had had a minster built to celebrate his victory there. This allows us another comparison with William, who had the much larger Battle Abbey built in the same circumstances.

Thurkill was banished in 1021, although he and Cnut became reconciled in 1023 when he was briefly appointed regent of Denmark and guardian of Cnut and Emma's young son Harthacnut, who was himself to become king of Denmark, then of England in his own right. Thurkill then disappears from the scene and Ulf, husband of Cnut's sister Estrith became regent of Denmark. Olaf Haraldsson had become king of Norway, and he and the king of Sweden induced Ulf to join them. In response to this, Cnut took a fleet to Denmark in 1026 but suffered a reverse. Cnut then took to subterfuge with the arrangement of the murder of Ulf, and outright bribery to unhappy Norwegian underlings, to undermine Olaf.

Cnut felt safe enough to undertake a visit to Rome in 1027 for the coronation of emperor Conrad II, and returned first to Denmark then England by sea. In 1028 a combined Danish and English force took Norway. Olaf Haraldsson took refuge in Sweden, but then tried to return to Norway in 1030. He was not welcomed and was killed. Cnut was now *de facto* king of England, Denmark, Norway and part of Sweden, a title he had assumed in 1027.

Cnut first appointed Hákon Ericson, son of Eric of Hlàthir, former earl of Northumbria, to be his regent in Norway, but soon afterwards Hákon either died at sea or was killed on Orkney, and was replaced by Cnut's oldest son, Sweyn Knutson, assisted by his mother Ælfgifu. This was not a success. Sweyn and his mother were driven into southern Norway by Magnus Olafson, son of Olaf Haraldsson, then by 1035 into Denmark, where Sweyn died in 1036. Magnus then threatened Denmark, where Harthacnut, Cnut's son by queen Emma, was by then old enough to be the full king of Denmark. This tale is told in Chapter 7 about Emma.

Another threat to Cnut's English kingdom had always been Malcolm II king of Scotland. Malcolm was long-lived and had always coveted Northumbria, making several incursions. In 1006 he had besieged Durham and ten years later in 1016 he tried again, but earl Eric of Hlàthir pushed him back. Soon after his return from

Cnut's North Sea Empire.
© Battle and District Historical Society

Rome in 1027, Cnut himself was forced to march north into Scotland and overcame Malcolm, forcing him to become his vassal. Malcolm died in 1034, and his successor Duncan caused no trouble to England. Duncan's personal claim to eternal recognition was to have been killed by the Macbeth of Shakespearian fame in 1040.

Relations with Normandy started to deteriorate in about 1030. Duke Robert of Normandy may have married Cnut's sister Margaret/Esthrith, but had repudiated or divorced her. This is not recorded by Norman writers, who naturally tended to avoid writing about things that their dukes might not wish to see, but both Adam of

Bremen, and Rodulfus Glaber (an 11th-century French historian) in his *Historiarum Libri Quinque*, both record (in a somewhat confused way) a marriage of a sister of Cnut to a duke of Normandy.

William of Jumièges says that duke Robert of Normandy sent envoys to Cnut, complaining of the long exile of Edward and Alfred. Cnut would do nothing and it is possible that Robert prepared an expedition to England. We are told a fleet was assembled at Fécamp in Normandy, but was blown off course and ended up ravaging Brittany instead. The same writer also says that in his final illness Cnut sent envoys to Robert, offering to restore half of the kingdom to the sons of Æthelred, to establish peace for his lifetime. Clearly nothing came of this, if it really occurred. Robert left on his pilgrimage to Jerusalem in early 1035, dying on the return journey.

Cnut died on 12th November 1035 at Shaftesbury, at the age of about 45, and was buried at Winchester. From the wording of his charter (S975) to Sherborne Abbey of 1035 it appears that he knew he was dying. He spent nearly 20 years on the throne, during which England was relatively peaceful after 1020 and free of Viking raids, plus had a growing economy. He helped fuse the two populations of England, the English and Danes, into a coherent whole, but with the loss of some legal and economic freedoms, and more taxation for the poor. He had stabilised and protected the country, and left a legacy of a strong central military guild. He had also created a new, powerful meritocracy, breaking lines of tradition. This meritocracy included earl Godwin, whose family would in time become too powerful for England's good.

Cnut had valued and rewarded loyalty, and dealt harshly and ruthlessly with dissent. He had supported and gifted the Church well, and had interfered with its functions and appointments very little. His marriage with Emma and his own background had kept the Vikings based in Normandy at bay. England remained at peace with Normandy, in spite of some possible end-of-life frictions with duke Robert. He had kept Emma's sons by Æthelred, Edward and Alfred, at arm's length, but sadly he left no able direct heirs. His North Sea empire would not survive long, and nor would his dubious sons by Ælfgifu, who died in their early 20s. Their deaths at last opened the door to the crown to Edward the Confessor, and the power of the kingdom to the Godwin family.

Just to set the record straight, the first telling of the story of Cnut and the tide was by Henry of Huntingdon in the 12th century. There is no contemporary record: '*Cnut set his throne by the sea shore and commanded the incoming tide to halt and not wet his feet and robes. Yet continuing to raise as usual the tide dashed over his feet and legs without respect to his royal person. Then the king leapt backwards, saying: "Let all men know how empty and worthless is the power of kings, for there is none worthy of the name, but He whom heaven, earth, and sea obey by eternal laws."'*

... he [Edward] was a very proper figure of a man – of outstanding height, and distinguished by his milky white hair and beard, full face and rosy cheeks, thin white hands, and long translucent fingers.

A monk of St. Bertin at St Omer,
Vita Ædwardi Regis, c. 1067

9

EDWARD THE CONFESSOR:
7TH SON, ÆTHELING, EXILE, KING OF ENGLAND

Keith Foord

King Æthelred II married Emma of Normandy, sister of duke Richard II, in spring 1002. It was not a marriage made in heaven, but to obtain a strategic alliance with Normandy and thereby try to contain the Viking threat. We can assume from the start that Emma would have had a powerful, resourceful and opportunistic personality ... it came with her genes, and the story of her association with events can be read in Chapter 7.

It was not Æthelred's first marriage. He had previously been married to Ælfgifu, daughter of an English earl, most likely earl Thored of Northumbria. From this marriage came six sons and three, possibly four, daughters. The sons were Æthelstan, Egbert, Edmund, Eadred, Eadwig and Edgar. The daughters were Edith (who would marry the to-be-infamous Eadric Streona *(the Acquisitor)*), Ælfgifu, Wulfhild and possibly another who entered a convent. So Æthelred did not seem to be short of heirs, nor daughters with whom to make strategic marriages.

So Edward, often *Eadweard* in charters, was nominally seventh in line of succession when he was born to Emma at Islip, most likely in 1005. His birth was followed by that of a brother, Alfred, and a sister Godgifu/Goda. Godgifu married Drogo of Mantes, count of Valois and the Vexin, in 1024, then when Drogo died in 1035, she married Eustace of Boulogne. Both husbands would have regarded marriage to a niece of the duke of Normandy as a benefit. Ralf, the second son of Godgifu and Drogo, would in time become earl of a large area of south Mercia centred on Hereford.

Only two of the sons of Ælfgifu survived their father. So, by the time Æthelred died in 1016, Edward had been promoted by default to third son in line behind Edmund (Ironside) and Eadwig. By 1017 Edmund had died after briefly co-ruling with king Cnut, who had conquered England by invasion, and Cnut had Eadwig executed after he had foolishly returned to England after being banished. The circumstances surrounding these events can be read in Chapters 7 and 8. So, in theory, Edward was suddenly heir, very presumptive, before his mother, Emma, married Cnut. Cnut already had sons, and was to have one more with Emma, plus a daughter, so Edward's claim went back into abeyance. In addition, Edmund Ironside had a son and grandson, who could have also have had prior regal claim, but had escaped from Cnut to safety in Hungary.

Emma and her children by Æthelred had fled to Normandy in 1014 when Cnut's father Sweyn had rampaged into England and seized the crown. Emma went first with the abbot of Peterborough, and the children followed with the bishop of London. They briefly returned when Æthelred was asked back after Sweyn's unforeseen death, but then fled back again, but not before Emma had transferred her support from her ill-counselled husband Æthelred to her stepson Edmund.

During the episodes of Danish invasions by Sweyn and then Cnut, Edmund Ironside and Eadwig did not flee, but tried with varying success to resist the Danes. It is recorded that Edward came back from Normandy – with the advance party when Æthelred was asked back – but also there is a record in *Óláfs saga helga* in the *Heimskringla* concerning the life of Óláf Haraldsson which says that, after the death of Æthelred, Edmund and Edward co-reigned, and that Edward fought defending London against Cnut alongside Edmund. This is possible, but Edward would have been only about 13 at that time and the *Heimskringla* may not be reliable. Whatever the situation, Edward is then presumed to have prudently returned to Normandy via Flanders in late 1016 to re-join his younger brother Alfred and sister Godgifu.

As nephews of duke Richard II of Normandy, Edward and Alfred were brought up in the ducal court, and eventually their sister Godgifu was married to count Drogo of Mantes. The brothers had many kinsmen in Normandy, were brought up as knights, but have no record of having been given estates or of marriage. Edward may have witnessed some charters of duke Robert I before the duke went on his fateful crusade (Chapter 5). The brothers probably moved around between courts, met many people and had many debts, both personal and monetary, to repay in the future. When Robert of Normandy and king Cnut both died in very different circumstances in 1035, Edward was aged about 30 and a survivor. He would have seen much duplicity, greed and fear, but was probably rather philosophical about his future, as Cnut's sons still lived.

In England king Cnut's death was somewhat unexpected. His oldest son Sweyn had been with his mother Ælfgifu in Norway acting as regent, but being deposed had fled to Denmark where he died in 1034. So he was out of the English succession issue. He was replaced in Norway by Magnus, son of Óláf Haraldsson.

Cnut's son by Emma, Harthacnut, was acting as regent in Denmark. Emma promptly manoeuvred on behalf of Harthacnut, her son by Cnut, but her stepson Harold Harefoot was in England. The Witan prevaricated and split over the succession, but Harefoot gradually gained ascendancy in England, except in Wessex where Harthacnut, through Emma as his regent and supported by earl Godwin of Wessex, was holding on. The split in rule roughly conformed to the old Danelaw line, which was not surprising as Harefoot was Danish/Northumbrian and Harthacnut half-Norman. Harefoot seized the royal treasure from Winchester in the heart of Wessex, and the Witan eventually made Harefoot 'protector' of all England, which made things very difficult for Emma. If Harthacnut had promptly returned from Denmark he might have gained all England for himself, but he was pinned down defending Denmark from Magnus, the new king of Norway.

At this point a letter asking for help was received by Edward and Alfred in Normandy, said to be from Emma living at Winchester, but possibly forged by Harefoot. She also repeated a rumour that Harefoot was not the son of either Cnut or Ælfgifu, but a changeling. It is possible that Edward was the first to respond, with Norman help, with a raid into Hampshire with 40 boats, landing near Southampton, presumably heading for Emma in Winchester. They were welcomed as a Viking raiding party, fought a small battle, took some booty, but had to retreat. The reports of this are entirely of Norman origin (or copied second-hand), and may not be entirely accurate. Then Alfred acted. He sailed from Flanders, possibly to Dover, was received by earl Godwin's men (Godwin had opportunistically switched allegiance to Harefoot), and was tricked into being handed over to Harefoot's minions at Guildford. They took him to their ships, and sailed round to Ely, blinding him at some time en route. They left him with the monks of Ely to die, rather horribly, from complications of his terrible treatment. This event would colour Edward's relationship with earl Godwin and his family in the future.

In 1037 Harefoot was finally recognised as king, and Emma fled to Flanders, as Normandy at the time was so unstable (see Chapter 6). She asked Edward for help, but he could do nothing. Harthacnut was still defending Denmark against Magnus, and also refused to be drawn into Emma's schemes, but in late 1039 he was able to visit her. This was after he had drawn up some sort of tontine treaty with Magnus, by which the survivor of the two if they had no children would rule both Norway and Denmark. It was never totally clear if England was also included in this pact, and later there was some confusion about this. Emma obviously thought it might be the case, as she would toy with the idea of supporting Magnus against Edward in the near future. Harold Harefoot then died suddenly at the age of 23 on 17 March 1040. The cause of death was some sort of illness, possibly suspicious, but the *Anglo-Saxon Chronicle* pithily says it was *'divine judgement'*. He certainly does not appear to have been a very nice person at all.

Negotiations between the English magnates and Harthacnut dragged on a while, but eventually he and Emma sailed just before midsummer with a moderately large escort of 60 ships (were they expecting trouble, or was it just a display of power?) to Sandwich, receiving a good welcome. Harthacnut is said to have had Harefoot's body exhumed and thrown into a ditch. Edward had a better reception. He was invited to join his half-brother and mother and to take an active role at court. Edward was probably accompanied by Robert, abbot of Jumièges, and his nephew Ralf, son of his sister Godgifu, plus a small group of other Norman supporters. Edward's fortunes were changing and changed even more the next year when Harthacnut died on 8 June 1042. He just dropped down dead with a convulsion according to reports. A sudden intracranial bleed must have been the cause, but he was drinking heavily at the time. He was only 24. His half-brother Harefoot had died aged 23. With no obvious love the *Anglo-Saxon Chronicle* (C version) says spikily of Harthacnut, '*And also he never accomplished anything kingly for as long as he ruled*'.

Edward was now about 37 and unmarried and as at one time he had been the seventh son found himself in a somewhat surprising position. For him to gain the crown was not quite as straightforward as it might seem. He was the only surviving male heir of Æthelred II or Cnut, but another Sweyn, Harthacnut's cousin by Cnut's sister Estrith Svendsdatter, also had a distant claim, and was also it seems the heir presumptive of Denmark, in spite of the above deal with Magnus. The surprising champion of Edward in the Witan was earl Godwin plus other southern magnates and bishops. Earls Leofric of Mercia and Siward of Northumbria who leant more to a Scandinavian outlook took somewhat longer to make their minds up.

Edward's mother behaved in a very strange way, which has never been adequately explained: suggesting Magnus of Norway as king of England, and holding on to the state treasures. Her relationship with Edward always appears to have been a cold one, and possibly stemmed back to her lack of regard for Æthelred II, plus a perceived lack of support for her schemes from Edward. Perhaps she saw a frailty in Edward. The Witan finally decided and Edward was eventually crowned at Winchester on 3 April 1043. Soon afterwards the treasures were removed from Emma, and she was left to live out the rest of her life at Winchester until she died in 1052.

There were almost immediate post-coronation challenges from Scandinavia which lasted several years. Magnus planned an invasion, but was held up by fighting with another Sweyn, a cousin of the Godwinsons, over Denmark. Sweyn asked for help from Edward, but was ignored. Sweyn was eventually chased out, and Magnus started to prepare his plans for England once more, only to die in late 1047. Sweyn returned, was re-crowned, and remained king of Denmark, and held it (just) against Harald Hardrada who had taken Norway, until he died in 1074.

Once more in 1048 there were Viking raids on England against Thanet, Sandwich and the Isle of Wight , all of which were chased off by Edward's navy. In 1049 Edward assisted the Emperor Henry III in his war against Baldwin V of Flanders, by using the English navy to blockade the Channel. No doubt many ships from Hastings and the other future Cinque Ports took part in these actions.

In the early years of his rule Edward had brought in Normans to advise and assist him. He also needed to keep the English great earls, Siward, Leofric and Godwin on-

Left: Edward being welcomed by the English barons on landing in England.
Right: The coronation of king Edward the Confessor.
From *Life of Edward the Confessor.* Reproduced by the kind permission of the Syndics of
Cambridge University Library

side, which was either helped or hindered by the earls' rivalries. Godwin rose to be much more influential than the others, and possibly to appease him Edward married his daughter Edith in 1045. But there were very clearly great tensions between the king and his father-in-law about the Norman influence. Normans and Norman abbeys had received grants of land from Edward and Edward's nephew, Ralf of Mantes, became earl of an area centred on Hereford. Tensions continued to rise. Two events in 1051 – the advancement of Robert Champart of Jumièges, who had already been made bishop of London, to the archbishopric of Canterbury over Godwin's candidate, and a secondary event involving Eustace of Boulogne (see Chapter 10) – caused a complete rift.

After an armed stand-off and near civil war, and with the support of earls Siward and Leofric, Edward banished Godwin and his family, and queen Edith was sent to a convent. These were extraordinary events. It can only be assumed that Edward had become almost completely in thrall to Godwin but actually detested him, possibly because of his role in killing his brother Alfred, but also because of his rising opposition to Edward's wishes. Edward had taken his first clear opportunity to rid himself of the Godwins. More details of this can be found in Chapter 10.

What is more astonishing is that the Godwins came back in force the next year and made a coordinated attack, again leading to near civil war. Things were appeased by the Witan with weaselly political words, and the essential withdrawal of Siward and Leofric from active support of Edward. This caused Edward to submit, although he had already taken Godwin's youngest son Wulnoth and grandson Hákon as hostages of Godwin's good faith and did not return them.

What happened in the year to change things so dramatically? Was it the possible visit of duke William II to England in 1051 and/or an indication to William via Robert Champart that he might be nominated by Edward as his preferred inheritor of the English throne the root cause of all this? We just don't know – records are contradictory, and much academic controversy has flowed over the issues.

Queen Edith was released from her convent and Robert Champart was sent packing to Normandy, somehow, it is believed, taking Edward's hostages Wulfnoth and Hákon with him. Godwin's protégé Stigand was inserted into Canterbury in Champart's stead. Stigand was promptly excommunicated by the pope, both as a usurper and also for plurality (holding on to other ecclesiastical appointments in addition to Canterbury). He could not consecrate bishops, nor could he crown kings. This situation was maintained by successive popes and William of Normandy would exploit it later.

Meanwhile the Godwins were firmly established back in power, and were now truly difficult to dislodge. Earl Godwin died in 1053 and Harold Godwinson became the pre-eminent earl, taking over Wessex, with East Anglia being transferred to Ælfgar, son of Leofric. In 1055 earl Siward died and Harold's brother Tostig became earl of Northumbria. Finally in 1057 Leofric of Mercia died, handing the earldom to his son Ælfgar. Ralf, earl of Hereford, a possible claimant to the English throne as the son of Edward's sister Godgifu, also died in the same year. Harold promptly added the lands of Ralf's earldom to Wessex. East Anglia, which Ælfgar had previously held, went to Gyrth Godwinson, and Leofwine Godwinson took over Buckinghamshire and Kent and the area in between. So virtually every earldom south of the old Danelaw line, plus Northumbria, was held by a son of earl Godwin.

During the period 1053–57 some thought must have been given to Edward's successor, and Edward, son of Edmund Ironside, was 'found' in Hungary where he had been since 1016, having fled from Cnut. The story was that, as a child, Cnut had sent him and his brother to the king of Sweden 'to be killed', but the Swede had refused to do Cnut's dirty work, and sent them to far-away Hungary, clearly placing them with a regal family. Negotiations for his return took place (discussed in Chapter 10), and he arrived in 1057 in some state, with some treasure and with the support of Holy Roman Emperor Henry III. He was accompanied by his wife and three children, Margaret, Edgar and Christina. Unfortunately he then died before he could meet king Edward. The children were placed in the royal household, and raised there.

Sources of information and charters become rarer post-1054. Edward was a nominal king now, and must have gone into a sort of semi-retirement. We are told that he spent much time praying and hunting. The *Vita Ædwardi Regis,* which is a strange document with Godwinian overtones, implies that before 1052 Edward was misguided, and that after this everything went well. The *Anglo-Saxon Chronicle* confirms that the king remained in good health. The names of people associated with the court become more Scandinavian, although French names do not totally disappear. Most in the church had English names. The role of queen Edith probably increased, and it is believed that she stirred up hostility to Ælfgar, who was banished, but then Ælfgar caused mayhem around the southern Welsh Marches having allied with the king of north Wales. Fortunately for him, he was able to regain his earldom through diplomacy. Edith may have also been implicated in some of Tostig's less savoury adventures. Edwin, eldest son of Ælfgar, took over Mercia on his father's death in 1062.

There were tensions between the Godwinson brothers, but as long as they co-operated and worked with, and nominally under, the king, the realm was strong. Foreign affairs were also surprisingly stable. The policy towards Wales and Scotland was defensive. Sweyn of Denmark was first cousin to the Godwinsons and the king was related to William II of Normandy. Tostig was married to Judith of Flanders, daughter of Baldwin IV and Eleanor of Normandy, a grand-daughter of Richard II. Eleanor's niece was Matilda of Flanders who married duke William II of Normandy.

It may have been the relationship of Edward to William II of Normandy was the reason behind the visit of Harold to Normandy in 1064 (possibly 1065). It may have been, at least in part, a diplomatic mission as part of the succession issue. Once again the true story behind this is obscured by post-Conquest history, fact, fiction and half-truths. Harold had previously operated in diplomatic mode in relationships with Mercia and Wales, and had also visiting Flanders and Germany in 1056, when he may have had something to do with the negotiations with Hungary concerning Edward Ætheling.

Tostig and Harold were clearly both gifted men who, as brothers of different character, could disagree very strongly. Some sources suggest that Edward preferred Tostig, but there was a revolt in 1065 against earl Tostig by the Northumbrians. The thegns of Northumbria seized and occupied York. The revolt involved *'all the thegns of Yorkshire'*, according to the *Anglo-Saxon Chronicle*. The rebels declared Tostig an outlaw and sent for Morcar, the brother of the new earl Edwin of Mercia, to be the new earl of Northumbria, and then they marched south.

Harold met them and, after discussed the issues with the rebels, he concluded that it was impossible for Tostig to remain earl of Northumbria. Harold returned to the king, and advised him to agree to the rebels' demands. Apparently Edward was furious, and took some time to be persuaded. Eventually Harold went to Northampton and told Morcar that he was now officially earl of Northumbria, and the rebels that they were pardoned. Tostig continued to argue with King Edward and found himself exiled to Flanders.

In November 1065 it became obvious that king Edward was dying. One possible heir was Edgar Ætheling and, with the approval of the Witan, he might have acceded with Harold 'Dux Anglorum' continuing as regent and running the country until the boy was old enough to rule on his own.

On 5 January 1066 Edward summoned the Witan to his deathbed. He had been semi-conscious for several days, but was roused. He 'commended' his kingdom and the protection of his queen to Harold. Discussion of this critical matter and what happened next, is covered at the end of Chapter 10.

Edward the Confessor's funeral from the Bayeux Tapestry.
From *The Bayeux Tapestry: The complete tapestry in full colour* by David M Wilson © 1985, Thames & Hudson, Ltd. London.

This Englishman (Harold) was distinguished by his great size and strength of body, his polished manners, his firmness of mind and command of words, by a ready wit and a variety of excellent qualities. But what availed so many valuable gifts, when good faith, the foundation of all virtues, was wanting?

Ordericus Vitalis, *c.* 1075–1143

You may not like William (who did?) but you have to admit that this hard, inflexible and unlovable man was politically the master of his world.

Michael Wood, 2014

10

HAROLD GODWINSON AND THE GODWINS

Keith Foord and Neil Clephane-Cameron

Harold Godwinson, born 1022, was the second son of Godwin Wulfnothson, earl of Wessex. Godwin himself had been born in 1001 and his parents and Harold's paternal grandparents are believed to have been Wulfnoth Cild, a thegn of Sussex, and Thyra Svendsdatter of Denmark (see Chapter 8).

His uncle may have been Æthelnoth, archbishop of Canterbury (appointed 1020 and who collected his pallium in 1022). Æthelnoth's appointment was possibly a gesture of appeasement, as another uncle, Æthelweard, had been executed by Cnut in 1017.

Harold may have been the great x5 grandson of Ælthelred I who had reigned 866–871, but this is unproven. His family obviously moved in the highest ranks of the English world, as thegns were one rank below earls in the Saxon hierarchy. Godwin Wulfnothson's talents must have been recognised as Cnut elevated him to earl, even though Godwin had supported Edmund Ironside in the struggle against Cnut in 1016. Godwin's brother had died in the bloody 1017 cull, but Godwin survived and had pledged his loyalty to Cnut. By 1018 he had campaigned with Cnut in Denmark and was made earl of the eastern part of Wessex.

Godwin became an extremely powerful figure in England, and after the death of Harthacnut (Hörthaknútr), second heir of Cnut by Emma, his second wife, in 1042 he was instrumental in getting the pro-Norman Edward (the Confessor, son of Ælthelred II and the same Emma) accepted by the Witan as king of England, instead of Magnus of Norway.

Godwin, although implicated in the murder of Edward's younger brother Alfred, had supported Edward against his mother, now Emma the queen dowager, who for her own reasons had flirted with the idea of supporting Magnus. Godwin also supported Edward in promoting abbot Stigand for the post of archbishop of Canterbury. Part of his reward was that one of Godwin's sons, Harold, was made earl of East Anglia in 1044 when he was about 25. There had been no earl of East Anglia since 1021, as Cnut was also king of Denmark and Norway, and Harthacnut had also been king of Denmark, so the area had been protected during their reigns. Harold was now the East Anglian representative of Edward with powers to act on his behalf in matters of law, and to raise a *fyrd* (army) from the earldom in war or emergency. To cover the costs of running the earldom there were extensive estates, the income from which was designed to cover the expenses of administration.

Cnut had deposed Olaf II as king of Norway in 1028, but Olaf's son Magnus I regained this throne from Cnut's son Sweyn, who had been placed as co-regent of Norway just before Cnut's death in 1035. Magnus I and Harthacnut, who had become king of Denmark on Cnut's death, had made a treaty in 1038–39 agreeing that if either died childless the other was to inherit the other's throne. So Magnus had promptly taken Denmark on Harthacnut's death in 1042, and reckoned that he should have England too, thus posing a significant threat from across the North Sea. Therefore Edward certainly needed to place a strong earl in East Anglia, and a year after his appointment Harold proved his strength as he led the English fleet out of Sandwich in manoeuvres to discourage Magnus, who had raised a raiding fleet.

The earls of England needed to work together, and by 1045 no fewer than four were Godwins: Harold himself; Harold's father Godwin of Wessex; Harold's brother Sweyn of south Mercia; and cousin Beorn of Northampton. The other earls were Leofric of Mercia, Ralf of Hereford and Siward of Northumbria. On top of this, Edward made Godwin's daughter Edith his queen in 1045.

Sometime after becoming earl of East Anglia, Harold took Edith Swanneshals (*Ealdgȳð Swann hnesce = Edith Gentle Swan, although more commonly known as Swan-neck*) as his partner. They were together for the next 20 years and had at least seven children. One of their daughters, Gytha, married the Grand Duke of Kiev and if the genealogies are correct, became an ancestor of the present British royal family via Philip IV of France whose daughter Isabella married Edward II of England and whose great-great granddaughter Catherine of France married Henry V of England. Catherine also had a liaison with Owen Tudor which made her grandmother of Henry VII, the first Tudor king.

The Godwins were known for their political acumen and talent, but they were also ruthless, headstrong and troublesome, some more than others. In 1046 earl Sweyn abducted the abbess of Leominster – and it took almost a year to make him release her. Sweyn was exiled for this offence, and his earldom was split between Beorn and Harold. Earl Godwin's support for Sweyn during this incident strained the relationship between Godwin and Edward. This was already difficult at times as Godwin disliked the large number of Normans that Edward had introduced into the court.

The influence of Normans on Edward cannot be understated. He had lived in Normandy in exile for 30 years since boyhood, and had only come back to England at about the age of 38 once Harthacnut was on the throne. He had acquired the tastes

Earldoms in 1045

and outlook of a Norman, spoke Norman-French and knew his Norman relations well, including his young first-cousin-once-removed William. He was unmarried, but then married Edith, daughter of Godwin in 1045 when he was about 43. There were no children, which may have disappointed Godwin, who may have wished to be grandfather to a dynasty. Edward had deep religious views and gained the nickname 'Confessor'.

1048 saw Harold once more in charge of the English navy, this time dealing with German raiders who managed to get through and raid Essex, part of his own earldom. Meanwhile the German emperor Henry was defending his own border from Magnus of Norway. Then Magnus's death saw his half-uncle Harald Hardrada claim Norway and fight Sweyn Ulfson, a cousin of Sweyn Godwinson, for control of Denmark. In these confused and turbulent years, emperor Henry had, by 1049, formed an alliance with Edward whereby the English fleet, part led by Harold Godwinson, was to contain the pirates by sea whilst the emperor dealt with them by land.

In the midst of all this, Sweyn Godwinson returned to England from Flanders where he had been in exile. He tried to reconcile formally with Edward, but the Witan, including Harold and Beorn, refused this, and Sweyn was given four days' safe conduct to leave England. Before he left there was news of pirates in the English Channel and the king ordered earl Godwin to take a fleet of 42 ships, some commanded by Harold, others by Beorn, to intercept them. The fleet became weather-bound at Pevensey, and Sweyn turned up and somehow persuaded Beorn to accompany him, the end result of which was Beorn's death. After this Sweyn was named '*nithing*', that is a person of no value, and he went back to Flanders. Some of his ships deserted him, but things had gone too far and two of these were nevertheless intercepted by ships from Hastings, their crews slain and the ships given back to the king. Over the winter of 1049/50 Godwin tried to persuade Edward to allow his son back and this was eventually allowed, under the condition that Sweyn would undertake a pilgrimage to Jerusalem. He eventually did this after the next events of 1051, but died in 1052 during his return at Constantinople.

In 1051 Edward blocked the appointment of a nominee of Godwin as archbishop of Canterbury, and instead appointed his own favourite Norman advisor, Robert Champart, who had been bishop of London from 1044, and a former abbot of Jumièges. This may have been the start of new tensions with Godwin, whom Edward still held responsible in part for his brother Alfred's murder. Also in the summer of 1051, Edward was visited by his former brother-in-law, count Eustace of Boulogne. Afterwards, travelling back to Flanders, Eustace demanded free lodgings for himself and his men at Dover. The people of Dover refused, and there was a fight with several deaths on both sides. Eustace returned to the king to complain, following which Edward angrily summoned Godwin, and ordered him to ravage Dover to punish the people. Godwin refused to ravage in his own earldom, Edward called the Witan to judge this refusal, and added in the issue of Godwin being involved in the murder of his younger brother Ætheling Alfred by Harefoot's men in 1036.

Godwin knew a trap when he saw one and gathered the Wessex fyrd, plus Sweyn and Harold with their troops. He also married off another young son, Tostig, to Judith, daughter of Baldwin IV of Flanders and his second wife Judith of Normandy, daughter of Richard II of Normandy, which created an alliance and a safe haven for himself. Edward in turn gathered his army plus Eustace, archbishop Robert and his nephew, Ralf of Mantes, and earls Leofric of Mercia and Siward of Northumbria. On 1 September, whilst Edward was at Gloucester news was brought that Godwin and his army were nearby. Godwin demanded an opportunity to refute the charges made against him concerning Alfred's murder. He also wanted Eustace to stand trial for his actions in Dover. Edward stalled, summoned the northern earls again and cried treason. Godwin's bluff was called when the earls with their fyrds arrived. Civil war loomed, negotiations took place, and Godwin's army dispersed.

Once more Edward commanded Godwin and Harold to appear before him. Godwin asked for guarantees but Edward refused. Godwin was again in an impossible position: if he went to Edward, his safety was at risk, but if he stood his ground it could come to conflict. In the end Godwin and the rest of his sons were declared outlaws and given five days to leave the country. Wulfnoth, Godwin's youngest son and Hákon, Sweyn's son, remained behind as hostages with Edward. Godwin, his wife Gytha, and his sons Sweyn, Tostig and Gyrth boarded ship at Bosham and went to Flanders. Harold and Leofwine Godwinson sailed from Bristol for the Norse stronghold of Dublin. Murchad, the new king of Dublin, allowed the Godwinsons to recruit for what seemed an inevitable struggle with King Edward.

Following this, the *Anglo-Saxon Chronicle* (D version only) briefly reports a visit by the 23-year-old duke William of Normandy and his entourage to Edward in 1051–1052 during the exile of the Godwins. This may have been a follow-up to the story about the appointment of Robert Champart as archbishop of Canterbury. Robert was a confidant of Edward, and en route to Rome to collect his pallium he is said to have conveyed an offer from Edward of the succession of England to duke William. He *may* have conveyed a promise to William of the succession during this visit, but historians disagree about whether the event even occurred and, if so, how seriously Edward meant the promise and whether he later changed his mind. He clearly knew that he would have no children, for his marriage to Edith of Wessex was a chaste political one. Whilst the Godwins were in exile she was sent to a convent at Wilton and Edward toyed with divorcing her.

In early 1051 Edward would have been drawn to a Norman successor. No precedent existed for English kings to nominate heirs, this being the duty of the Witan, but this was not the case in Normandy. In Normandy, from the time of Rollo, it was usual for the incumbent to name his successor before his death. Usually it would have been the eldest son, but not always. The logic was that the nobles would swear an oath of allegiance to him before the present incumbent died. This process of grooming was less developed in England. But this was how it was done in Normandy, so William would probably have seen nothing wrong with the process. Possibly, neither would Edward who had spent so many years in Normandy.

At that time Edward had other living male relatives – his nephew earl Ralf (the Timid) and his brother Walter count of Mantes – and there was also an exiled descendant of Edmund Ironside living in Hungary, who would have had little knowledge of England. No one wanted another Scandinavian king (neither Magnus nor Harald Hardrada, uncle and heir of Magnus, who claimed England on the basis that Harthacnut and Magnus had agreed that if either died childless the other would have his throne, and also that he was a successor of Cnut), nor the return of a Viking dynasty, and the power struggles between the earls would have made it difficult for any to be successful. A Norman succession would ensure that the Channel was kept closed to Vikings.

This was all before the return of the Godwins and their gradual re-establishment of a powerbase. On 24 June 1052, earl Godwin made a sortie from his exile in Flanders across the Channel possibly to see what support he could count on from Wessex. After recruiting (no doubt vigorously) at Winchelsea, Rye and Hastings he retreated to Pevensey, as king Edward's fleet sallied forth from Sandwich to find him. A storm covered Godwin's further retreat to Bruges, after 'acquiring' additional ships from

Pevensey, but soon after that he returned to England, landing on the Isle of Wight.

Harold and Leofwine left Dublin with nine ships full of mercenaries. They ravaged Porlock and entered the river Severn to provoke Odda, who now had responsibility for the area. The local fyrd was called out, but they were easily defeated. This was Harold's first military action, and it was a small-scale success. The Godwin brothers then sailed round Land's End and joined their father off the Isle of Wight, after which they went to Portland where Godwin re-imposed his authority as earl of Wessex. From there the combined fleet sailed up the Channel to London, gathering men and ships (again no doubt including from Pevensey, Hastings *et al.*) as they went.

Once more Edward summoned the earls. Ralf and Odda responded, but Leofric and Siward were this time noticeable by their absence, and Edward found himself outnumbered. Arriving in London earl Godwin talked directly to the citizens and persuaded them to support him. As in 1051, two English armies faced each other, but bishop Stigand acted as an intermediary, a truce was made and a meeting of the Witan called. The missing party was Sweyn Godwinson who had died during his return from the pilgrimage initially imposed in 1050.

The Witan, when it met, included Leofric and Siward. Godwin cleared himself, on oath, of involvement in the Ætheling Alfred's death and of treasonable intent by himself and family in 1051. The Witan and the reluctant king accepted the oath. Following this Godwin and his family were restored to their lands. The Witan, in a political fudge, had held that the crisis of 1051 had been caused by 'bad counsellors', that is Edward's Norman advisors!

Following the temporary eclipse of his family, earl Godwin did not enjoy his return to favour for very long, for Ordericus Vitalis reports that in 1052 he promptly dismissed, or at least caused to flee, the above controversial archbishop of Canterbury. Champart may have somehow taken Edward's hostages, Wulfnoth Godwinson and Hákon Sweynson, with him and handed them over to William of Normandy. Stigand was appointed as archbishop but Robert Champart appealed to the pope, who reinstated him. Then Champart died at Jumièges on the way back from Rome.

This incident does show just how confident Godwin felt. He was clearly prepared to manoeuvre around Edward, although never to overthrow him. But a new pope still refused to recognise Stigand and removed his pallium so that he was unable to perform archiepiscopal functions such as the consecration of bishops. Stigand also held the see of Winchester and some abbeys. This pluralism was forbidden by a series of popes. Edward could have dismissed Stigand, but he did not.

Soon afterwards, during a feast, earl Godwin suffered a stroke and died three days later. This must have been with the knowledge that he would never be grandfather to a dynasty via Edward and Edith's marriage. King Edward then made a surprise political move and appointed Harold as the new earl of Wessex. He also created him Dux Anglorum. This was a new title, indicating not that he had been designated heir but the military deputy of the king.

Godwin about to take the oath and Edward accepting Godwin's oath
From the *Abbreviatio of Domesday Book c.* 1241   E 36/284 f2v
© National Archives

At this point Northumbria started to cause trouble. It had always been semi-detached from the rest of England and had a residual Danish-Saxon law structure, so king Edward appointed another of Harold's brothers, Tostig, to the earldom. Undoubtedly this was with the instruction to convert the earldom to Anglo-Saxon law.

Earl Ælfgar of East Anglia thought that the earldom of Northumbria should have been his and his complaints riled king Edward, who promptly outlawed him. Following the familiar former example of the Godwins, the discarded Ælfgar fled to Ireland where he raised a force of mercenaries which sailed to Chester. He then tried to get the king of North Wales, Gruffydd ap Llewellyn, to join him to attack England. The Welsh king, however, had another issue to deal with first: Gruffydd ap Rhydderch of South Wales. With the help of Ælfgar's 18 shiploads of mercenaries, Gruffydd ap Llewellyn raided South Wales, which resulted in the killing of his rival. They now turned on the southern Welsh Marches, the area previously known as Hwicce, but avoided conflict with Ælfgar's father, Leofric of Mercia. Ralf the Timid, earl of Hereford, was sent against them. He decided to use cavalry and had a monumental defeat, so king Edward had to look elsewhere for a force to defend England. He called on Harold. Harold moved cautiously, making a feint at Wales to draw Gruffydd back, and then opened negotiations with the invaders. Ælfgar was reinstated as earl of East Anglia, Gruffydd gained some borderlands, and Ælfgar accepted Tostig as earl of Northumbria. Although it was not an ideal solution, it broke the alliance of Ælfgar and Gruffydd. Shortly afterwards more problems broke out with Gruffydd. Earls Harold and Leofric, gathered an army, and with this at their back sat down with Gruffydd to talk. This ended up with Gruffydd recognised as king of Wales in exchange for him recognising Edward as his overlord.

Edward had started to think about his successor again, and tried to find Edward Ætheling, the son of Edmund Ironside, who had fled with his family to Hungary. Bishop Ealdred of Worcester set out in 1054 to track him down but was unsuccessful. In 1056 Harold, in diplomat mode, may have travelled to visit Baldwin of Flanders and on to Cologne then to Regensburg, met the Hungarian king there, found Edward Ætheling and negotiated his return to England as a possible heir for king Edward. Walker proposes a scenario for this, but it is not directly recorded. Whatever happened, Edward Ætheling arrived in England with his family in 1057, coinciding with the death of earl Leofric. Edward Ætheling also died soon after arriving, but he had a young son, Edgar, and other children whom king Edward took into the royal household. Earl Leofric's son, Ælfgar, succeeded him in Mercia and a new earl of East Anglia was appointed – yet another Godwinson, Gyrth.

On 21 December 1057, Ralf the Timid, earl of Hereford, died. To replace him the earldom which actually covered much of south-west Mercia was divided in three: Harold gained the Welsh border counties, and Ælfgar and Leofwine split the more eastern counties. Of all the earls of England, now only the unsettled Ælfgar was not a Godwinson. In 1057 Ælfgar made another alliance with Gruffydd ap Llewellyn of

Wales, which Edward saw as a threat and banished him. Again Harold in diplomatic mode arranged for Ælfgar to be given back his earldom and Gruffydd more English borderlands. The alliance ended when Ælfgar died sometime after August in 1062. As soon as Christmas was over, Harold as military commander struck at Gruffydd, determined to smash him once and for all and to regain the lands the English had had to concede to him over the years. Harold and his brother Tostig undertook a joint land/sea operation. By the spring of 1063 Gruffydd and his shrinking forces had fled inland to the fastness of Snowdon, where he continued to harass the English. On 5 August Cynan ap Iago, who was the son of Iago ab Idwal, ruler of Gwynedd from 1033 to 1039, brought Gruffydd's head to Harold, who took it and laid it at the feet of king Edward. His response is not recorded.

In the autumn of 1064, possibly early 1065, Harold visited Normandy. The early records suggest that he was to inform William that he was Edward's preferred heir, but the sources of information are Norman and written after 1066, so the storyline may be more than suspect. Interestingly, Douglas considered that the early Norman accounts were 'reasonable'. All the sources concur that a visit happened, although vary in describing what transpired. Another theory is that this was an attempt by Harold to retrieve his young brother Wulfnoth and nephew Hákon, who were still being held hostage in Normandy (see above for the possible story of how they came to be there), although why he should suddenly decide to do this 12 years after they became hostages is not clear.

He had sailed from Bosham, and may have been aiming for Flanders to use count Baldwin as an intermediary or tried to sail directly to Normandy. Wherever his projected landfall, his ships were caught in a storm and ended up north of Normandy. Harold became a hostage of the count of Ponthieu, a vassal of Duke William, and was held to ransom himself. William of Normandy found out and had Harold released to his 'care' at Eu where he met him himself with a troop of armed horsemen and took him to Rouen.

Harold stayed at the Norman court for some time, and during this he took part alongside William in a campaign against Conan II of Brittany who was besieging Dol. William knighted Harold, which as an English earl he may have regarded as no more than an act of gratitude, but to the Normans it would clearly have been taken that Harold had accepted William's lordship. In addition there was the possible oath on (hidden?) holy bones that Harold would do all he could to make William king of England. If he did take this oath, it might have been to secure his own release or to protect his own future position in the event of the duke's success in gaining the throne of England. William had agreed that as part of the deal, Harold would marry one of his daughters (possibly Agatha or Adeliza), and that one of William's related magnates would marry Edith, Harold's sister, who would by then be Edward's widow. Harold returned to England in late 1064 with Hákon, but still without his brother, Wulfnoth, who remained a hostage.

The story is told in the Bayeux Tapestry, which is chiefly a tale of Harold's double dealing and his denouement as seen from the Norman viewpoint. This is in some pictorial detail, but we should be wary of over-interpretation of it, and of taking specific scenes too literally. As with all things related to the Conquest it has been academically dissected. Cowdrey gives an interesting view of the nuances of the tapestry imagery, and also points out some sub-tales in the border images which, whilst often decorative, sometimes appear to give commentaries (sometimes not very complimentary and sometimes obscene) on the events related in the adjacent main panel, and also refer to Middle English fables, particularly in the first section (Chefneux).

Did Harold take an oath?

From *The Bayeux Tapestry: The complete tapestry in full colour* by David M Wilson © 1985, Thames & Hudson, Ltd. London.

As J Campbell has said, there was probably no smoke without fire about all this. Edward's many years in Normandy must have counted for something. Although Edward was about 28 when William was born, Edward had been brought up, educated and lived 'like a son' in the Norman court through the difficult years when William's father died and William only just survived. He must have known the dukes of Normandy well, and William as a boy.

Edward clearly detested the Godwins but was at first powerful enough to use them, although after 1052 his position was much weaker. Also he had found that he could not trust his own mother. For a man who was supposed to be deeply religious he also held deep opinions and had a fierce temper. His situation must have led to deep frustrations.

There was a revolt in 1065 against earl Tostig by the Northumbrians. Tostig had increased taxes, never a popular thing to do, but there were deeper-seated reasons for the revolt. He had curbed the power of local landholders through intrigue and murder, and his men were using arbitrary justice to enforce tax collections. In the autumn of 1065 this led the thegns of Northumbria to seize and occupy York and kill Tostig's retainers. The revolt involved 'all the thegns of Yorkshire', the *Anglo-Saxon Chronicle* says. They took back what they deemed theirs by right, then declared Tostig an outlaw and sent for Morcar, the younger brother of earl Edwin of Mercia, to be the new earl. Lead by 'earl' Morcar they were joined at Northampton by earl Edwin (Edwin and Morcar were sons of Ælfgar), and moved south looking to find recompense from Tostig's holdings. Harold met them but, after he had discussed the issues with the rebels, he concluded that it was impossible for Tostig to remain earl of Northumbria.

Harold returned to the king, counselled against military action against Morcar and his thegns, and acceptance of the rebels' demands. Edward was angry, as Tostig had been another favourite, but was finally swayed. For the first time since Sweyn's death, the Godwinsons were divided. Harold went to Northampton and told Morcar he was now officially earl of Northumbria, and the rebels that they were pardoned. Tostig continued to argue with king Edward and in the end took himself off to Flanders, or, as was usually the case with Godwinsons, found himself exiled. He went to Bruges to join his brother-in-law, count Baldwin V.

It was now November 1065 and it became obvious that king Edward would soon die. New kings of England were normally drawn from the royal family but not necessarily by primogeniture. A possible heir was Edgar Ætheling, and normally, with the approval of the Witan, he might have succeeded with Harold 'Dux Anglorum' continuing as regent, and running the country until the boy was old enough to rule on his own. There were also aggressive claims from Harald Hardrada of Norway and William of Normandy, the latter having a family claim through his great-aunt, Emma of Normandy. The meeting of the Witan and celebrations held at Christmas saw all five earls, the archbishops of York and Canterbury, eight bishops and many leading thegns gathered in London. On 5 January 1066 Edward summoned the Witan to his deathbed. He had been semi-conscious for several days, but was roused. He 'commended' his kingdom and the protection of his queen to Harold, and bound his Norman servants to take oaths of loyalty to Harold.

The Witan soon afterwards unanimously acclaimed Harold king of England, perhaps taking into account that to appoint a child king in such circumstances would be too dangerous, but also wishing to have an English king. What has never been clearly ascertained, and never will be, is whether Harold expected and manoeuvred for this. He had been Edward's right-hand man, protector, advisor, diplomat and fixer for over 10 years: did Edward mean to hand over to him as a caretaker regent, not as king? Would Harold have been just as content serving Edgar Ætheling, now 13? He would not have wished to serve William.

The main contemporary English source – the *Anglo-Saxon Chronicle* – observes a prudent post-Conquest silence about Harold's elevation, but later English writers such as John of Worcester and Roger of Hovenden (the latter drawing on the much earlier work *Historia Saxonum sive Anglorum post obitum Bedae*) say that Edward before his death chose Harold for his successor.

William of Malmesbury says, *'he (Harold) said, that he was absolved from his oath, because his (William's) daughter, to whom he had been betrothed, had died before she was marriageable.'*

The half-English Ordericus Vitalis has the most to say: *'There is no doubt that Edward had bequeathed the realm of England to his kinsman William, duke of Normandy, announcing it, first by Robert* [Champart], *archbishop of Canterbury, and afterwards by Harold himself, and, with the consent of the English, making the duke heir to all his rights. Moreover Harold had taken the oath of allegiance to duke William at Rouen, in the presence of the nobles of Normandy, and doing him homage had sworn on the holy relics to all that was required of him. ... This Englishman was distinguished by his great size and strength of body, his polished manners, his firmness of mind and command of words, by a ready wit and a variety of excellent qualities. But what availed so many valuable gifts, when good faith, the foundation of all virtues, was wanting? Returning to his country, his ambition tempted him to aspire to the crown, and to forfeit the fealty he had sworn to his lord. He imposed upon King Edward, who was in the last stage of decay, approaching his end, by the account he gave of his crossing the sea, his journey to Normandy, and the result of his mission, falsely adding that Duke William would give him his daughter in marriage, and concede to him, as his son-in-law, all his right to the throne of England. The feeble prince was much surprised at this statement; however, he believed it, and granted all the crafty tyrant asked.'*

No time was wasted. Ealdred, archbishop of York, crowned Harold the following day (Stigand of Canterbury was still under interdict.) Sometime afterwards Harold formally married Ealdgyth, daughter of earl Ælfgar, sister of earls Edwin and Morcar and widow of the Welsh king Gruffydd ap Llewellyn. This considerably strengthened Harold's ties with the north of England.

After this Malmesbury records: *'William, in the meantime, began mildly to address him by messengers, to expostulate on the broken covenant; to mingle threats with entreaties; and to warn him, that ere a year expired, he would claim his due by the sword, and that he would come to that place, where Harold supposed he had firmer footing than himself. Harold again rejoined, concerning the nuptials of his daughter, and added, that he had been precipitate on the subject of the kingdom, in having confirmed to him by oath another's right, without the universal consent and edict of the general meeting, and of the people: again, that a rash oath ought to be broken; for if the oath, or*

Harold's coronation. It was not the Archbishop of Canterbury, Stigand, who performed the coronation, but the Archbishop of York (see above).

From *The Bayeux Tapestry: The complete tapestry in full colour* by David M Wilson © 1985, Thames & Hudson, Ltd. London.

vow, which a maiden, under her father's roof, made concerning her person, without the knowledge of her parents, was adjudged invalid; how much more invalid must that oath be, which he had made concerning the whole kingdom, when under the king's authority, compelled by the necessity of the time, and without the knowledge of the nation. Besides it was an unjust request, to ask him to resign a government which he had assumed by the universal kindness of his fellow subjects, and which would neither be agreeable to the people, nor safe for the military.'

William of Poitiers records that shortly before the Battle of Hastings, Harold sent William an envoy with a message admitting that Edward had promised the throne to William, but argued that this was over-ridden by Edward's deathbed promise to Harold. In reply, William did not dispute the deathbed promise, but argued that Edward's prior promise to him took precedence. It seems that in Normandy he might have been correct, but this was England.

Harold needed to be sure of the support of the leaders of Northumbria, including that of Oswulf who was subordinate to Morcar, so by marrying the sister of earls Morcar and Edwin he had reassured northern England that Tostig would not be welcomed back. He also created Waltheof Siwardson-earl of Northampton – an area somewhat larger than Northamptonshire is today, in the south-east midlands – and confirmed the positions of Edward's Norman civil servants.

In May Tostig returned. After landing on the Isle of Wight he raided along the south coast to Sandwich. Harold called out the fleet plus the Wessex fyrd and Tostig retreated. He turned north and raided along the coast of East Anglia and along the Burnham river in Lincolnshire, in an area under the control of Edwin. Together Morcar, the earl of Northumbria and Edwin of Mercia expelled the weakened Tostig, who fled to Scotland and the protection of king Malcolm III.

Harold remained well informed about William's actions across the Channel, and all summer of 1066 held ready the fyrd and navy in Hampshire and the Solent. Harold had to stand down his army and navy on or about 8 September 1066. The men were at the end of their period of service and harvests had to be gathered in, and it was also getting late in the year.

Meanwhile Tostig plotted with Harald Hardrada, who had his own ideas about becoming king of England, the outcome being an attempted invasion from the north and the Battles of Fulford and Stamford Bridge. The weather at the same time turned in favour of William. Disaster for Harold Godwinson was just around the corner.

11

NORMANDY AND DUKE WILLIAM II: 1042 TO INVASION

Keith Foord and Neil-Clephane-Cameron

We left Chapter 6 about William at the end of 1041, which was the point at which Edward, prince of England, left exile in Normandy to travel to England. This was after Emma and Harthacnut's journey to England from Flanders and Harthacnut's accession to the throne of England.

Nicholas, son of Richard II and cousin of William, who had allowed William to sideline him from inheriting the duchy by pushing him into the church, became abbot of St Ouen in 1042. Mauger and William, the sons of duke Richard II by Papia and half-brothers of William, now gradually increased their profiles. Mauger became archbishop of Rouen and William count of Arques. They and Nicholas became prominent in the ducal court and other members of the ducal family gained in authority and placements.

William's personal authority remained weak and depended a great deal on the backing that he could obtain from the factions around him, as well as the support of his overlord, king Henri I of France and the administrative functions of the loyal viscounts (sheriffs). He was also helped by the continuing rivalry between dissenting families. Somehow much of the traditional authority and machinery of government survived through to 1047.

Then the western areas revolted. The chaos started to become more organised into a potential coup against William, led by Guy of Burgundy who had received the fiefdoms of Vernon and Brionne on the death of Gilbert, who had himself succeeded Alan II of Brittany. Guy was seeking to become duke. He involved other leading feudal families in this quest, including Nigel, viscount of the Cotentin, and Rannulf I of the Bessin. They nearly caught William, but he escaped and eventually found sanctuary at Falaise. He then directly appealed to king Henri to help him. Henri decided that the threat to his vassal was also a significant threat to France and led an army into Normandy, advancing towards Caen and on to the plain of Val ès Dunes. There he and William, who had gathered a small force of his own, met the rebels who had come from the west and crossed the River Orne. The battle of Val ès Dunes, from the sparse reports available, was a somewhat chaotic, spread-out affair with multiple engagements. But it turned out to be a decisive event and a comprehensive defeat of the rebels. In the final rout the rebels were chased into the Orne and many drowned. Val ès Dunes was the king's victory, not William's. William was on the winning side, but he still had much to overcome. He was about 19 and his minority was now over.

The anarchy of Normandy still had to be dealt with. Later in October 1047, an ecclesiastical council met with William and the chief churchmen of Normandy, including archbishop Mauger of Rouen and abbot Nicholas. A 'Truce of God' was proclaimed and sworn to on Holy relics. This meant that private war was prohibited from Wednesday evening until the next Monday morning and during all the seasons of Lent, Easter, Pentecost and Advent. This only left 36 hours a week for private wars, and a full rest from these during the Holy seasons! How easy would this be to enforce? The chief penalty was to be excommunication and denial of spiritual benefits, but the king and duke were specifically excluded, and could maintain troops and use them in the interest of all.

The period of 1047 to 1060 has been called William's 'war for survival'. From 1047 there was a continuing crisis until 1054. First, Guy of Burgundy had to be dealt with; he had been wounded in, but survived, the battle of Val ès Dunes, and fled to his fortress at Brionne. William had to lay siege to this massive castle on an islet in the Risle valley, and it took three years to force Guy to surrender, when he was banished from Normandy. This delay was also to hold up William's ability to rule all of Normandy, but he must have decided at around that time that it was important to amalgamate Upper and Lower Normandy. As part of this he encouraged the growth of Caen, which would become the second city of Normandy. It was also the place where he and his wife Matilda would build twin abbeys, the Abbaye aux Hommes and the Abbaye aux Dames.

More problems occurred from 1051, which would see a significant change in allegiances. The count of Anjou started to press northwards into Maine, occupying its capital in 1051, and war spread to the southern border of Normandy. King Henri felt obliged to act and, with his consent, William entered Maine, besieging Domfront but also suddenly storming Alençon. He allowed terrible atrocities to be carried out there, and the terrified inhabitants of Domfront, having seen what happened, surrendered. The war between Anjou and the king dragged on, and they eventually reconciled, in spite of efforts by William to prevent this.

This changed the pattern of alliance and, in the face of yet another revolt, William, who was somewhat disconcerted by the turn of events, found himself opposed by the king. Henri had become concerned that William was becoming too powerful and therefore dangerous to the kingdom of France. William had married Matilda of Flanders at about that time, and Henri may have also been concerned about a possible alliance between Flanders and Normandy. At the same time, duke William's uncle,

William of Arques, decided to desert him and duke William then promptly besieged his uncle at Arques. In spite of some help to William of Arques from king Henri of France, William of Arques finally had to surrender and fled to Eustace of Boulogne. He and his family were never restored.

1051 was also the year William is supposed to have visited Edward the Confessor in England. This event is recorded in only one version of the *Anglo-Saxon Chronicle* (D), corroborated by John of Worcester, who says that Edward *'gave earl William many gifts'*. William does seem to have been rather busy in Normandy, but it is just possible that it did happen, and that during his private discussions with Edward the succession to the English throne was discussed. Further messages about this possibility may have been received by William from Robert Champart, who had been appointed by Edward to the archbishopric of Canterbury, when en route to Rome to receive his pallium. In 1052, when the said Robert was chased out of England by earl Godwin, Edward may have transferred the Godwin hostages to him. He is believed to have brought to William as hostages Wulfnoth, the youngest son of earl Godwin and brother of Harold, and Hákon, the nephew of Harold and son of Sweyn Godwinson, his dead brother.

William had to face another, this time two-pronged, assault towards Rouen from king Henri in early 1054. But this time he was able to generate a wide response to his call to arms, and having taken Arques had no hostile force within Normandy to deal with at the same time as this incursion. William's force was large enough to deploy on each side of the Seine, to confront Henri's approaches, with the count of Eu and Walter Giffard commanding the east and William the west. Eu and Giffard caught their opponents unprepared early in the morning, and this resulted in a complete rout of the French to the east. To the west, hearing this result, Henri withdrew. This was the Battle of Mortemer, where William himself did not need to engage, and after this William would never again be faced with so strong a direct threat to his power. In 1054/5 an ecclesiastical meeting deposed Mauger, another uncle of William, as archbishop of Rouen and appointed a reforming archbishop. William seemed to be firmly back in control, and supported by the Church.

Once again in 1057 Henri and the count of Anjou attacked, entering the Hiémois along the Orne valley and pushing towards Bayeux and Caen. William massed a large force near Falaise and watched. As the enemy reached the Dives marshes west of Caen they crossed the Dives estuary at a narrow ford near Varaville but were caught by the incoming tide. William opportunistically pounced and massacred the part of the army that had not crossed. Henri, king of France, having lost half his army, beat a hasty retreat. This was not a pitched battle, more a very large ambush, although for convenience it has been recorded as the Battle of Varaville.

In 1058 William felt strong enough to take on his previous overlord who had turned against him. He opened hostilities in the southwest, but the affair moved to stalemate. Then William had some good fortune with the deaths of two of his main adversaries. On 4 August 1060 Henri I died, and his young son Philip inherited under the guardianship of Baldwin V of Flanders, who was William's father-in-law. As a bonus, the count of Anjou, Geoffrey Martel, died on 14 November of the same year with no direct heir, and his nephews immediately squabbled, not sorting things out until 1068. The last count of Maine, Herbert II, then died in 1062 without a male heir, and William promptly strategically married Herbert's sister Margaret to his son Robert Curthose.

The pattern of power was changing and William conquered Maine, eventually taking Le Mans following a prolonged period of terror across northern Maine during 1062/3, laying waste the land and burning towns, at the same time seizing or creating strongholds. His main opponent was Geoffrey of Mayenne whose castle he destroyed by fire in 1063. There is a little story told that William had smuggled two children with pyromaniac tendencies into the castle to do this.

The pattern of William's warfare was clear. He was prepared to wait and watch, to sow terror, make alliances through marriages, banish (and worse) those who rebelled, take opportunities and be brutal. It was very effective. He may have remained relatively inexperienced with respect to large set battles, but Gillingham has pointed out that he must have engaged in some kind of fighting at least 13 times between 1047 and 1065.

William was now in his thirties. That he had survived all the above and more must have been down to a huge strength of character, luck, and to some extent the underlying established ducal system of Normandy that he had inherited, plus the power of the Norman church. Now he turned his attention to Brittany and its duke, Conan II, who was besieging Dol, held by an ally of William's. This was the occasion when he took with him Harold Godwinson, earl of Wessex. The siege of Dol was lifted, Conan weakened, and the Normans progressed as far as Dinan, possibly Rennes, but they soon returned to the duchy.

Normandy's southern and south-western borders were now tranquil, and William could consider the situation in England, particularly after Harold's visit. The story behind Harold Godwinson's visit to Normandy in 1064 is covered in Chapter 10, but it is thought that Harold's involvement in the Brittany expedition was deliberate on the part of William, as he became clearly subordinated to the duke. William's view was clear: Harold was his vassal, pledged on oath to support William in his claim to the English throne. He may also have become betrothed to one of William's daughters, Adeliza or Agatha during his stay: as we have seen, William used alliance through marriage a great deal.

Edward the Confessor died on 5 January 1066 and what seems to have been William's long game came to the fore. What was (retrospectively) at stake was the position of England *vis à vis* Scandinavian and Latin Europe, plus the ecclesiastical and political structure of western Christendom for the rest of the middle ages – not to mention William's own ambition. What he did not envisage, however, was that Harold

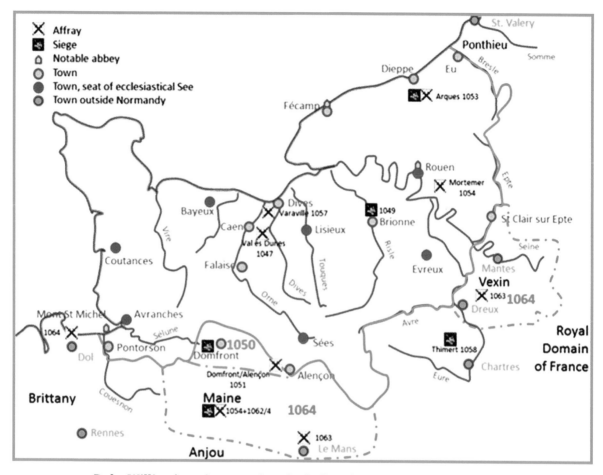

Duke William's main campaigns including the annexations 1050–1064
© Battle and District Historical Society

would be crowned king of England within 24 hours of Edward's death. To William this must have been astounding and an affront, given the understanding that he had thought he had reached with Edward and the events of 1064 when Harold was his 'guest'. What William with his Norman heritage possibly did not understand was the role of the Witan in the selection of a new king.

William's first step was an immediate protest, which received the normal response to such formal protests. This was all a formality as he immediately realised that force was going to be required. He moved to obtain the support of his vassals and to split his rivals. He met with his magnates who had shared his rise to power, who at first were sceptical of the prospects of a successful invasion of England, but they became persuaded otherwise.

The duke then held a series of assemblies at Lillebonne, Bonneville-sur-Touques and Caen and presumably there were more, as this was a grand war plan, which required full cooperation and 'ownership'. Being of Viking descent the prospect of extending their estates and possible plunder would not have been far from Norman minds.

William also ensured that the duchy would be in good hands during his absence or, in the worst case, his non-return. Duchess Matilda, in association with his oldest son Robert (then 14), took on special responsibilities, and Robert was proclaimed heir to the duchy. Roger of Beaumont, Roger of Montgomery and Hugh, son of the viscount of the Avranchin, were to assist Matilda and Robert. The Church was not forgotten, and was anxious to have confirmation of grants and ratifications and settlement of disputes before the departure of William. Lesser men also gave grants to local churches in similar vein, which showed how the enterprise was affecting all.

The Pope was sent a mission led by the archdeacon of Lisieux to ask for his favour. Although no papal record of the actual case has survived, pope Alexander II proclaimed his approval and a papal banner was carried at Hastings. Ordericus Vitalis writes '*On hearing all the circumstances, the pope favoured the legitimate rights of the duke, enjoined him to take up arms against the perjurer, and sent him the standard of St Peter the apostle, by whose merits he would be defended against all dangers.*' It must have helped that the archbishop of Canterbury, Stigand, who had been placed there by the Godwins, had been excommunicated, and undoubtedly the unpleasant case of Alfred Ætheling, the events in England of 1051–1052, plus Harold's supposed oath on Holy relics were all mentioned.

Men from Flanders, France and Brittany and further afield joined the Normans in the invasion force, many simply mercenaries, but the expedition was regarded in some European circles as almost a crusade, having tacit support from France, the Pope and the Holy Roman Empire. These men had to be created into a disciplined force and merged with the forces of the duchy so that they could fight together.

Ships were also needed, and to those available were added many newly built for the occasion. Considerable numbers of various sized ships were required from the magnates of Normandy. The quota list of ships adds up to 776, but maybe some more were added by William himself, and small vessels were added to make the fleet up to about 1000. That these were acquired or made from new and then assembled at Dives was a triumph of organisation in a duchy that was now united. The south-east Sussex interest in this is that the original ship list probably originated from Fécamp abbey in 1067–1072, and was copied in the Battle Abbey scriptorium sometime between 1130 and 1160. This and the preparations discussed above are well described by van Houts (1987). During these preparations William could receive reports on what was happening around the North Sea, and must have had spies watching Harold on the south coast. Once Harold disbanded on or about 8 September 1066 the time was ripe. All William needed was a south wind.

The Ship List of William the Conqueror

William fitzOsbern, the steward	60 ships
Hugh, later earl of Chester	60 ships
Hugh of Montfort	50 ships & 60 soldiers
Romo (Remigius), almoner of Fécamp Abbey, later bishop of Lincoln	1 ship & 20 soldiers
Nicholas, abbot of St. Ouen	15 ships & 100 soldiers
Robert, count of Eu	60 ships
Fulk of Anjou	40 ships
Gerald the steward	40 ships
William, count of Evreux	60 ships
Roger of Montgomery	60 ships
Roger of Beaumont	60 ships
Odo, bishop of Bayeux	100 ships
Robert of Mortain	120 ships
Walter Giffard	30 ships & 100 soldiers

Apart from these ships which totalled 1000 (?), the duke had ships from others according to their means

Duchess Matilda provided a ship for William called 'Mora', with on the prow a statue of a child pointing to England with his right hand and with the left hand blowing an ivory horn

The Ship List: The data is transcribed from translations from the Latin of a copy (dated 1130–1160) from the Battle Abbey scriptorium which is held at the Bodleian Libraries (MS E Museo 93 fo.8v (p16). The original was probably written at Fécamp Abbey between 1067–1072.

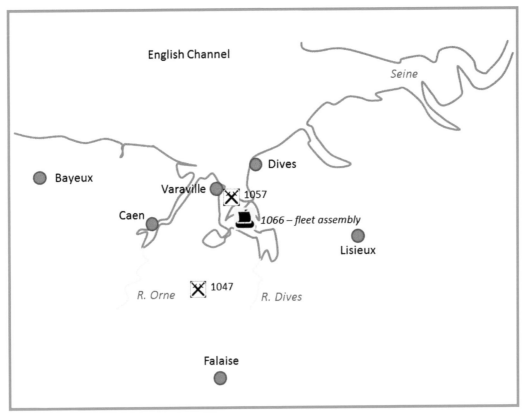

Assembly of the invasion forces at Dives. The coastline is shown as in 1066, with a shallow wide harbour (not unlike Pevensey was at that time) at the mouth of the River Dives, east of Caen. Note the proximity of previous battle sites.
©Battle and District Historical Society

... the comet sightings of 1456, 1531, 1607 and 1682 were so similar that they must have been the same comet returning every 75–76 years.

Edmond Halley (1656–1742),
A Synopsis of the Astronomy of Comets, 1705

Halley's comet will next appear in mid-2061

The Normans are a race inured to war, and can hardly live without it, fierce in rushing against the enemy, and, where force fails of success, ready to use stratagem, or corrupt by bribery.

William of Malmesbury *c.* 1125

Nothing happens in a vacuum in life: every action has a series of consequences, and sometimes it takes a long time to fully understand the consequences of our actions.

Khaled Hosseini, 2013

12

STRATEGIC MOVEMENTS IN 1066: BATTLES OF FULFORD and STAMFORD BRIDGE; WILLIAM'S VOYAGES and LANDING; HAROLD'S RETURN SOUTH

Keith Foord and Neil Clephane-Cameron

D uke William's invasion of England had been expected all summer. When all was ready the departure of the fleet was delayed for two weeks or more by wind and weather conditions in the Channel. But this was not to be the only challenge to king Harold Godwinson during 1066.

Another claimant to the English throne struck first – Harald Hardrada of Norway, supported by Harold's banished brother Tostig Godwinson. This led to the first battles of 1066 at Fulford and Stamford Bridge. The only truly trustworthy record we have of the preliminaries to and immediate aftermath of these events is from the *Anglo-Saxon Chronicle* (C, D and E versions).

The story starts on or about 24 April 1066 when Halley's Comet appeared, as it does every 75–76 years, enough of an interval for its re-appearance to be taken mythically to portend great events. This time it was to be true, but the date of its supernatural appearance coincided with the relatively unwelcome re-appearance of the banished Tostig Godwinson 'with as great a fleet as he could get', who landed on the Isle of Wight with a band of mainly Flemish men (Gaimar). There he demanded money and provisions. Tostig had originally sailed from Flanders after agreeing with Harald Hardrada on a plan to invade England later in the year. After leaving the Isle of Wight he proceeded eastwards and 'did harm everywhere along the sea coast where he could get to' until he reached Sandwich. As he went he pressed sailors into service, no doubt calling at Hastings to do so. Ordericus Vitalis states that he was joined at Sandwich by a lieutenant, Copsi, with seventeen vessels from Orkney. This was the first open indication of the involvement in this escapade of Norway, which ruled the Orkney and Shetland Islands.

At Sandwich he was seen off by Harold's gathering army and navy. He then turned northwards with his 50–60 ships up the east coast, raiding as he went. He made a brief landing on the south coast of the Humber, but he was met by earl Edwin of Mercia at Lindsey, in Lincolnshire. Much of his army was lost, and the pressed

Halley's Comet from the Bayeux Tapestry – it could be seen in England for only six days in 1066, between 24–30 April.

From *The Bayeux Tapestry: The complete tapestry in full colour* by David M Wilson © 1985, Thames & Hudson, Ltd. London.

boatmen deserted after earl Morcar prevented his landing on the north coast of the Humber. He retreated to Scotland with only 12 ships remaining. He was allowed to stay all summer and was assisted and supplied by king Malcolm III.

This is in the initial story. We also have the *Heimskringla* or *The Chronicle of the Kings of Norway* by Snorri Sturlason (*c.* 1179–1241) to give us the Norwegian version of the events. Snorri's tale was written down more than 150 years after the event and is based on oral histories; therefore it is entertaining but unreliable (except where it agrees with the *Anglo-Saxon Chronicle*). Interpretations of the events it describes enter and confuse later stories, but there is so little mention of the events in the post-Conquest Norman chronicles – after all the Normans had no wish to praise Harold, or by allusion diminish their triumph, that we do need to refer to it! Below, where we use direct extracts from Snorri, they are in *italics* so that the reader is aware of their provenance.

The *Heimskringla* tells us that with over 300 ships (the *Anglo-Saxon Chronicle* C version says '*a very great raiding ship-army*', the E version agrees with 300, Florence says 500). Hardrada's force voyaged from Solund on the Sognafjord in Norway, probably sometime in August, via the Shetland and Orkney Islands where, we are told, he dropped off his wife and daughters on Orkney for a holiday (!), picked up reinforcements and also met more reinforcements from Iceland before meeting Tostig, possibly in the Firth of Forth or on the River Tyne. The Norwegian army was added to by Tostig's force which he had managed to enhance a bit. After meeting, Hardrada's and Tostig's forces landed at the Cleveland district in the Tees area in early September 1066.

'When king Harald was clear for sea, and the wind became favourable, he sailed out into the ocean; and he himself landed in Shetland, but a part of his fleet in the Orkney Islands. King Harald stopped but a short time in Shetland before sailing to Orkney, from whence he took with him a great armed force, and the earls Paul and Erlend, the sons of Earl Thorfin; but he left behind him here the Queen Ellisif, and her daughters Maria and Ingegerd. Then he sailed, leaving Scotland and England westward of him, and landed at a place called Klifland [Cleveland]. *There he went on shore and plundered, and brought the country in subjection to him without opposition. Then he brought up at Skardaburg* [Scarborough], *and fought with the people of the place. He went up a hill which is there, and made a great pile upon it, which he set on fire; and when the pile was in clear flame, his men took large forks and pitched the burning wood down into the town, so that one house caught fire after the other, and the town surrendered. The Northmen killed many people there and took all the booty they could lay hold of. There was nothing left for the Englishmen now, if they would preserve their lives, but to submit to king Harald; and thus he subdued the country wherever he came. Then the king proceeded south along the land, and brought up at Hellornes* [Holderness], *where there came a force that had been assembled to oppose him, with which he had a battle, and gained the victory.'*

So we are told by Snorri that Harald Hardrada and Tostig had raided down the north Yorkshire coast, with skirmishes at Scarborough, and a small battle with the local forces at Holderness, which are estimated by Laporte to have taken place on or about 12–14 September. They then sailed up the Humber estuary as far as Riccall on the River Ouse, fully invading the earldom of Northumbria on or about 16–17 September (Laporte).

'Thereafter the king sailed to the Humber, and up along the river, and then he landed. Up in Jorvik [York] *were two earls, earl Morukare* [Morcar], *and his brother, earl Valthiof*, *and they had an immense army. While the army of the earls was coming down from the upper part of the country, king Harald lay in the Usa* [Ouse]. *King Harald now went on the land, and drew up his men.'*

*The *Heimskringla* is erroneous on this point confusing earls Edwin and Waltheof.

BATTLE OF FULFORD

The northern earls, Edwin of Mercia and Morcar of Northumbria, failed at the Battle of Fulford on 20 September to repel the invaders. York (*Jorvik*), which may have had some residual Danish sympathies, then surrendered rather than be ravaged, and promised to support Hardrada and Tostig against Harold Godwinson. A few days later Hardrada arranged a meeting with the citizens for the next morning and the delivery or exchange of some hostages, just in case, so to speak. Little was he to know that he would only hold York for another 24 hours.

Fulford is sometimes thought of as a minor battle. This cannot be so, for it must have caused significant losses for the northern English army. It may be that if Edwin and Morcar had known that Harold was on the way, they might have instead retreated behind the walls of York and awaited reinforcement.

'When king Harald [Hardrada] saw that the English array had come to the ditch against him, he ordered the charge to be sounded, and urged on his men. He ordered the banner which was called the 'Landravager' to be carried before him, and made so severe an assault that all had to give way before it; and there was a great loss among the men of the earls, and they soon broke into flight, some running up the river, some down, and the most leaping into the ditch, which was so filled with dead that the Norsemen could go dry-foot over the fen.

Then the king advanced to take the castle, and laid his army at Stanfordabryggiur [Stamford Bridge]; and as king Harald had gained so great a victory against so great chiefs and so great an army, the people were dismayed, and doubted if they could make any opposition. The men of the castle therefore determined, in a council, to send a message to king Harald, and deliver up the castle into his power. All this was soon settled; so that on Sunday the king proceeded with the whole army to the castle, and appointed a Thing [meeting] of the people without the castle, at which the people of the castle were to be present. At this Thing all the people accepted the condition of submitting to Harald, and gave him, as hostages, the children of the most considerable persons.'

A second Thing was arranged with Hardrada early on Monday morning, where king Harald was to name officers to rule over the town, to give out laws, and bestow fiefs.

The main English army had been on invasion alert standby on the south coast all summer, but was disbanded on or about 8 September to allow its members to bring in their harvests. We do not know the precise dates of the initial Norwegian landing, or the precise date on which Harold received that news. However, once he heard about the events happening near York, Harold Godwinson had to march north with an army that he hastened to gather, but with a strong core of housecarls.

There was also a problem with the English fleet. If he had had enough ships Harold might have avoided much of the fatigue of his troops, as well as the logistic problems of a march to the north. The English fleet had been backing up the army, having been on watch in the Solent all summer, and had also been stood down. It had been sent to London, but unfortunately lost many vessels as it made its way around the south coast during late summer storms, the same that had prevented William of Normandy from crossing the Channel earlier. The losses from Harold's fleet may have been one reason that the king did not sail en masse for the north instead of making the arduous overland journey.

It was likely that Harold's throng was composed mainly of mounted warriors in view of the remarkable speed they were able to achieve in getting to Yorkshire. He managed to travel some 185 miles (300 km) in only four days, an extraordinary feat. He followed the quickest route via Ermine Street, and north of Lincoln took the alternative inland route to avoid a fording of the Humber. On the way he must have recruited from the areas he passed through, and then rallied his own and the remnants of Edwin and Morcar's army at Tadcaster on the Sunday 24 September (*Anglo-Saxon Chronicle* C).

Some soldiers may have enshipped, as the *Anglo-Saxon Chronicle* (C) writes *lið fylcade* (marshalled the fleet) when talking of the mustering at Tadcaster – so a few ships may have sailed up the River Wharfe. Given favourable winds and tides a voyage could have taken about three days. Jones confirms this interesting interpretation – that some English ships had reached Tadcaster on the River Wharfe, which joins the River Ouse south of Riccall, before the Vikings got there. Presumably a few ships had been sent north from the depleted navy as a precaution, once it had returned to London from the Solent or as soon as news had reached Harold Godwinson of Hardrara's and Tostig's landings at Cleveland.

This might indicate that Harold may have had rather more than four days' warning of their arrival, but that he may initially have thought that it was a Viking raid, rather than a full-scale invasion.

BATTLE OF STAMFORD BRIDGE

Harold's arrival was unexpected. He could have been expecting to need to attack York, but found York undefended, thanks to the deal that had been done. No doubt he 'forgave' the citizens of York their acceptance of an offer they could not refuse from Hardrada, and so was able to engage Hardrada and Tostig the next day.

Hardrada had sent one third of his army back to the ships at Riccall, and many of his soldiers were un-armoured (it was reported to have been a hot day). Instead of an exchange of governance details with the cowed citizens of York he met a rather angry Harold Godwinson.

'A Thing [meeting] *was appointed within the castle early on Monday morning, and then king Harald was to name officers to rule over the town, to give out laws, and bestow fiefs. The same evening, after sunset, king Harald Godwinson came from the south to the castle with a numerous army, and rode into the city with the good-will and consent of the people of the castle.'*

King Harold Godwinson went on to soundly defeat the Norwegians and their allies on 25 September (Florence, *Anglo-Saxon Chronicle* (D) says 28 September, *Anglo-Saxon Chronicle* (E) says 29 September) at Stamford Bridge, a few miles east of the city. Harold's success was helped by his use of cavalry – and as noted many of Hardrada's men were without their armour, as they had been caught by surprise. Harold Godwinson used 'hit and run' tactics throughout the battle – much as the Normans were to do three weeks later at Hastings.

'King Harald Godwinson had come with an immense army, both of cavalry and infantry ... Twenty horsemen rode forward from the Thing – men's troops against the Northmen's array; and all of them, and likewise their horses, were clothed in armour. One of the horsemen said, "Is earl Toste in this army?" The earl answered, "It is not to be denied that ye will find him here." The horseman says, "Thy brother, king Harald, sends thee salutation, with the message that thou shalt have the whole of Northumbria; and rather than thou shouldst not submit to him, he will give thee the third part of his kingdom to rule over along with himself." The earl replies, "This is something different from the enmity and scorn he offered last winter; and if this had been offered then it would have saved many a man's life who now is dead, and it would have been better for the kingdom of England. But if I accept of this offer, what will he give king Harald Sigurdson* for his trouble?" The horseman replied, "He has also spoken of this; and will give him seven feet of English ground, or as much more as he may be taller than other men."

Now the battle began. The Englishmen made a hot assault upon the Northmen, who sustained it bravely. It was no easy matter for the English to ride against the Northmen on account of their spears; therefore they rode in a circle around them. And the fight at first was but loose and light, as long as the Northmen kept their order of battle; for although the English rode hard against the Northmen, they gave way again immediately, as they could do nothing against them. Now when the Northmen thought they perceived that the enemy were making but weak assaults, they set after them, and would drive them into flight; but when they had broken their shield-rampart the Englishmen rode up from all sides, and threw arrows and spears on them. Now when king Harald Sigurdson saw this, he went into the fray where the greatest crash of weapons was, and there was a sharp conflict, in which many people fell on both sides. King Harald then was in a rage, and ran out in front of the array, and hewed down with both hands ... King Harald Sigurdson was hit by an arrow in the windpipe, and that was his death-wound ... before the battle began again Harald Godwinson offered his brother, Earl Toste, peace, and also quarter to the Northmen who were still alive; but the Northmen called out, all of them together, that they would rather fall, one across the other, than accept of quarter from the Englishmen.'

So Harald Hardrada was already dead, and Tostig was killed in the final stand. Very few Vikings escaped back to Scandinavia. The *Anglo-Saxon Chronicle* reports: *But Harold let the king's son, Edmund, go home to Norway with all the ships. He also gave quarter to Olave, the Norwegian king's son, and to their bishop, and to the earl of the Orkneys, and to all those that were left in the ships; who then went up to our king, and took oaths that they would ever maintain faith and friendship unto this land. Whereupon the King let them go home with twenty-four ships* (they came with 300, or so).

*Note the *Heimskringla* uses Hardrada's patronymic to distinguish the two Harolds.

PREPARATION FOR INVASION

In order to understand some sequential events, it is necessary to have a very brief résumé of the Godwin family, and its relationship to Edward the Confessor after 1052. For many reasons, earl Godwin of Wessex, Harold Godwinson and the rest of Godwin's sons were all declared outlaws by king Edward in early October 1051. Godwin left for Flanders and Harold and Leofwine Godwinson sailed to Dublin. On 24 June 1052 earl Godwin made a sortie across the Channel, possibly to see what support he could count on from the men of Wessex. After recruiting (no doubt vigorously) in Winchelsea, Rye and Hastings he retreated to Pevensey, as king Edward's fleet sailed out of Sandwich to find him. A storm covered Godwin's retreat to Bruges, but soon after that he landed on the Isle of Wight, where he was joined by Harold from Ireland, after which they went to Portland where he re-imposed his authority as earl of Wessex.

Following this Godwin and his family were restored to their lands. The Witan, in political fudge, held that the crisis of 1051 had been caused by 'bad counsellors'. Godwin did not enjoy his return to power for very long. Soon afterwards, during a feast, he suffered a stroke, and died three days later. King Edward then made the decision to appoint Harold as the new earl of Wessex. He even created a new title for him: Dux Anglorum. Suddenly Harold was king Edward's right hand man. Parts of his duties were diplomatic, and by design or error he found himself in Normandy in 1064/5. Fuller explanations of these events can be found in Chapters 7, 9, 10 and 11.

What follows from this is the background to the invasion of England by duke William of Normandy, about which much has been written. In essence Edward the Confessor died childless on 5 January 1066. William had a claim to the throne through his great-aunt, queen Emma, and believed that Edward had promised him the throne of England and that Harold had sworn allegiance to him during his sojourn in Normandy in 1064. Harold's claim was based on being in power; accepted by the Witan and getting himself promptly crowned. The other two possible contenders were Harald Hardrada who claimed that he was an heir of Cnut; and Edgar Ætheling, grandson of Edmund Ironside, who was still very young. William clearly believed, using Norman feudal logic, that the throne of England was his by right, and prepared an invasion. Best evidence suggests that he obtained, or had built, between 700 and 1000 ships, of varying sizes, and mustered an army of about 8,000. How this was done is covered in Chapter 11.

The ships were gathered together and loaded at Dives (near Caen), waiting for a favourable wind from the south. It is thought that from Dives he would have wished to cross to the Isle of Wight and the adjacent mainland, but direct routes to landing beaches west of Brighton and to the shallow harbours east of Beachy Head but west of the Fairlight Cliffs were other possibilities. Sailing in those days was hazardous and it was normal to take the most direct or fastest route with optimal wind directions and favourable tides.

SAILING FROM DIVES TO ST VALÉRY-SUR-SOMME

There are two possible explanations as to why William first sailed his fleet eastwards from Dives along the hazardous Côte d'Albâtre to St Valéry-sur-Somme before crossing to Sussex.

The first is that William, having waited in vain for a south-west wind to take the fleet across to England, on or about 13 September 1066 made the decision to use an incessant west wind to sail along the Norman coast to the haven of St Valéry at the mouth of the Somme which, at the very least, would reduce the distance the fleet would need to cross to England.

The second is that on about 13 September the awaited southerly wind appeared, and the fleet departed. The wind soon turned westerly and much stronger, and the endangered fleet which must have gone too far out to run back into the Seine estuary, ran before the wind for whatever safety could be sought, up the dangerous coast to St Valéry-sur-Somme in Ponthieu, fortunately the land of William's vassal.

As almost always in accounts of these events it is difficult to be certain which story was more accurate. Even before embarkation, morale in William's army was deteriorating and desertions occurred; indeed his decision to embark at this time may have been a deliberate attempt to remedy this. Unfortunately for William, losses were incurred on the voyage (some reports estimate as many as 100 ships), and this only added to morale loss, to the extent that William ordered any burials to be done secretly. At St Valéry-sur-Somme William gave prayers and vows, even processing the body of St Valéry in front of his army to induce God to send a favourable wind. Somehow William kept the army and navy on-side, but now had to aim for a specific landing place with room for his ships to re-muster on the English side of the Channel.

CROSSING THE CHANNEL, LANDING IN ENGLAND

Eventually a light southerly arose again. High tide on 27 or 28 September was at about 1500, and they set sail on the falling tide between then and sunset at 1730, aiming for the lands of the Abbey of Fécamp – between what are now Eastbourne and Rye. The English coast would have come into view of the leading ships at 0600, and the fastest boats held their anchors in the offshore shoals, waiting for the slower boats to catch up, so that they could enter harbour on the rising flood tide from about 0900 on 28 or 29 September.

Landfall is said to have been at Pevensey, but even 700 ships would have required a lot of space. Allowing only 10 metres between boats that have run to the shore bow first, and not very differently if there had been multiple parallel mooring, would have required a landing zone 7km [4½ miles] long, and if there were 1000 ships 10km [6¼ miles]. It would seem entirely logical, if William was heading for the Hastings

Above: Loading the horses and men onto the ships
Below: William's ship, the 'Mora' at sea
From *The Bayeux Tapestry: The complete tapestry in full colour* by David M Wilson © 1985,
Thames & Hudson, Ltd. London.

peninsula, that as many as possible would have landed on the eastern side of the bay of Pevensey (i.e. the Hastings side near Hooe and Ninfield), and some into the much smaller Bulverhythe harbour, and the even smaller Priory harbour, both nearer Hastings, and even directly onto the beaches. But it would also have been important to land enough men and matériel to secure the western flank and the Roman shore fort and to build and then defend a new Norman wooden castle at Pevensey.

The wind was light southerly, and the ships would have sailed at varying speeds. They would have been much influenced by the strong tidal flows in the English Channel – so the landings may have been over a wider area than just Pevensey and Bulverhythe, maybe extending to the shingle bar across the Rye Camber and more beach landings. We know that two ships ended up as far east as Old Romney, which was the main entrance to the Rye Camber and that their crews met a sticky end.

If the weather had remained favourable, some of the ships may well have returned to Normandy for further supplies, men and horses, whilst the army 'dug in' at Hæstingaceastre. During the two weeks before the Battle of Hastings they built pre-fabricated wooden forts at both Pevensey and Hastings, rested, foraged the local area, and created a strong defensive forward supply position.

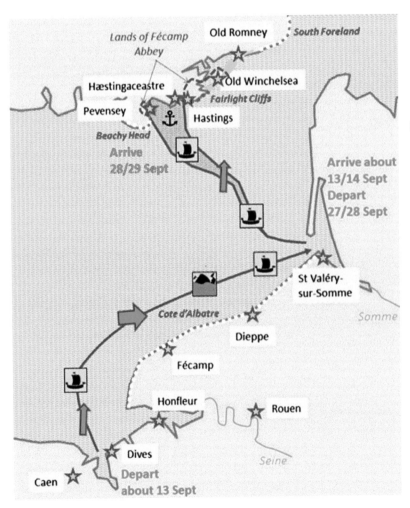

William's voyages: From Dives to St. Valéry-sur-Somme, followed by St. Valéry to Pevensey.

Wind directions as red arrows. Cliffs shown as dotted lines.

The fleet would have spread out during the crossing of the Channel due to tidal flows and boat speed variations

©Battle and District Historical Society

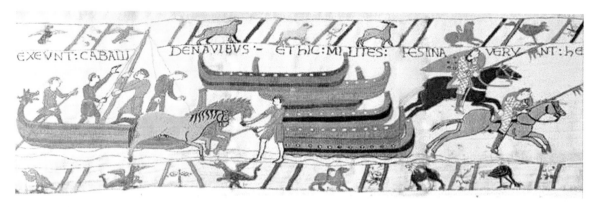

The landing. The steersmen with their side steer boards direct the crews, trim the sails and finally 'pole' their ships bow on to the shore. The sail and mast are lowered. The beached ships, in shallow water, appear bow on to the shore. All the rigging is down and the ornamental posts at the bow and stern have been removed. The horsemen gallop off.

From *The Bayeux Tapestry: The complete tapestry in full colour* by David M Wilson © 1985, Thames & Hudson, Ltd. London.

HAROLD'S RETURN TO THE SOUTH

As the English rested after the battle of Stamford Bridge, Harold's concerns about duke William came back with the news of William's landing, and he hastened south again, leaving Morcar and Edwin to sort out things in Northumbria.

We do not know exactly when Harold arrived back in the south – it is some 250 miles (400km) from Stamford Bridge to Battle – but he would have come by horse using the quickest route, and once again reinforced en route and from around London. This was another great feat, though probably not achieved at quite the speed of the journey north. He may have arrived in London on or about 5 October, and he lingered gathering what army he could for about a week. We do not know exactly how many fighting men Harold was able to bring all the way from the north, or collect on the way, or what condition they were in. What was available of the navy was sent to the seas off Hastings to try to prevent Norman reinforcements arriving, but the much depleted English navy may not have been too much of a nuisance to the Normans (although Ordericus Vitalis says it was 70 ships, which could have been significant – this appears a little considered issue in the histories). It has also been noted that the English had no cavalry at Hastings although the *Heimskringla* says that they had used this with success at Stamford Bridge. It is possible that their horses were 'blown out' after an arduous journey to Yorkshire followed by a pitched battle at Stamford Bridge and the return, and were in no condition to be used.

After rallying at London, Harold is believed to have marched impetuously southwards towards Hastings on 11 October without gathering his full strength, reaching what became Battle on the evening of 13 October. The route taken by Harold from London toward Hastings has received very little consideration by historians, perhaps because the sources are silent on the matter, although one does give a frustrating hint. Even after 600 years, the old Roman road network still formed the main routes and Lemmon held that Harold was faced with two options: either that from London to what is now Lewes (a section of this road can still be visited south of the A264 at Holtye, East Sussex) from which, in the vicinity of Maresfield, he would turn east on to the Uckfield–Rye ridgeway to Caldbec Hill (98km, 61 miles); or London to Rochester, then turning south via Maidstone and Bodiam to Cripps Corner where he would turn west onto the Rye–Uckfield ridgeway to Caldbec Hill (103km, 64 miles).

Based to a degree on excavations conducted by BDHS at Bodiam, which showed continuous use of the Roman road into the medieval period, Lemmon favoured the eastern route. By contrast, Dunlop considered a third route – that of a pre-Roman track way which became the London–Rye road (via Tonbridge) and would have been upgraded to a main route by 950. He favoured it as presenting the shortest route for Harold to take. Tyson in arguing the case for an alternative battle site by the river Brede necessarily adopts the eastern route, citing in support lines 321–322 of one of our earliest sources:

Where he advances there he lays planks of wood
And by this means makes dry crossings of rivers.

She applies this to the waterlogged and flooded nature of the ground south of the Rother at Bodiam in the eleventh-century.

There is however a strategic weakness in the 'eastern' route in that, if William had had time, it potentially left William clear to exit the Hastings peninsula and strike out west – toward the ancient capital of England, Winchester, with Harold's army then in pursuit. Pillaging as he went and supplied from the sea, it offered an escape route if needed as well as the attractive possibility of both a return to William's 'Plan A' (if indeed his original intention had been to sail from Dives to the Isle of Wight, then use it as a base from which to attack Winchester) and the psychological victory which the undefended sack of the ancient capital would achieve. Earl Godwin had used the Isle of Wight in 1052 as a secure base on his return from banishment, from which to ravage far and wide, and thus both William and Harold will have been entirely aware of its strategic importance.

A 'western' route by Harold (London to Maresfield) would have had the effect of checking any such move and thus left William bottled up in south-east Sussex, only able to choose between A) movement by land along the narrow gap between

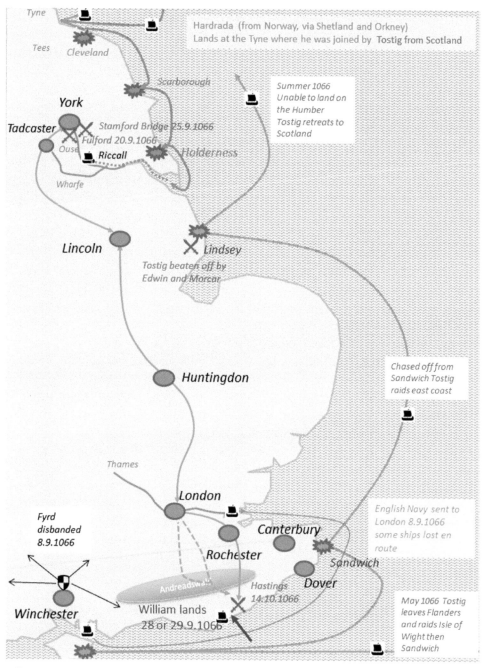

Military and Naval movements around England during May to 14th October 1066. Harold's (land movements green [alternative routes dashed], English naval movements blue lines), Hardrada's (red lines), Tostig's (orange lines)

© Battle and District Historical Society

the Andreadsweald and the Rye Camber with the English in hot pursuit until finally he runs out of land at Dover, B) re-embarkation and return to Normandy or C) stand and fight. Of course, if Harold's instructions to the southern fyrd had been promptly followed (as it appears they were) or indeed if local commanders had already taken their own initiative, then it is possible that William was already bottled up in the Hastings peninsula with local English units established at the nodal point of Caldbec Hill. In such a case Harold could use the eastern route with confidence.

Much as we may conjecture, identification of the route that Harold took from London to Hastings is a problem to which there appears no definite answer. Harold's rapid response, by whatever route, found William still encamped on a fortified Hastings peninsula, and there was no question of William's army moving out either way, and then manoeuvring in front of a chasing English army.

Harold's brother Gyrth may have offered to lead the army at Hastings, and advised less haste and different tactics. Ordericus Vitalis writes that Gyrth said, *'It is best, dearest brother and lord, that your courage should be tempered by discretion. You are worn by the conflict with the Norwegians from which you are only just come, and you are in eager haste to give battle to the Normans. Allow yourself, I pray you, some time for rest. Reflect also, in your wisdom, on the oath you have taken to the duke of Normandy. Beware of incurring the guilt of perjury, lest by so great a crime you draw ruin on yourself and the forces of this nation, and stain for ever the honour of our own race. For myself; I am bound by no oaths, I am under no obligations to Count William. I am therefore in a position to fight with him undauntedly in defence of our native soil. But do you, my brother, rest awhile in peace, and wait the issue of the contest, that so the liberty which is the glory of England, may not be ruined by your fall.'*

Harold's rush may have been an attempt to catch William whilst still bottled up in the Hastings peninsula. In this he succeeded, whichever route he chose for the march from London. In spite of all the above adventures, the English were sufficient in foot-soldier numbers to fight a long battle on 14 October, and to come close to victory, but in the bloody end they failed to keep the bottleneck corked.

13

THE BATTLE OF HASTINGS

Neil Clephane-Cameron

T he Battle of Hastings which took place on 14 October 1066[1] has been much written about with variable accuracy, usually presented with a rarely justified air of certainty.

Judgement is required to assess the reliability of each interpretation, but the very basic outline of the battle is agreed upon: duke William of Normandy led an invading army of Normans, Bretons and French/Flemish; king Harold II led the defending English army; duke William made numerous attacks which failed to break the English shield wall, on at least one occasion narrowly averting disaster when the Bretons on his left flank retreated. The battle, unusually for battles at that time, lasted all day, albeit with inevitable natural pauses not recorded in the sources, e.g. to enable the Normans to replenish their supply of arrows, William to review his tactics and both armies to refresh and reform, until Harold was killed and the English line broke.

This simple summary highlights the deductions which are presented as fact by modern historians. For example, Harold being hit in the eye by an arrow (the iconic image of the battle) has been questioned as a misinterpretation of the Bayeux Tapestry. Such a wound is indeed at odds with the immediate written records that survive. The eye story is first explicitly stated by Henry of Huntingdon[2] about 60 years later.

Although no guarantee against embellishment – as with the press today, chroniclers often pandered to patrons or followed the principle of 'never let the facts get in the way of a good story' – the narrative below focuses solely on directly combining those texts written within approximately 12 years of the battle,[3] the writers of which would have been able to directly access information from living witnesses and participants. A particularly graphic source is the *Carmen de Hastingæ Prœlio*, written *c.* 1067, and to it we owe the detail of Harold's death given below.

When told that duke William had landed and moved to Hastings, king Harold began assembling a large army at a place only located in an English source and described as 'the hoary apple tree', hoping to take duke William unawares by the speed of his response.[4] However, before Harold's army was fully assembled William seized the initiative, leaving Hastings in a surprise manoeuvre.[5] Harold chose to give fight even though he lacked many of his troops (a later source[6] states as much as one third of his total force), and the limited battlefield space available between marshland and steep slopes at what was then the neck of the Hastings peninsula meant that some of Harold's army actually left before the battle as there was not enough space for them to deploy.[7]

Harold deployed his army on foot and as a single dense body with the shields of the front rank overlapping in the traditional Anglo-Nordic manner. He set up his standard at the highest point of the hill. William deployed in three bodies: Bretons (left), Normans (centre) and French & Flemish (right). Archers were in front, then infantry, then the mounted knights.

The archers shot into the English line and over the infantry which advanced up hill in the face of a storm of missiles and into hand-to-hand contact with the English. But the English line stood firm. William possibly paused the fighting at about this time to consider his next move and it was perhaps during such a pause, or at the start of the battle, that a juggler called Taillefer sought to give heart to the Normans and demoralise the English by riding out between the two armies, throwing his sword high into the air and catching it. An English soldier attacked, but was killed by him with his lance then beheaded and Taillefer displayed the trophy head for all to see. A great cheer arose from the Normans, battle proceeded but no progress was made by the Normans, the English line remaining so solidly packed that there was not even room for the dead to fall and they remained upright preventing those behind from taking their place.

Initial attacks.
From *The Bayeux Tapestry: The complete tapestry in full colour* by David M Wilson © 1985, Thames & Hudson, Ltd. London.

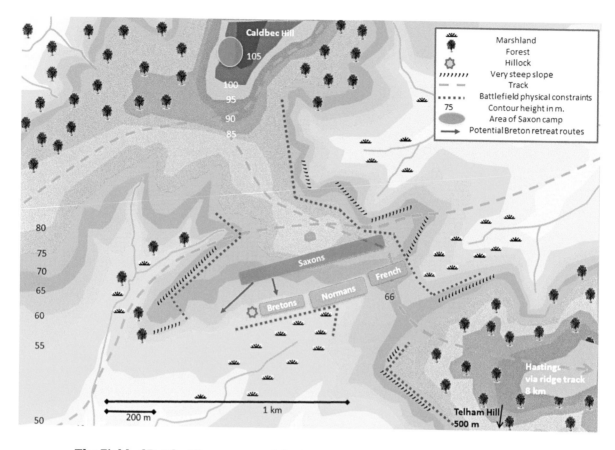

The Field of Battle. The way out of the Hastings peninsula was a bottleneck and the battle lines relatively short. © Battle and District History Society

It was at about this stage that Robert de Beaumont distinguished himself leading his men on the right flank of the Normans, attacking with great boldness and bringing down many English. But still they made no headway and some or all of the Norman army then broke – with the result that many English chased after them. The fleers then turned on their pursuers and cut them down in large numbers before they could regain their line. Whether it was a ruse or not it worked, and the resulting release of pressure on the English line gave room for the dead and wounded to fall. The Normans pushed on once more to assault the shield wall but the English, feeling a sense of desperation as their numbers reduced, fought with redoubled vigour.

The Norman army three times turned in genuine or feigned panic; two retreats were feigned but one was genuine. It is unclear whether this genuine rout was the first or second of the flights, but during it many Normans turned in disorder, their shields covering their backs. William, enraged, removed his helmet to show his fury and despairingly laid into his own retreating men with his lance and fist to stop the

Norman catastrophe by the hillock.
From *The Bayeux Tapestry: The complete tapestry in full colour* by David M Wilson © 1985,
Thames & Hudson, Ltd. London.

rout. The English killed many Normans during these retreats and, even when the Normans counter-attacked a group of them, made a bloody stand on the hillock above the marshy ground of the valley.

Rallying his army, William personally led the next attack, killing many English himself until his war-horse was killed by a javelin thrown by Gyrth (one of Harold's brothers), forcing William to fight him on foot. Having slain Gyrth, William looked around for a horse but when refused he grabbed the knight by the nasal bar of his helmet and pulled him to the ground. William then mounted the horse and continued the fight, only to be soon unhorsed once more by a javelin from the son of Helloc. William quickly recovered himself and thrust his sword into the Englishman's groin. Eustace of Boulogne arrived and gave William his horse, accepting one of his men's for himself. The two commanders then fought side-by-side when William spotted Harold, who was slaying all who came near him.

William and Eustace, together with Hugh de Ponthieu and Giffard, now targeted (the possibly wounded) Harold. The first to arrive thrust his lance through Harold's shield and into his chest, the second took off his head below the protection of the helmet, the third thrust his lance into Harold's belly and the fourth took off Harold's leg at the thigh and carried the trophy away, for which act of wanton butchery he was later dismissed from William's service.[8]

The remnants of the English army now appeared routed and many more English were slain as they ran or collapsed through exhaustion or injury, only to be butchered or trampled by the victors where they lay. Yet the English force maintained some cohesion. During the final pursuit, duke William saw in the fading light a body of English which he took to be reinforcements. Eustace of Boulogne with fifty of his men retreated from contact with this group and urged William not to go on. Whilst the two

King Harold's death.
From *The Bayeux Tapestry: The complete tapestry in full colour* by David M Wilson © 1985,
Thames & Hudson, Ltd. London

were arguing Eustace was struck between the shoulder blades and blood streamed from his nose and mouth. The fate of the English warrior may be easily guessed and, while Eustace was carried away half dead, William led an onslaught against the last resistance.[9]

The battle, with breaks, had lasted all day and there were heavy casualties on both sides. William himself may have been unhorsed as many as three times; Harold was killed as were two of his brothers, Gyrth and Leofwine, together with most of the English leaders. For an army which we are told spent the night before in drunken singing, the English had shown none of the symptoms of sleep deprivation and hangover which one might expect. It was a close-run thing.

Following the battle, duke William waited a while, burying his dead, resting his army, collecting arms and materiel from the battlefield, consolidating his base and waiting to see what the English response would be. Having received no response and needing to avoid a dangerous march north through the Andreadsweald (a forest which extended across much of Kent and Sussex) he left Pevensey and Hastings garrisoned and led his army eastward toward Dover, en route slaughtering the citizens of Old Romney in revenge for killing the crews of two ships from his invasion fleet.

Notes

1   The event is dated by the Julian calendar, which was in use at that time. Today we use the Gregorian calendar, which gives a difference of six days from the Julian calendar's 14 October 1066, so it was 20 October 1066 by today's (Gregorian) reckoning.

2   Henry of Huntingdon, *History of the English*.

3   The early source texts: *Anglo-Saxon Chronicle* (versions D & E);
Guy, Bishop of Amiens, *Song of the Battle of Hastings* ;
William of Jumièges, *Deeds of the Dukes of the Normans*;
William of Poitiers, *Deeds of William, Duke of the Normans and King of the English.*

4   For consideration of Harold's character on this point this see Chapter 14.

5   For consideration of William's character on this point this see Chapter 14.

6   Florence of Worcester, *The History of the English from the Invasion of Julius Cæsar to the Accession of Henry II.*

7   For consideration of the size of the armies see Chapter 14.

8   For consideration of the *Carmen*'s account of Harold's mutilation see Chapter 14.

9   For consideration of the Malfosse incident see Chapter 14.

14

THOUGHTS AND POSTSCIPTS

Neil Clephane-Cameron

Nothing occurs in a vacuum: there is a context to everything.

We understand these simple and commonsense truths in our everyday lives, yet they tend to be overlooked when we view major political and historical events. For whatever reason there is a tendency to 'over-intellectualise': to apply higher motives and objectivity to the decisions and behaviours of key (particularly historical) figures.

Historians are not immune from this frailty, particularly when faced with interpreting epoch-marking events, and often a pause to reflect upon the human dimension – that these were indeed real people with all the frailties that entails – can shed an appreciation of how mundane domestic occurrences might bear upon the international stage.

The family associations chart on the next page and notes below are not assertions that such relationships caused the Battle of Hastings, but it does demonstrate how the drama and relationships were as complex as in any popular television drama.

Theories abound about the size of the armies concerned at Hastings; what happened to Harold after his death; the Malfosse incident and medieval battle tactics; and here you will also find a few thoughts about these.

CONCERNING HAROLD'S CHARACTER

One of the outstanding features of Harold's behaviour in the campaigns of 1066 was the lightning speed of his reactions. He saved the north through a rapid march toward York from London, a feat which he repeated a week later when returning to London following the news of William's landing. It then appears that a few days later he made a dash toward Hastings, intent on achieving the same surprise against William as he had achieved against Harald Hardrada. But how believable is this? And why did it fail against William?

Harold was a Godwin through-and-through, but combined his father's raw ambition with the qualities of an astute and innovative military commander. As king

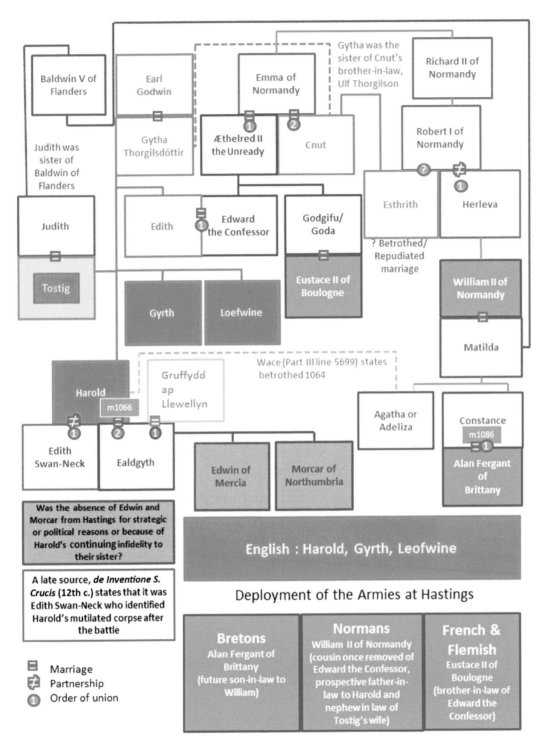

Baldwin V of Flanders

Judith was sister of Baldwin of Flanders

Judith

Earl Godwin

Gytha Thorgilsdóttir

Æthelred II the Unready ①

Emma of Normandy

Cnut ②

Gytha was the sister of Cnut's brother-in-law, Ulf Thorgilson

Richard II of Normandy

Robert I of Normandy

Esthrith ?

Herleva ① ≠

? Betrothed/ Repudiated marriage

Edith ①

Edward the Confessor

Godgifu/ Goda

Tostig

Gyrth

Loefwine

Eustace II of Boulogne

William II of Normandy

Matilda

Harold ≠
m1066

Gruffydd ap Llewellyn

Wace (Part III line 5699) states betrothed 1064

Agatha or Adeliza

Constance
m1086 ①

Edith Swan-Neck ① ② ①

Ealdgyth

Edwin of Mercia

Morcar of Northumbria

Alan Fergant of Brittany

Was the absence of Edwin and Morcar from Hastings for strategic or political reasons or because of Harold's continuing infidelity to their sister?

A late source, *de Inventione S. Crucis* (12th c.) states that it was Edith Swan-Neck who identified Harold's mutilated corpse after the battle

English : Harold, Gyrth, Leofwine

Deployment of the Armies at Hastings

Bretons	Normans	French & Flemish
Alan Fergant of Brittany (future son-in-law to William)	William II of Normandy (cousin once removed of Edward the Confessor, prospective father-in-law to Harold and nephew in law of Tostig's wife)	Eustace II of Boulogne (brother-in-law of Edward the Confessor)

⊟ Marriage
⇄ Partnership
① Order of union

A Dysfunctional Family? The Relationships of the Hastings Protagonists.
©Battle and District Historical Society

Edward's military right hand, Harold had, in 1052, led what is generally regarded as an undistinguished reprisal action against the Welsh king, Gruffydd, but which may only have had as its objects the checking of Welsh aggression and bringing of Gruffydd to the negotiating table. These it achieved.

By contrast in 1063, when the political landscape was much changed, Harold (increasingly now the elderly king Edward's military leader) used the death of earl Ælfgar of Mercia – ally and father-in-law of Gruffydd ap Llewellyn – after Christmas 1062 to launch a mounted lightning strike against Gruffydd's power base at Rhuddlan, perhaps before the news of Ælfgar's death reached him. The strike was a qualified success, immediately achieving destruction of Rhuddlan and much of Gruffydd's fleet. Come the spring, Harold then personally led naval raids whilst his brother Tostig made a land incursion. Gruffydd had been forewarned of Harold's raid on Rhuddlan and had fled with part of his fleet, but in concert these actions together prompted the murder of Gruffydd by his disaffected followers.

From his earlier Welsh foray of 1052 Harold appears to have learned well the need to destroy an evasive enemy without being drawn into an unwinnable guerrilla war of attrition. His victory was complete and lived for generations in legend, Giraldus declaring it was to Harold that the early Norman kings owed the subjection of the Welsh, while the *Anglo-Saxon Chronicles* (D & E versions) rejoice in Harold's use of combined naval and land operations.

CONCERNING WILLIAM'S CHARACTER

William became duke of Normandy aged about eight, following the death of his father who was on pilgrimage to the Holy Land. Almost immediately political instability ensued and William lived in hiding with the shadow of near constant violence and fear of an assassin's knife – a guardian even being murdered in the room in which the young William slept. In 1047, when he was about 20 years old, a turning point at last arrived, with victory over his rivals at the battle of Val-ès-Dunes and from which his authority as duke may be dated. Being raised in this way it is not surprising that he should be a determined survivor: ambitious, strong-willed and adept both in military command and the forming of alliances.

Whatever its origins may have been, William had by 1064 – the probable year of Harold's controversial 'embassy' to Normandy – acquired a definite ambition for, or expectation of, the crown of England. He knew, of course, that without the support of the Godwin family, and specifically its dominant member Harold, a peaceable fulfilment of such ambition was impossible. By 1064 William will have been well-versed in the tales of Harold's military prowess, and not least his conduct of operations and victory against Gruffydd only the year before.

The conundrum must have appeared impossible to resolve, when by accident or design (see Chapter 10) Harold appeared at his court. It gave William his first opportunity to get the true measure of Harold in person and, if we take into account the early and later sources, he employed all his experience to test Harold: first wooing Harold with an extravagant welcome, then taking Harold on campaign to Brittany where he witnesses Harold's skill as a military leader and personal valour, perhaps 'honouring' Harold as a Norman nobleman (so that Harold owed him fealty) and next the betrothal of one of his daughters to Harold (securing familial alliance), then finally orchestating the controversial oath to support William's claim as Edward's successor. Ultimately the details are not material – Harold would have regarded any oaths or undertakings as acts of necessity given under duress (one of his own brothers and a nephew were long-term prisoners of the Normans, and Edward's nephew had recently died a Norman prisoner) whilst William had gained the valuable first-hand insight into Harold that he needed, with the bonus of any political benefit that perjured oaths might (and indeed did) later bring.

When William waited at Hastings he was fully aware of Harold's likely rapidity of response, and his harrying of the neighbourhood may have been a deliberate ploy to ensure it – news may even have reached him of Harold's lightning strike against Hardrada in the north. Armed with his knowledge and experience of Harold, and his own childhood memories of danger at every turn, it would appear inconceivable that William would not have posted piquets at the head of the Hastings peninsula to give warning and, having received this, act with matching speed to steal the initiative for himself.

CONCERNING THE SIZE OF THE ARMIES AT HASTINGS

That the armies were of more or less equal size has not been seriously questioned, the length and apparent evenness of the battle being taken as the convincing factor for the balance. Of course, this is not a definitely reliable method of assessment – the English had the advantage of defending their homeland and the height advantage given by the ridge whilst the Norman army had also to contend with the generally swampy ground at its base; therefore the English could have held their ground with fewer men. On the other hand, the Norman army had the sole use of mounted troops and a superior amount of long-distance missile men (archers) to wear down the English without fear of effective retaliation; thus the advantages and disadvantages to both sides may be felt to balance out.

The long-adopted consensus is for small numbers, about 7,000–10,000 men per army; however, the sources are generally non-specific or obviously exaggerated on the matter of numbers. Wace gives a very specific 696 as the number of ships; others give generally similar and some higher numbers. From this some creditable attempts have been made to estimate the size of the Norman army by reference to the numbers of men capable of being accommodated in the examples of few longships which still survive from Scandinavia. The difficulty here of course is in not knowing the exact sizes of the ships in William's fleet, nor the amount of accommodation 'lost' due to horses, arms and forage.

The impossibility of the calculation therefore led some historians to accounts of later medieval campaigns such as English chevauchées (a raiding method of medieval warfare for weakening the enemy, focusing mainly on ravaging and pillaging enemy territory) to France during the Hundred Years' War, in which records of indenture reliably provide for armies of up to circa 14,000 men – Edward III leading c.15,000 men (and assembling a fleet of c. 700 ships) in his 'Crécy' campaign of 1346 and Henry V leading c. 12,000 (and a fleet of c. 1,500 ships) in his 'Agincourt' campaign of 1415. But these were exceptionally large expeditionary armies even for their times, being as much as double the size of forces normally deployed (see below), and Ramsay rhetorically invited the reader to decide whether a duke of Normandy in the eleventh-century could muster greater resources than a king of England in the 14th century. So from then the 'small numbers' consensus reigned. However, this overlooks two material factors. First, during the fourteenth-century English armies were increasingly mounted with the appearance of a new type of soldier – the hobelar (mounted infantry) – and for the Agincourt campaign the English army was entirely mounted save for a very small number of 'special' archer units (i.e. even those who usually fought on foot, such as the bulk of the archers, were required to provide a mount for use on the march) which would impact upon shipping logistics, as seen above, and necessarily thereby reduce the numbers of men. Secondly, in terms of the late fourteenth-century chevauchées, the Black Death (1348–1349) led to appalling crises in manpower and the economy, consequences that impacted upon English society for more than a generation after and which would have made unattainable mustering of expeditionary forces on a scale much larger than the range generally achieved – Curry noting that during the twenty years from 1369 to 1389 no expedition had been larger than 6,000 men. Additionally, if instead of looking forward those historians had looked back, they would have seen that Julius Cæsar had landed with perhaps some 25,000 men from about 800 ships and established camp easily within a single day.

A further difficulty with the small numbers theory is that the early sources are explicit in terms of the lack of space for the English to deploy and the effect of the extreme press of men preventing the dead from falling. In order to have sufficient depth (8–10 men) to provide the bulwark of defence that held so long, only about half of the ridge (to about opposite the hillock – see 'Field of Battle' map in Chapter 13) could have been occupied, and so is at odds with the overcrowding of which we read. At this point a tactical consideration then presents itself: with the English fighting on foot an entirely defensive, static battle, why did William not send a detachment to take the unoccupied section of ridge and assault the English from there, thus denying them a key topographical advantage – height – rather than, as happened, throwing his forces relentlessly against a solid front. But perhaps it was simply that the early reverses of the Breton flight on his left flank had left him too wary of splitting his army, part of which, due to the presence of the hillock, would have had to operate as an independent command.

Freeman makes no specific estimate, but the deployments shown in his work would have demanded a force of perhaps 20,000, and Lawson does much to rehabilitate the 'large numbers' theory. Given that the answer is unlikely ever to be determined perhaps the last word should be given by Hilaire Belloc, who, in a letter to C T Chevallier dated 7 July 1935 and held in the archive of BDHS wrote:

> The small numbers often given by modern writers are absurd. If the Dons were made to hold close to a mile of line without missile weapons and with heavy cavalry charging at them they would find out in the first few minutes what xxxxxxx they had been talking.

CONCERNING THE *CARMEN*'S ACCOUNT OF HAROLD'S MUTILATION

The language of the *Carmen* has led to speculation that it was not a leg in fact which was hacked off, but a more intimate member. I doubt this, for I entirely see that a good swipe with a sword could remove a leg, which would present as a large, ready target for a mounted opponent; however emasculation would surely require the assailant to dismount, expose Harold's genitals, change weapon to a knife (a sword being too unwieldy for the job), do the deed, re-mount and gallop off – all in the heat of battle which was still apparently raging all around – not a course of action to be undertaken lightly! By way of illustration the emasculation of Simon de Montfort's corpse (*'a torment never before heard of'*) took place in the calm *after* the battle at Evesham.

CONCERNING THE MALFOSSE INCIDENT

The final resistance by the English has become known as Malfosse (evil ditch) and its location – even its occurrence – has been the subject of much debate for more than a hundred years. Not all of the early sources mention it (William of Poitiers is one who does) and some of the later ones (notably William of Malmesbury), perhaps confused by differing accounts, refer to a similar incident during the battle at around the time of the Breton retreat, and which is so graphically shown in the Bayeux Tapestry. However, if the incident occurred other than at the end of the battle, the injury sustained by Eustace de Boulogne would clearly rule out any possibility of him undertaking the energetic role which the early sources unite in recording. So we are left with an incident at the end of the day.

The natural line of retreat away from the enemy is northerly and topographically two possibilities present themselves: first, what today is known as Lake Field, immediately to the rear of the left flank of the English army. This was favoured by Freeman writing in 1869; second, Oakwood Gill which forms the northern base of Caldbec Hill and is crossed by the modern A2100. Oakwood Gill was first suggested by Chevallier in 1953 and accepted in 1963 following publication of his examination into the medieval deeds relating to the town of Battle. These show that an area was known as 'Malfosse' for as much as 200 years or more after the battle and from which a location was identified. The difficulty with Oakwood Gill, however, is that it would be too far (approx. one mile (1.6 km), from the English position) for the English on foot to outrun their mounted pursuers if, as we are told, the English line held firm and only broke at the last when Harold was dead. This is however resolvable if:

1. There was a gradual desertion during the later stage of the battle;
2. There were a series of stands as part of a semi-structured withdrawal (as described by William of Malmesbury);
3. The English were late arrivals, as duke William himself believed.

There may also be a flaw in part of Chevallier's deduction, i.e. the area between today's Marley Lane and Caldbec Hill is known as Little Park (which was the 'Little Park' of Battle Abbey – its 'Great Park' lay between the abbey itself and Catsfield). The deeds consulted by Chevallier describe the land in Malfosse as *'lying in the old park'*. Although accepting this gives initial endorsement to Freeman's Lake Field location, Chevallier concluded that 'old park' must refer to an earlier abandoned park. Knowing the land to be off the North Road (i.e. the ancient track to London) he looked around and found – Oakwood Gill.

CONCERNING MEDIEVAL BATTLES

We have referred to Viking and Norman battle tactics in other chapters, which in common with most military strategy at that time showed an avoidance of situations which were not likely to lead to victory. We see this in William's tactics at the Battle of Varaville and also at the Battle of Mortemer – which both utilised situations in which the foe was ill-prepared and caught by surprise (Chapter 11). There now appears to be a consensus amongst medieval scholars about 'battle avoidance strategy', and great set-piece battles such as Hastings are acknowledged to be relatively rare events.

A view that somehow medieval warfare lacked strategic rationale was replaced by new thinking by the end of the twentieth century. This has led to a change in views about the importance and relevance of the Roman writer Vegetius' works. This consensus has been referred to as the 'Gillingham Paradigm', following on from Gillingham's researches into medieval leaders such as William Marshal and Richard I of England. They seemed to use the principle of avoiding direct battle, playing a waiting game but still keeping close enough to the enemy army to minimise ravaging.

Harold, in dealing with William's invasion and knowing that the Norwegian threat had gone (at least for the time being), should certainly have used this tactic, which was spelled out during the late 4th century CE by Flavius Vegetius Renatus, in his *De Re Militari* [*Concerning Military Matters*]. This influenced how war was waged during medieval times, as it contains tactics and strategies used very successfully by the Roman legions when building and holding their vast empire. The books are not intellectual works, but emphasise thinking over 'heroism' and reliance on 'fortune -seeking' victory by manoeuvre, diplomacy or starvation. Gillingham says that: *when on military campaigns 'cautious mastery of the logistics of Vegetian warfare' allowed even a 'romantic hero' like Richard the Lionheart to show his real competence as a general.*

On the other hand, as Abels points out, earlier English kings from Alfred to Harold Godwinson had mainly fought limited defensive battles upon their own soil and seas, or undertaken smaller scale incursive operations against the Welsh and Scots. So, in defence of Harold and the English they did not, at that time, have the military experience of living off an enemy's territory and of minimising the plundering for food and other supplies of an army which did have that experience. An army that was unable to plunder was an army that was going to run into difficulties. This in retrospect appears to have been a strategic deficiency before and after Hastings, which demonstrated some military inexperience of those in power in England and was fatal to the England as known before 14 October 1066.

15

AFTERMATH

Keith Foord

After the battle, only the Hastings peninsula and Pevensey were held by William. According to William of Poitiers, the streets of London remained teeming with the soldiers who had answered Harold's call to arms too late and had been left behind, plus those who had been lucky enough to escape from the battlefield. But with Harold and his brothers slain there was no experienced military leader.

As we have seen in previous sections, the direct way from Hastings to London was obstructed by the dense Andreadsweald forest. It may not have made sense for William to go west towards Winchester through the difficult terrain between the north of Pevensey harbour, then between the South Downs and the Andreadsweald. Also Wessex and Winchester were known strongholds of Harold. So the geography of the area would have dictated that William would move out from Hastings to the north-east following the old Roman road, leaving a protective rear-guard and a supply base. He would have had the choice of moving directly northwards to the Medway area and then to London, or to first go east towards Dover and Canterbury. There is some discussion of the possible alternative routes in Chapter 14.

The invaders' departure from their bridgehead was delayed for up to two weeks. We can only assume that this was because William was preparing Pevensey and the Hastings peninsula to be a continuing stronghold and supply route. The fortifications would have been further strengthened during this time. When the weather was favourable, some of the ships must have been making return journeys to bring more supplies, men and horses from Normandy. Whilst William stayed on the Hastings peninsula, he was waiting for a contact from the English. It did not come. As far as he could know he might still be faced with another English army.

There was no immediate rush to Hastings to offer the crown to William. With Harold dead there was still one more potential candidate for king living in England – Edgar Ætheling, half-great-nephew of Edward the Confessor, who had been born and had grown up in Hungary until he was about four years of age. When he came to England with his family in 1057 his father had died soon after their arrival, and he had been brought up in the royal court together with his sisters. He was still a boy of about 13. The two young northern earls Edwin and Morcar 'promised to fight for him' says the *Anglo-Saxon Chronicle,* and Edgar Ætheling, rejected as Edward's heir in January 1066 probably because of his youth and inexperience, now attracted some support from both archbishop Ealdred (*Anglo-Saxon Chronicle* (D)), the new abbot of Peterborough (*Anglo-Saxon Chronicle* (E)) and others in London who might now choose him for king (*Anglo-Saxon Chronicle* (D); *Gesta Willelmi*). William of Poitiers says '*They had chosen Edgar Ætheling, of the noble stock of king Edward, as king*', but perhaps he overstated the case.

From William's battle experience, he would have expected to fight further conflicts to take England, and to have been 'shadowed' by the English as discussed in Chapter 14, so he must have been somewhat surprised and perplexed by the lack of appearance of the English. So William set off to test them, possibly to draw them in, using terror tactics that he had refined in Maine. He marched the army first briefly northwards then east, avoiding crossing the Andreadsweald. His first 'visit' was to Old Romney , where he '*inflicted such punishment as he thought fit*' for the slaughter of his men who had landed there by mistake. He then proceeded to Dover with its English fortified settlement centred on the 10th century church of St Mary de Castro which still stands, although now much restored by the Victorians in the late 19th century.

Instead of defending Dover the townspeople surrendered, presumably having heard about what had happened recently at Romney, and in the past at Alençon. The burgesses of Dover met William as he marched towards their town and surrendered their castle's keys. William billeted his men in the town and halted for at least a week, possibly up to a month, meanwhile sending demands for tribute from the English: the city of Canterbury being first to respond. The length of this halt at Dover may have been deliberate to allow reinforcements from Normandy and responses from the English, but an epidemic of dysentery or gastro-enteritis due to contaminated food and/or water blighted William's army, which was still living off the land, and this delayed his departure. There was some burning of the town, probably secondary to plundering, which was severe enough to still be an economic factor of Dover recorded by *Domesday* 20 years later. During the stay at Dover he would have strengthened its defences and probably received more seaborne reinforcements. There is one uncorroborated source which says that William may have sent a detachment to take and hold the Royal Treasury at Winchester. This would have seemed attractive, but militarily might have been foolhardy as it would have split his army.

Leaving Dover, he set off towards London. Canterbury and other cities such as Rochester submitted on terms that would have involved tribute. On the approach to London the Normans did meet some heavy resistance south of the Thames. London was mainly on the north bank of the Thames at that time, and William baulked at a direct assault across the river bridges against the heavily defended city. This was in accordance with the way he had normally fought wars up until Hastings: not to take on a strong opponent but to seek an easier route. This strategy was the norm of the age: what was unusual for him was the type and ferocity of the battle at Hastings. So he continued to do what he had done many times before in Normandy and most recently in Maine. He burnt what he could south of the Thames and swung westwards, then northwards, harrying around London, laying waste *'wherever he wished'* all before him across Surrey, Hampshire (at this point maybe sending a smaller force to receive the keys of Winchester from Harold's widow), then through Berkshire to south Oxfordshire. In all he covered perhaps 350 miles. Why did he do this? It certainly created fear. It was also a 'come and get me if you can' taunt.

He eventually arrived sometime in late November 1066 at the river Thames at Wallingford, the first point where he could ford the river upstream of London without the need to use boats or build bridges. He had still not met an English army. Wallingford was an old Anglo-Saxon burgh. King Alfred had constructed massive earthen ramparts in a parallelogram fronting the Thames on one side, covering some 41 hectares (100 acres) of land. This was the second largest burgh in England, and the ramparts can still be seen today. At one time it is thought to have been a housecarl base and was a large settlement for its time. There is a large entry for Wallingford in *Domesday,* at the start of the Berkshire section, in which it is estimated to have had a population of 2,000–3,000.

Hedges writes about a Wigod (sometimes Wigot) of Wallingford, who may have been sheriff of Oxford and a kinsman of king Edward (Harmer), who held the town from king Edward before 1066. He may have supported William's cause from the first, and it has been postulated that he may have met him in 1051, at the meeting between William and king Edward, if it had actually occurred in that year. The *Anglo-Saxon Chronicle* does not mention the crossing at Wallingford, but it is mentioned by

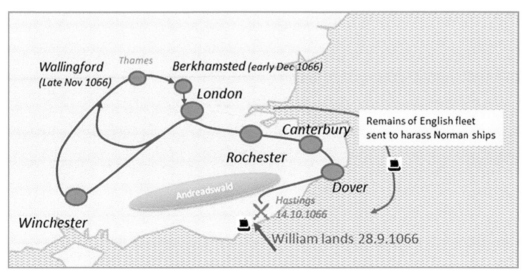

William's route from Hastings to London
©Battle and District Historical Society

the Norman chroniclers who would have understood that the river crossing was a key event. None of these sources mentions Wigod who appears only in the *Domesday Book*, but references to Wigod in *Domesday* suggest that, unlike many English thegns, he survived 1066 in the service of William. His daughter Ealdgyth later married Robert D'Oilly, one of William's Norman knights.

William stopped for a few days and received the first emissaries from London. William of Poitiers said that Stigand, archbishop of Canterbury, came and paid homage, renouncing the Ætheling. Clearly he did not speak for all, for the resistance from London continued and therefore so did the harrying, on through Buckinghamshire and Hertfordshire.

John of Worcester describes the situation of earls Edwin and Morcar at this point. They *'withdrew their support and returned home with their army'*. This appears not so much a desertion as an assessment of reality, and clearly they did not go very far as they were back in early December. Maybe they were trying to persuade all to accept defeat and negotiate; maybe they could not rally more to the cause. The *Anglo-Saxon Chronicle* briefly describes a further short period of prevarication by those around the Ætheling. Finally there was loss of hope, which eventually led to surrender. Florence of Worcester goes on to say, quoting and slightly expanding from the *Anglo-Saxon Chronicle* (D): *'Edgar Ætheling , with Archbishop Ealdred of York, the earls Edwin and Morcar and a group of bishops including Wulfstan, bishop of Worcester, and Walter, bishop of Hereford and other leaders went the 25 miles from London to Berkhamsted in early December to meet William, out of necessity, after most damage had been done … and it was a great piece of folly that they had not done it earlier'.* They *'gave hostages and swore oaths to him and he promised them that he would be a gracious lord'.*

The Ætheling had never been crowned, although he had been 'considered'. So in Norman eyes he had never officially been king, but he must have been a very frightened 13-year-old. After some minor hesitation on William's part (which appears to have been about the military situation, as he was only really in control of the south-east), William consented to be crowned at Westminster Abbey on Midwinter's day/ Christmas day, 25th December (the *Anglo-Saxon Chronicle* uses Midwinter/Christmas Day interchangeably throughout) using the full rites of an English coronation, led by archbishop of York Ealdred in Old English and the bishop of Coutances in French (*William of Poitiers*). Note that the tainted Stigand did not officiate.

Why did the English not manage to muster an army against William after Hastings? The main reason must have been a power vacuum. The Witan, an informal advisory council of no fixed membership, was headless and full of talkers, not doers nor warriors. The Witans of 1051 and 1052 had shown how inconsistent a mechanism it could be when they allowed the Godwins to return and emasculate the king, and permitted the Godwin family to become all powerful, thus helping to set up the situation of 1066. Earl Godwin had failed to be the grandsire of a new English dynasty via Edward's marriage with his daughter Edith which was, for whatever

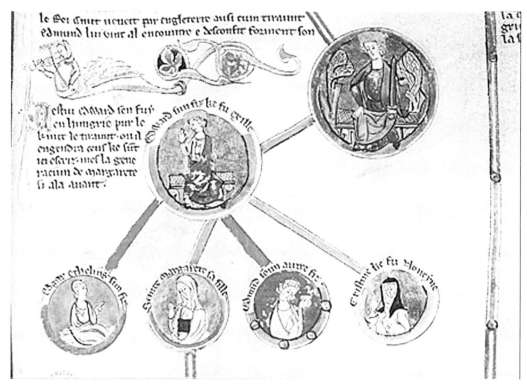

Edgar Ætheling (bottom left): From a genealogical document of Edmund Ironside's family in the British Library. Detail from the roll of six roundels of Edmund II Ironside and his descendants: Edward Ætheling, Edgar, Margaret, Edmund, and Christine.
British Library Royal 14 B V Membrane 3 Edmund II Ironside

reason, childless. The Godwinson earls – Tostig, Harold, Gyrth and Leofwine – who had so dominated England for many years were gone, the first killed fighting his brother and the northern earls at Stamford Bridge, the other three killed in battle at Hastings. Edwin and Morcar were still young (estimated to have been around 19 and 17 years old). They had no power base in southern England and their northern thegns were still recovering from the battles near York and remained on guard against more Vikings. Harold, Gyrth and Leofwine's housecarls would have been severely depleted. The Ætheling was too young, unknown and inexperienced to rally an army or do anything else.

The Godwinsons had been all-powerful: too powerful. Harold, full of the memories of his recent trip to Normandy, had a personal point to settle with William. He is said to have ignored Gyrth's request to delay to build a bigger army and for Harold's brothers to lead the field at Hastings, so that if necessary Harold could organise a scorched-earth policy and muster a second army in London to back them up. With the three brothers all dead on the field of Hastings there were no replacements of note. The two northern earls had been weakened by losses at Fulford and Stamford Bridge.

They may have thought that they could 'do business' with the Normans. If so, they were very wrong.

After years of internal strife, and wars on their borders the Normans had evolved into an efficient, terror-striking, lean, mean, fighting machine with added political acumen. There were problems ahead for the Normans, but the English would learn, sometimes in a very cruel way, that their new masters were not going to go away.

Miniature of William I enthroned, and below, his children seated at a table.
British Library   Royal 20 A II f. 5v William I
http://www.bl.uk/catalogues/illuminatedmanuscripts/ILLUMIN.P?Size=mid&IIIID=46334

16

THE BATTLEFIELD AND BATTLE ABBEY

Keith Foord and Neil Clephane-Cameron

T he question of the actual site of the Battle of Hastings has been particularly controversial in the last twenty to thirty years, and has spawned a number of books and websites. However this polemical issue has been argued over for centuries, and has engaged the best academic minds. Some of the debates both academic and generalist have been fierce indeed.

English Heritage has stood fast in supporting the accord – based on the available historical written record and the unusual physical location of Battle Abbey – that the high altar of Battle Abbey's church is on the spot where Harold fell. This is in the face of other ideas and proposals which also lack supporting archaeological evidence, and usually contain selective and sometimes 'imaginative' interpretations of the available written evidence. Other proposals for the site have been at Crowhurst (Austin, 2012), Caldbec Hill (Bradbury, 2010; Grehan/Mace, 2012), 'three miles to the east' (Tyson, 2014). The last is based on her own translations rather than Barlow's 1999 scholarly re-examination with a revision of Morton and Muntz's translation of the near contemporary 835 line epic poem the *Carmen de Hastings Proelio*, plus Roger of Howden's much later '*De viis maris*' portulan (navigational text) of 1190, which we discuss in some detail in Chapter 3. There are inevitably even more theories, some reasonable, some bizarre.

Later texts, such as Wace's *Roman de Rou*, were often based on the earliest sources, such as the Carmen, so it is worth discussing more of some the other earliest written sources.

Firstly the *Brevis Relatio de Guillelmo Nobilissimo* which was written after 1114 but before 1120 at Battle Abbey, during the abbacy of abbot Ralph of Bec, a monk and later prior of Caen and prior of the bishopric of Rochester who was appointed abbot in 1107, and died 17 years later at the age of 84. Ralph, aged 30, had come to England from Normandy in 1070 with Lanfranc, the new archbishop of Canterbury, and had previously been one of William I's chaplains. He was a go-between for

Lanfranc and William and knew both personally. He would have had at least excellent second-hand information about the battle and probably friends and acquaintances that were present on 14th October 1066. The monk of the Battle Abbey scriptorium notes twelve times that he is directly writing down recent oral memories. The *Brevis* states shortly and factually that the abbey stands '*on the site where the Lord gave him victory over his enemies' and 'in memory of that victory and for the absolution of the sins of all those who were killed there'*.

Secondly the *Chronicle of Battle Abbey* written in about 1170 reinforces this with an account that the monks initially began to build in a nearby different and to their minds better location, but that William flew into a rage insisting that it be built where he had instructed and with the high altar of its church marking the site where Harold was killed. This is allegorically illustrated in the 'Battle Tapestry' made to commemorate the 950th anniversary of the Battle of Hastings in 2016. There is no evidence of course that William ever came to Battle on horseback as shown to deliver the rebuke, but it artistically improves the panel.

Thirdly, a slightly earlier source than the *Brevis,* is the *Anglo-Saxon Chronicle* (*E – i.e. the version written at Peterborough*) in its entry for 1086, which from its textual content must have been written before 1100 and thus within 34 years of the Battle of Hastings. This says 'In the same place (*OE*: 'On ðam ilcan steode') *where God granted him that he might conquer England he raised a famous minster'*. As Marc Morris comments this was '*a contemporary witness – an English witness – from the time of William the Conqueror himself'*.

To those who remain sceptical of the 900 plus year old writings of monks, there is further rebuttal – in the remains of the abbey itself and in the local landscape. The abbey's location on the edge of a ridge required much work to the foundations and a complex architectural design, as is still visible today in the remains of the dorter range, with its arrangement of stepped under-crofts, difficulties which would have been avoided by a more hospitable location.

It has also been demonstrated by reference to the contemporary network of tracks and roads, together with the extent of the then, and sometimes now, flooded and marshy watersheds to east and west (see map on page 149), that duke William's route of march from Hastings would have had to pass along the ridgeway from Hastings and across a saddle or shallow col through to what is now the town of Battle. This was endorsed by LIDAR mapping as recently as 2013. The site of the high altar of the abbey's church is located at a high point of the ridge north of the col and near an ancient crossroads formed by two local tracks, one east–west, which to the east is the old track down Marley Lane then through Bathurst Wood (Battle Great Wood) to Kent Street on the present A21 and which Lemmon names as the 'Wasingate', and the other the south–north ridgeway (the latter the Normans' route out of the Hastings peninsula).

The needs of 'Command & Control' (to use modern military parlance) made such a place a natural location for Harold to plant his standard and from which to direct the battle as explained by Willing. The static nature of both the English defence and Harold's personal conduct as described by the contemporary writers (see Chapter 13) indicate that Harold was killed at his command post, which remained static throughout the battle.

What is also of interest is that in 1994 Reuben Thorpe gave a talk to BDHS which was recorded by Audrey Swan in the BDHS Transactions. There are also some related unpublished English Heritage papers all relating to an archaeological study of the present courthouse of Battle Abbey in the early 1990s. Some insubstantial but interesting finds were found at a deep level within the previous courthouse floor, which had been raised 1.3m in the 16th century at the time of replacing the original stone building on the foundations of its predecessor, which is believed to have been a hall with a low undercroft, which itself probably replaced an original timber building. In a ditch related to the last were found two fragments of Saxon pottery with nearby slightly deeper evidence of clay churned and stained by animals. Even deeper were found fragments of Bronze Age flints and hammer stones. This at least raises the possibility that this was a known ancient rendezvous point perhaps for the sale and exchange of animals and maybe even the site of the 'hoary/grey apple tree' of the Anglo-Saxon Chronicle (D version) entry for 1066. But that is all that can be said and further extrapolation seems impossible.

From the Battle Tapestry showing an ecclesiastical meeting between William and the papal legates, William on horseback (see note above) ordering the monks to build where they had been told to and the first formal abbot of Battle (Gausbert)
© Tina Greene   Photograph Peter Greene

Porter has reviewed all the available evidence and made a strong case against the views expressed by the authors mentioned in paragraph 2 of this Chapter. Nevertheless, whilst status quo is the recognised position, no good historian has a totally closed mind and new evidentially based ideas must be closely dissected and evaluated. The whole debate has been made difficult by the lack of archaeological evidence of a battle in spite of the attentions of the televisual 'Time Team' with some supervision by Dr Glen Foard in 2013. Foard was the archaeologist behind the detection of the true location of the Battle of Bosworth – a discovery which moved the site of Richard III's defeat two miles from its assumed location. At Battle three sample trenches were cut across the sloping field south-east of the abbey site in order to remove modern contamination. Deep to this recent layer some medieval artefacts were found – but nothing related to the events of 1066. 'Time Team' also undertook a metal detecting survey on nearby Cadlbec Hill and no battlefield archaeology was recovered at that site.

The lack of archaeological evidence may be because of the nature of the acid soils around the Battle area, which have a chemistry which does not preserve artefacts at all well. Bone, wood and natural fabrics rot and disintegrate, and metal corrodes in it at an alarming rate. It would be quite consistent that no significant finds have been made, as anything could quite literally have dissolved and disappeared in the last 950 years. Possibly the only chance of finding anything will be deep in nearby persisting waterlogged marshy areas which may have preserved some objects in anaerobic conditions. As far as we are aware this has never been attempted.

In any case anything recyclable or of use or value made of leather or metal and discarded weapons would have been methodically stripped from the dead and the battlefield by the victors, who had one or two weeks to search the area before William decided to move on, so we should be looking for 950 plus years old leftovers. It is also clear from a 2016 review paper by Curry and Foard that the dead of mediaeval battles are indeed very difficult to find. They report that: '*Modern archaeologists have so far drawn a blank in finding human remains at virtually all English and French battlefields of the fourteenth and fifteenth centuries*'. And at the field of Hastings we are looking back 300 plus years more – at the eleventh century.

In January 2013 the Battlefields Trust reported that, after spending several months consulting with archaeologists and historians, it '*could not support the suggestion that the Battle of Hastings was fought at Crowhurst, or that the evidence suggests that any detailed archaeological investigation into the battle should focus on the Crowhurst area.*' A synopsis of the case for Crowhurst is available in the members section of the Trust's website. Their officers clearly considered that they had not yet seen sufficient evidence from any source to establish that the traditional site was incorrect. They added that '*archaeology must be conducted to the highest standards and finds must be properly identified and recorded and subject to expert scrutiny.*'

English Heritage is to be commended for responding to the questions raised, and in trying to define an answer, however there is scope for further archaeological work. Nevertheless if, as seems probable, little or nothing is found, the arguments would without doubt still rage on; but if it came up with startling conclusions, then parts of this book and many others may need to be extensively re-written.

Meanwhile, in discussing issues the status quo is accepted in this and other chapters of this book. So it is worth repeating and expanding on the description of the foundation of the abbey given in Foord's previous book. The story of the foundation of the abbey has two versions. One or neither may be true. The first is that William, duke of Normandy, vowed on the eve of the battle that if God gave him success he would found a monastery upon the place of victory. The second is that pope Alexander II's legate, on confirming the re-coronation of William I in 1070, reminded him of his promise or demanded that William do penance for the English and Norman lives lost, not just on the battlefield of Hastings but during the truly bloody progress of the Conquest after that. This, or just before it (see below) was when the vow was made to build the abbey on the site of the battle, with the high altar of its church at the place where Harold had not just fallen but was hacked to pieces on Saturday, 14 October 1066. The second explanation does seem more likely as thoughts of the future must have been far from William's mind when the battle was imminent.

The second explanation is backed up by reports from the three papal legates – John Minutus, Peter the Bibliothecarious, and Ermenfrid, who had been sent by Pope Alexander in 1070. These legates ceremonially re-crowned William during the Easter court at Winchester, which may be seen as a papal 'seal of approval' of the conquest. The legates and the king then held a series of ecclesiastical councils dedicated to reforming and re-organising the English church. As part of this, Archbishop Stigand was deposed from his archbishopric of Canterbury and replaced by the above Lanfranc of Bec, a long-standing advisor to William I. Also a Penitential Ordinance was issued by bishops from Normandy and approved by the chief papal legate, Ermenfrid, cardinal bishop of Sion (a diocese near Geneva in what is now south-west Switzerland). This interesting and valuable document is generally held as being issued by the legates during their visit to England in 1070. However, this may be the date of formalisation of a document which some believe may have been compiled as early as 1067. If the earlier date is correct, then the Penitential Ordinance was compiled at about the same time as The *Carmen de Hastingæ Proelio* and the extreme differences in tone between the documents give us a fascinating glimpse into the competing contemporary cultures: the *Carmen*'s vivid celebration of military triumph and the pacific morality of the Penitential Ordinance. The latter cannot have been welcomed by those subject to it, especially as the expedition had received papal sanction in the first place.

So it is very likely that in 1070 William founded Battle Abbey, a new royal monastery at the site of the Battle of Hastings, partly as a penance for the deaths in the battle and partly as a memorial to those dead, but of course it also undoubtedly marks his victory. He may have decided to do this even before the ecclesiastical councils, but it does appear that building did not start until 1070. Another insight into William's motives for founding the abbey is also suggested by the author of the *Brevis* when writing that Battle Abbey was built *'to the memory of this victory and for the absolution of the sins of all who had been slain there'.*

The Penitential Ordinance is not unique, but it is rare. Many such Ordinances were issued by the Church, usually in respect of acts committed over (sometimes extended) periods of time; Ermenfrid's is rare because it deals with a specific event of conquest (the battle and subsequent subjection of the English). There had been no similar ordinance for killing in battle since the Battle of Soissons in 923, but on that occasion both sides were required to atone for the bloodshed; Ermenfrid's only applied to the Norman army, it being deemed that the English had suffered enough already

ERMENFRID'S PENITENTIARY

This is an institution of penance according to the decrees of the bishops of the Normans, confirmed by the authority of the Pope through his legate Ermenfrid, bishop of Sitten [Sion, Switzerland]. It is to apply to those men whom William, duke of the Normans, led and who gave him military service as their duty.

[Killings & wounding – at the Battle of Hastings]

Anyone who knows that he killed a man in the great battle must do penance for one year for each man that he killed.

Anyone who wounded a man, and does not know whether he killed him or not must do penance for forty days for each man he thus struck (if he can remember the number), either continuously or at intervals.

Anyone who does not know the number of those he wounded or killed must, at the discretion of his bishop, do penance for one day in each week for the remainder of his life, or, if he can, let him redeem his sin by a perpetual alms, either by building or by endowing a church. [William's building of Battle Abbey may have been as a consequence of this, or fulfilment of a promise made beforehand.]

The clerks who fought, or who were armed for fighting, must do penance as if they had committed these sins in their own country, for they are forbidden by the canons to do battle. The penances of the monks are to be determined by their rule, and by judgement of their abbots.

Those who fought merely for gain are to know that they owe penance as for homicide. But those who fought as in a public war have been allotted a

penance of three years by their bishops out of mercy.

The archers who killed some and wounded others, but are necessarily ignorant as to how many, must do penance as for three Lents.

[Killings – after the battle but before William's coronation]

Apart from the actual battle, anyone who before the consecration of the king killed those who resisted as he was going through the countryside for the sake of food, must do penance for one year for each man he so killed. But if it was not for food, but merely for plunder that he was foraging, he must do penance for three years for each man he then killed.

[Killings – after William's coronation]

Those who have killed men after the consecration of the king must do penance as for homicides wilfully committed, always with this exception that if the men thus killed or wounded were in arms against the king, then the penalties will be as before stated.

[Other crimes]

Those who committed adulteries or rapes or fornications must do penance as if these sins were committed in their own country.

Concerning the violation of the church likewise. Let those who stole from churches restore what they stole to the church they robbed if they can. If they cannot, let them restore it to some other church. And if they will not restore it, then the bishops have decreed that they may not sell it, nor may anyone buy it.

The task of supervising the construction of the abbey was given to the Benedictine abbey of St Martin of Tours at Marmoutier, near Tours on the banks of the Loire (not to be confused with Marmoutier in Alsace). This abbey had been founded by St Martin in late Roman Gaul in 372, and it had been raided and pillaged by Vikings in 835. The abbey had recovered, and become one of the richest abbeys in Europe. Poignantly, it was disestablished and demolished in 1819 after the French Revolution. A convent built a new chapel there in 1856 and established a school which still exists. Part of the site of the ruins now belongs to the city of Tours, and is under archaeological study. It can be seen on looking east from the northbound carriageway of the A10 autoroute as it leaves Tours.

William sent William Faber 'the Smith', a monk in his service, to recruit from Marmoutier and he and four other monks, Theobald 'the old', William Coche, Robert of Boulogne and Robert Blancard (who was designated to be the future first abbot) came to start the new community. However, when the five saw the constricted site which was on top of a dry scrubby sandstone ridge, much as in Ashdown Forest today, with no nearby water supply and surrounded by waterlogged heavy clay valleys, they considered it unsuitable, and tried to build it further to the west at a place called Herst, *'further down the hill to the west'*. This was possibly in the area below the present Asten Fields, but herst is a very common Old English descriptive name for a copse or patch of woodland, and several other sites including Crowhurst have therefore been suggested.

Benedictine and Cistercian monasteries are most often found placed in well-watered valleys, on the border of a river or stream (think of Fountains and Tintern abbeys). Either that, or for other more austere orders, they are ascetically placed in high, remote places such as Montserrat monastery near Barcelona, or on rocky islands, such as Skellig Michael off the coast of Kerry in Ireland. The chosen site for Battle Abbey does not conform to either description, certainly not for an abbey of the status proposed. This has always been the argument about the siting of the abbey as decreed by William himself – and therefore by logic the location of the battlefield – *'with the high altar of its Church at the place where Harold fell'.* To reinforce this we are told that when William I was informed of the monks' first site they were told in

The substantial remains of the three most eastern crypt chapels of the extended Abbey church. St Mary's parish church is in the background. © Keith Foord

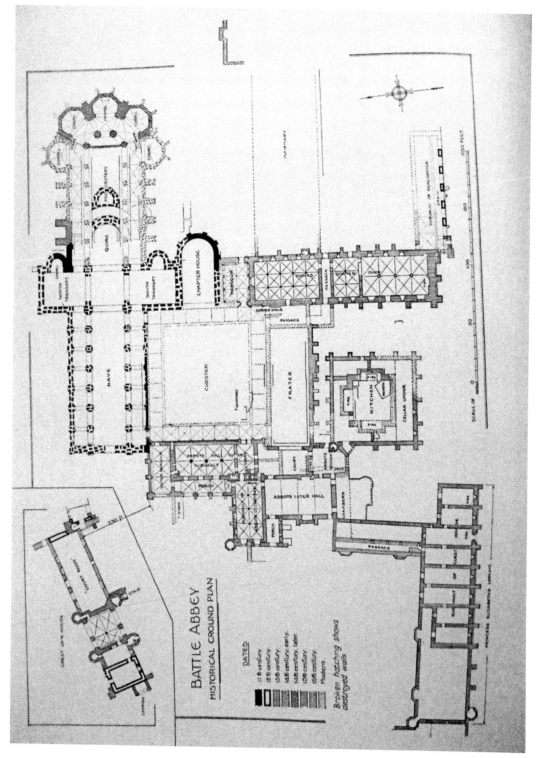

Sir Harold Brakespeare's plan of Battle Abbey.

no uncertain terms to build it where he had commanded. Upon the monks pleading a scarcity of water at the site he is said to have replied, *'If God spare my life I will so amply provide for this place that wine shall be more abundant here than water is in any other great abbey.'*

The abbey was built mainly of locally quarried stone. After complaints from the monks that they would like some Caen stone, a limited amount was imported, and also some Purbeck stone, and even some of the rarer Sussex limestone was used for later more decorative stonework for which the local sandstone would have been unsuitable. Local sandstone is very soft and friable, but there is a blue-stone variety which hardens after quarrying and cutting, and this must have been extensively used. There are several old quarries around the area of the old abbey's Great Park, but the nearest quarry is described to the east south-east of the abbey church, which would have placed it somewhere near the top end of the present Lower Lake.

The *Chronicle of Battle Abbey* states that the dedication of the abbey was to *'the Holy and indivisible Trinity and the blessed Mary, forever virgin also the blessed Martin, confessor of Christ'*. As William 'the Smith' is said to have suggested the name, this must be St Martin of Tours, who was a Roman soldier in Gaul. He converted to Christianity and became Bishop of Tours in 372 and became known as the Apostle of Gaul. Confusingly, there is also a St Martin the Confessor who was the last pope of Rome to be martyred, in 655. He was clearly not the same person as St Martin of Tours. The fact that William I regarded St Martin of Tours as 'his' saint, as did many Norman soldiers, and that the founding monks of Battle Abbey came from the Abbey of St Martin of Tours, must confirm the dedication to be truly to this St Martin, but the word 'confessor' leads to brief minimal disquiet.

The monks at Battle Abbey, as at Marmoutier, wore the black habit of the Order of Saint Benedict (*c.* 480–*c.* 547). It was at Monte Cassino after 530 that Benedict finalised his *Rule for Monks*, basing it on earlier monastic literature as well as his own original material. Today, the Rule of Saint Benedict is considered one of the most important factors in the development of Christian Europe. The monks took a vow of obedience, to lead a simple and self-denying life, be celibate and own no property. The simple celebration of the daily services in praise of God was their first duty; work and reading took up the rest of their time.

The abbot of St Martin of Tours at Marmoutier made an early attempt to make the abbot of St Martin at Battle go to Marmoutier to be consecrated, and hence subservient. William had made it very clear from the start that in no way was his abbey to be beholden to anyone else but the monarch and he ordered Marmoutier to desist from this claim. The abbey was a 'Royal Peculiar' of the same status as Canterbury and within its banlieu (the area around the abbey) the rule of abbot was absolute. Bishops and royal officers could not interfere there and taxes and other dues were not levied. To fund and finance the new abbey, William bestowed his foundation with all the land within a radius of a league (the banlieu or leuga or lowey), the estate of

Alciston in Sussex, the royal manor of Wye in Kent with its lands of Dungemarsh on the coast (this amounted to about 20% of Kent according to Lambarde), Limpsfield in Surrey, Hoo in Essex, Brightwalton in Berkshire, Crowmarsh in Oxfordshire, and churches in Reading, Cullompton and Exeter. The banlieu of the abbey is mentioned in the *Domesday* book of 1086 variously as 'Sancti Martini de Labatailge' or 'Abbatia Sancti Martini de loco belli' or 'Æcclesia de la Batailge', but the area around was 'part of the hundred of 'Hailesaltede' (later renamed Netherfield hundred), still of little value at that time, what little there was having been 'wasted' in 1066.

By *Domesday* in 1086, the only 'populous' area of this hundred not directly associated with the abbey was to the north with households numbering 4 at Uckham, 11 at Mountfield, 13 at Netherfield and 12 at Brightling. The other adjacent areas with any significant numbers of households were in the hundreds of Baldslow, Ninfield and Bexhill, around the lower lying coastal areas of Bulverhythe at Filsham (89 households), Crowhurst (22), Wilting (14), Cortesley (27), Bullington (38) and at Bexhill hundred (with '63 ploughs', suggesting a moderately large population) and on the east side of the Pevensey haven at Hooe (73). The coastal zones would have been much easier to farm. But if the area around the abbey was not rich, *Domesday* nevertheless recorded that the gross annual income of the abbey was £212 3s 2d (£212.16). This was the largest income at that time of any religious house in England and larger than the English income of the abbey of Fécamp (which held adjacent lands around Brede and Rye) or of any other Norman abbey.

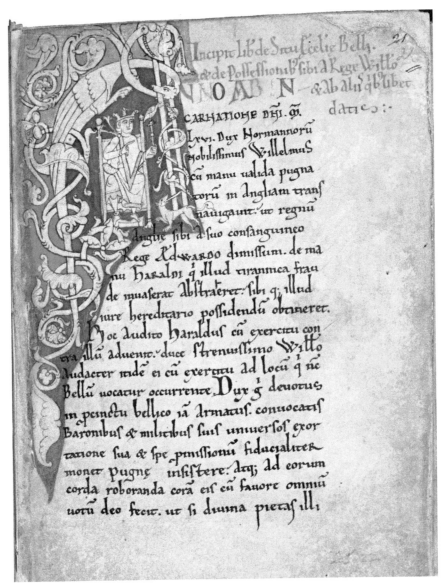

From the Chronicle of Battle Abbey – the illustration shows the Conqueror on his throne. British Library Cotton MS Domitian II, fol. 22r. ©The British Library Board

'If God spare my life I will so amply provide for this place that wine shall be more abundant here than water is in any other great abbey.'

William I (*Chronicle of Battle Abbey*)

17

WHAT DID THE NORMANS DO FOR US?

Adrian and Sarah Hall

NOT A CONQUEST ...

The Battle of Hastings had major consequences for the ensuing centuries, and some of them are still to be observed today. Yet the term 'Norman Conquest' implies that England, a country of two million people in 1066 (some historians think as many as six million) could be changed suddenly by a small number of Normans – perhaps fewer than 7,000 in 1066 after discounting mercenaries, and perhaps only 25,000 when William died in 1087. The reality was more complex and nuanced. William, for example, insisted that there was continuity with the past because he was Edward the Confessor's true heir.

... BUT A NEW TOWN AT LEAST

However the impact of the Normans nationally is assessed, for the town of Battle, the Norman arrival meant the difference between it being a piece of land on a sandy ridge at a crossroad, but with no settlement of note, to being a thriving abbey town which by 2016 will have stood the test of time, 950 years after the battle which it commemorates. The town owes its name to William who, tradition has it, personally named it La Bataille.

ARCHITECTURAL LANDSCAPE CHANGES

Superficially, several changes to the landscape made by the Normans would have been evident within one or two generations of 1066. The English had few castles; by 1087 William had overseen the construction of 86 royal castles, built of stone to show that the Normans were here to stay. Castles built by other Normans by 1100 are thought perhaps to number 500. Norman churches with characteristic semicircle arches and zigzag patterns went up all over the country, in the vast majority of cases replacing the Saxon equivalents. By 1087 nine of the 15 English cathedrals had been demolished and replaced by Norman ones. The great church of Battle Abbey, and the accompanying peoples' church of St Mary – finished in 1095 and begun sometime between 1102 and 1107 respectively – were the *raison d'être* of Battle, and the abbey would have dominated it.

The Norman cathedrals of the late eleventh and early twelfth centuries were vast in scale by standards of that period. They gave visual expression to the power of the Normans as well as to their reform of the church in the conquered realm. Buildings such as Durham cathedral were built to impress and awe.

Royal forests were established arising, among other reasons, from William's interest in deer hunting: trespass by unauthorised people, e.g. poachers, was usually punished by death.

STILL A MEDIEVAL TOWN TODAY

The grant of land to the first abbot of Battle in the late eleventh century created a 'banlieu' or 'leuga' with significant delegation and power for the abbot which lasted until the dissolution of the monasteries in 1538. It was this which resulted in the highly unusual preservation of early medieval plot structures in Battle, still visible today – in the town centre the plots have recently been re-measured in perches, and remain as they would have been in medieval times.

LAND TENURE AND ITS MEDIEVAL CONSEQUENCES

The Norman 'feudal' system was a semi-rigid system of land-based obligations between nobles, knights and villeins, which we previously discussed on pages 77 and 78. In England, William changed the system of land tenure so that it drew its source from the king, who could remove it from the nobles if he so chose – and he often did. This seemed a shrewd move in the years after 1066 when grants of land rewarded effort in the Norman cause. But in the view of some scholars, in later centuries of the medieval era, the removal of land as a punishment to nobles and the promotion of individuals through grants of land became one of the causes of disputes between the ruling élite and the king, notably in the reign of king John. After the Black Death shortages of people created new labour markets which undermined the feudal system.

From the point of view of those working on the land, Norman rule would have been noticeable to the extent that slavery – widely practised by the English – was less common. This was a gradual process – for example in 1086 Battle had twelve slaves – and it was not until 1130 that historians think slavery was absent from England. Some attribute this change to the Norman belief that serfs paying rent and covering their own costs was better financially than having slaves who had to be fed and housed. On the other hand, others point to evidence that some parts of Norman society considered slavery morally unacceptable. But at the same time there were fewer freemen who could move from one property to another. Most labourers were villeins under the Normans: they were obliged to provide their services to a specific land owner or tenant.

WHAT'S IN A NAME?

Another consequence of the Normans' strong focus on land ownership was that in due course some settlements were to bear the owners' names: Helions Bumpstead in Essex, Milton Keynes in Buckinghamshire, and very many more – although this is not the case in south-east Sussex. Herstmonceux is unusual as it sounds very French. It was called Herst (a common OE word for a copse or wood) in *Domesday* and was transferred to Drogo of Monceux later. He married Idonea de Herst, and their son was known as Walleran de Herst Monceux, so the name is an Anglo-Norman hybrid.

The names given to children tended to be Norman up to the eighteenth century – Robert, Emma, William, Alice, Geoffrey. Only later did some OE or ON Germanic names such as Alfred and Harold return for boys. Wulfnoth and Leofwine remain virtually unused. Girls' names are even now predominantly of mainly Norman origin, with a strong sprinkling of 'Celtic' or biblical names. Maybe OE/ON girls' names are too complex, or a little difficult for modern English tongues. Names such as Aelgifu, Ealdgyth and Ethelfreda hardly trip off the tongue and remain dormant.

DOMESDAY – NEW RULING ÉLITE

Another change in land tenure was to date titles of land from the time of Edward the Confessor (referred to in *Domesday* by the acronym TRE) or William himself as a means of legitimating land seizures since 1066. As well as formidably demonstrating Norman willpower and reach, the *Domesday Book* gave form to, and drew a line under, the Norman takeover of land tenure. *Domesday* showed that by 1087 56% of the major landholdings were in the hands of the Norman nobility; and of that 56%, 40% belonged to ten families. William himself owned 17% of the land in England (double that of Edward the Confessor) while the Church owned 26%, including the large holdings of 12 members of the clergy. Only four major landholdings were in

English hands. This preponderance of Normans in land ownership was reflected in the virtual absence of English from the ruling élite. In Battle, there may have been more of a mix: at the time of *Domesday*, the three main landowners apart from the abbey appear to be Reibert, Geoffrey and Alvred, the last presumably English.

CONTINUITY OF GOVERNANCE

Ironically, some think, the information for the *Domesday Book* was collected by means of a network of local officials which was invented by the English. The previous financial systems were retained as well – England was attractive to William among other reasons because there was an established system for levying taxes. In general the Normans did not seek to impose centralised systems unless the local ones were dysfunctional. Most notable amongst established systems were the counties or shires which the Normans inherited from the English. The endurance of these, still important to the present day, contrasts with developments in mainland Europe. In their self-interested preservation of the machinery of English government, the new Norman rulers learnt to be English.

At his level, William used a Great Council which was similar to the English Witan, although it met more frequently with more pomp and ceremony. One area of governance where William did make an innovation was in the creation of a Chancellor in charge of and coordinating the royal clerks: although this role was nothing like as significant as that of later holders of the office, Herfast is the first person who can be proved to have been appointed Chancellor, around 1068. Another reform was the breaking up of the massive earldoms which had dominated and by their nepotistic abuse eventually damaged political life under the English.

LAW AND ORDER

William enforced law and order with energy. He clarified the respective roles of ecclesiastical and civil courts. Otherwise the law was much as it had been under the English. The great leap forward in the law of England was to be less than a hundred years later in the reign of Henry II, who from 1154 oversaw the codification of laws – Anglo-Saxon largely, albeit with Norman laws on land tenure – in what came to be known as the Common Law. Henry left us the legal term 'from time immemorial', referring to the law as it was before his death in 1189. He also strengthened the old shire courts and weakened the baronial courts brought in by the first generation of Norman invaders.

THE MILITARY

Not much changed in the first few decades in respect of the system of calling up infantry: the fyrd. William used the English system, requiring his Norman lords who had supplanted the English to provide fyrd troops, well beyond the 1080s. In 1079 William's life was saved by Toki, son of an English thegn, Wigod of Wallingford, whom William would have met in 1066 when crossing the Thames, but may also have first met during his supposed visit to Edward the Confessor in 1051.

LANGUAGE

It was not until the late 12th to 15th centuries that it could be said that a Middle English language recognisable in modern times emerged from some 350 years of incremental admixture of Norman and Old English families; and hence of the Norman-French and OE tongues. By then Chaucer was on the scene. Henry IV would become the first king to address Parliament in English, in 1399. To begin with, however, the signs for this fusion did not seem promising, because from 1070 the Normans required official documents to be in French or Latin, not Old English, which reverted to being an oral instrument for use by those outside the Church and the ruling élite. Intermarriage however, with thousands of Norman men looking for wives, caused an intermingling of Norman and English.

Nevertheless some fragments and reminders of Norman-French remain. The royal motto is: *Honi soi qui mal y pense.* When Acts of Parliament are approved by the queen, Parliament is told *'La reyne le vault'.* We talk of mutton from a sheep and pork from a pig, using a French derived word for the meat and the OE/ON derived word for the living animal. Also we use French derivations for many freshwater fish and OE/ON for sea fish.

Within a hundred years of Hastings, some of the most creative minds such as William of Malmesbury, Ordericus Vitalis and Henry II himself had English ancestry. By 1220 the biographical poem of 22,000 lines which commemorates the life of William the Marshal – a fourth son of a minor noble who was regent of England in 1216/17– was written in a form of OE/ME which begins to look a little like the ME language of Chaucer almost 200 years later.

In the late 1170s the royal treasurer, Richard FitzNeal, wrote that *'with the English and Normans living side-by-side and intermarrying, the peoples have become so mingled that no-one can tell – as far as free men are concerned – who is of English and who of Norman descent.'*

The bringing together of Norman and English proceeded during the twelfth century along another track as well: in that century kings were referred to as kings of the French and English, while Magna Carta in 1216 refers only to the English. This, however, did not stop English kings (until 1801) from claiming the French throne, and including the *fleur de lys* in their coat of arms. The post-John crisis of 1216–18 was a turning point in Englishness, it could be argued, as the conflict forced the nobility in England to choose whether they were French or English due to the loss of French lands through the king's incompetence. In 1244 Henry III decreed that no Englishman could hold lands in France, thus cementing the separation.

WILLIAM AND EUROPE

From 1066 William pursued a policy of close involvement in European affairs: he and the Normans were an integral part of shifting alliances in Europe. The English recognised its situation as an island which had four times been invaded and accommodated cultural changes – by Romans, Anglo-Saxons, Vikings and then the Normans themselves. To guard against a recurrence of invasion a standing naval force was set up, and it was necessary to maintain alliances with neighbouring countries also opposed to the enemies of England.

A further consideration was that the papacy had helped William in his efforts to win the English throne, declaring the invasion a holy war on the grounds that Harold had defied Edward the Confessor's wish that William should succeed him. This meant that William fostered close ties with the Church when he was king, at home and abroad: he was personally devout, but at the same time the Normans returned the backing they had received from the pope in the form of assistance with campaigns across Europe, notably in Sicily. This change of emphasis should not, however, be stressed too strongly, because Harold was not without his own European connections, but the change did mean that England now looked more across the English Channel than it did across the North Sea.

RELIGION

William replaced Stigand – generally seen as corrupt at the time – as archbishop of Canterbury with Lanfranc in 1070, with the result that the customs of the English church were tightened up and regularised. Lanfranc was suspicious of local saints, often related to the royal families of the old tribal kingdoms. Monastic practice was standardised and uniformity of ecclesiastical buildings encouraged.

English bishops and abbots were gradually replaced during William's reign, so that by 1087 only two were not Norman. According to William of Malmesbury the English resented the Norman Romanesque style of church building, and in some places the monks persisted in the old liturgical practices. At Canterbury opposition to Norman innovations caused riots and at Glastonbury observance of the new religious order was encouraged by the stationing of archers in the organ loft. The presence of bishop Wulfstan, however, one of the two surviving English bishops/abbots, also led to the preservation of tenth-century monastic reform. In general, the Normans re-stimulated religious observance in England.

DRINK

Some authors think that the Normans had a preference for wine and that this changed the previous preference for mead and ale in England. The evidence for this is scanty. Wine would have been the privilege of the few in both English and Norman times; mead and ale have been drunk in England from time immemorial. William of Malmesbury writes in his *De Gestis Regum* that in 1066 the English were '*accustomed to eat until they became surfeited and to drink until they were sick'*: perhaps echoed in some of today's behaviour?

Amusingly in the 1966 programme for the Battle of Hastings commemoration, there is an advertisement suggesting that during the battle Harold would have regretted the absence of a certain dark beer to strengthen the resolve of his men.

SELECTED SOURCES

Listed by Chapter

2

Beach Sustainability and Biodiversity on Eastern Channel Coasts. Interim Report of
the Beaches At Risk (BAR) Project January 2006. http://www.sussex.ac.uk/
geography/reserachprojects/BAR/publish/Interim%20Report.pdf
Cleeve, J and Williams, R. 'Cliff Erosion in East Sussex'. *Sussex Studies* No.5. 1987
http://www.hurstwic.org/history/articles/manufacturing/text/norse_ships.htm
Robinson, DA and Williams, RBG. 'The Sussex Coast, Past and Present'. *Sussex:
Environment, Landscape and Society*, The Geographical Editorial Committee,
University of Sussex. 1983
Romney Marsh Research Trust Monographs 1–5 (1988 – 2011) http://rmrt.org.uk/
monographs/
Steers, JA. *The Coastline of England and Wales.* 1964
Smyth, C and Jennings, S. 'Mid-to late Holocene Forest Composition and the effects
of Clearances in the Combe Haven Valley, East Sussex'. *Sussex Archaeological
Collections* 126 (1988):1–20.
Williamson, JA. *The Evolution of England.* 1931

3

Al-Idrisi, M. *The Book of Roger* [Kitab Ruyar]. 1154
Anon. *Sussex Archaeological Collections (SAC)* 14 xiii 1862
Armstrong, JRA. *History of Sussex.* 1976
Austin, N. *Secrets of the Norman Invasion.* 2012
Baines, JM. *Historic Hastings* 1955
Baines, JM. *Sussex Notes and Queries* 11 (1946)
Ballard, A. *The Domesday Boroughs.* 1904
Baring, FH. 'Hastings Castle 1050–1100, and the Chapel of St. Mary' *SAC* 57 (1915)
Boxell, G (U. Waikato, NZ): 'Harold Godwinson – Last King of the English') http://
geoffboxell.tripod.com/harold.htm
Brodribb, G and Cleere, H. 'The Classis Britannica Bath-house at Beauport Park, East
Sussex'. *Britannia* 19 (1988)
Brooks, NP. 'The unidentified forts of the Burghal Hidage.' *Medieval Archaeology* 7
(1964)
Campbell, J (ed.). *The Anglo-Saxons.* 1982
Cleeve, J and Williams, R. 'Cliff Erosion in East Sussex.' *Sussex Studies* 5 (1987)
Chevallier, CT. 'The Frankish Origin of the Hastings Tribe'. *Sussex Archaeological
Collections* Vol. 104 (1966): 56–62
Cole, T. *The Antiquities of Hastings and the Battlefield: With Maps, and a Plan of the
Battle.* 1884
Cornwall, K and Cornwall, L. 'Roman Coins from the HAARG Area'. *HAARG Journal* New

series 27 (2009): 8–11

Cousins, H. *Hastings of Bygone Days and the Present.* 1920

Darby, HC and Campbell, EMJ (eds). *The Domesday Geography of South-East England.* 1971

Davison, BK. 'The Burghal Hidage Fort of Eorpeburnham: a suggested identification'. *Medieval Archaeology* 16 (1972)

Dawson, C. *History of Hastings Castle.* 1909

Eddison, J, Gardiner, M and Long, A (eds). *Romney Marsh: Environmental Change and Human Occupation in a Coastal Lowland.* OUCA Monograph 46 1998

Gautier Dalché, P. *Du Yorkshire à l'Inde.* 2005

Gardiner, M. 'Saxo-Norman Hastings, Reflections on its Development'. *HAARG Journal* New Series 8 (1999)

Gardiner, M. 'Shipping and Trade between England and the Continent'. *Anglo-Norman Studies* XXII (1999): 71–93

Harris, RB. *Pevensey Historic Character Assessment Report. Sussex Extensive Urban Survey* (EUS), East Sussex County Council, West Sussex County Council, Brighton & Hove City Council 2008

Haslam, J. 'King Alfred and the Vikings: Strategies and Tactics 876–886 AD'. *Anglo-Saxon Studies in Archaeology and History* 13 (2005). Oxford University School of Archaeology

Hill, D. *An Atlas of Anglo-Saxon England.* 1981

Hill, DH. 'The Burghal Hidage – the establishment of a text.' *Medieval Archaeology* XIII (1969)

Hodgkinson, J. *The Wealden Iron Industry.* 2008

Hughes, P. 'Roger of Howden 's sailing directions for the English coastline'. *Historical Research* vol. 85 no. 230 (November 2012)

Johnston, RDE (ed.). 'Research Report No 18 – The Saxon Shore'. The Council for British Archaeology 1977

Jones, G A. *History of the Vikings.* 1975

Laing, L and Laing, J. *Anglo-Saxon England.* 1979

Leslie, K and Short, B. *An Historical Atlas of Sussex.* 1999

Loyn, HR. *The Governance of Anglo-Saxon England 500–1087*

Loyn, HR. *The Vikings in Britain.* 1977

Maitland, FW. *Domesday Book and Beyond.* 1896

Margery, ID. *Roman Ways in the Weald.* 1965

Morillo, S. *The Battle of Hastings.* 1996

Morris, J (ed). *Domesday Book – Sussex.* 1976

Padgham, D. 'The Lost Settlement of Bulverhythe'. *HAARG Journal* New Series 12 (2001)

Parish, WD. *A Dictionary of the Sussex Dialect and Collection of Provincialisms in Use in the County of Sussex.* 1875

Robinson, DA and Williams, RBG. 'The Sussex Coast, Past and Present' in *Sussex: environment, Landscape and Society.* The Geographical Editorial Committee, University of Sussex. 1983

Romney Marsh Research Trust Monographs 1–5 (1988–2011) http://rmrt.org.uk/monographs/

Rotuli Chartarum. 7 February 1205

Rotuli Litterarum Patentium. 9 April 1206

Ruding, D. 'Roman Rural Settlement in Sussex: Continuity and Change' Ruding, D (ed.)

The Archaeology of Sussex to AD2000. 2003

Rushton, NS. 'Parochialization and patterns of patronage in 11th-century Sussex'. *Sussex Archaeological Collections* Vol. 137 (1999): 133-52

Salzman, LF (ed.) *The Victoria History of the County of Sussex.* Vol. 9 1937

Sawyer, PH. *Anglo-Saxon Charters: an annotated list and bibliography.* 1968 – also see the 'E-sawyer' www.esawyer.org.uk

Stevenson, W H. 'The Old English Charters to St. Denis'. *English Historical Review* vi (1891)

Stenton, F. *Anglo-Saxon England.* (1943)

Swanton, M (ed.). *The Anglo-Saxon Chronicles.* 2000

Thorpe, L. *The Bayeux Tapestry and the Norman Invasion.* 1973

Tyson, K. *Carmen de Triumpho Normannico.* 2014

Vidler, LA. *A New History of Rye.* 1934

4

Davis, N. *Europe – a History.* 1997

Friðriksdóttir, SD. 'Old Norse Influence in Modern English – The Effect of the Viking Invasion, University of Iceland' (2014) skemman.is/stream/get/.../Old_Norse_ Influence_in_Modern_English.pdf

Leslie S, Winney B, Hellenthal G, *et al.* 'The fine-scale genetic structure of the British population'. *Nature* (March 2015)

Magnusson, M. *Viking Expansion Westward.* 1973

Oppenheimer, S. *The Origins of the British.* 2007

5

Anscombe, A. 'The Pedigree of Godwine.' *Transactions of the Royal Historical Society.* 37 (1913): 129–50

Bates, D. *Normandy before 1066.* 1982

Crouch, D. *The Normans – The History of a Dynasty.* 2007

Christiansen, E (tr. and notes). *Dudo of St. Quentin – The History of the Normans.* 1998

Douglas, DC. *William The Conqueror.* 1964

Fauroux, M (ed.). *Recueil des actes des ducs de Normandie de 911 à 1066.* 1961

Jones, G. *A History of the Vikings.* 1968

Neveux, F. *A Brief History of The Normans.* 2008

Searle, E. 'Fact and pattern in Heroic History – Dudo of St. Quentin.' *Viator – Medieval and Renaissance Studies* Vol. 15 (1984)

van Houts, EMC. (ed. and trans.). *The Normans in Europe.* 2000

6 (see 11)

7

Campbell, A (ed.). *Encomium Emmae Reginae.* 1949

Fisher, DVJ. *The Anglo-Saxon Age.* 1973

Jones, G. *A History of the Vikings.* 1968

Lawson, MK. *Cnut, England's Viking King 1016–35.* 1993

Morris, M. *The Norman Conquest.* 2013

Swanton, M (ed. & trans.). *The Anglo-Saxon Chronicles.* 1996

8

Bolton, T. *The Empire of Cnut the Great: Conquest and the Consolidation of Power in*

Northern Europe in the Early Eleventh Century. 2009

Campbell, A (ed.). *Encomium Emmae Reginae.* 1949

Darlington, RR (ed.), McGurk, P (ed. & trans.), Bray J (trans.). *The Chronicle of John of Worcester*: Volume II: The Annals from 450–1066 Vol 2. 1995

Fisher, DJV. *The Anglo-Saxon Age.* 1973

Giles, JA. *William of Malmesbury's Chronicle of the Kings of England.* 1847

Hooper, N. 'The Housecarls in England in the Eleventh Century.' Strickland, M (ed.): *Anglo-Norman Warfare.* 1992

Keynes, S 'The Æthelings in Normandy.' *Anglo-Norman Studies* 13 (1991)

Larson, LM. *Canute the Great.* 1912

Larson, LM. *The King's Household in England before the Norman Conquest.* 1904

Lawson, MK. *Cnut – England's Viking King 1016–1035.* 2011

Loe, L. *Given to the Ground.* 2014

Schama, S. *A History of Britain: At the Edge of the World 3000BC–AD1603.* 2000

Stenton, F. *Anglo-Saxon England.* 1971

Swanton, M (ed. & trans.). *The Anglo-Saxon Chronicles.* 1996

9

Barlow, F. *Edward the Confessor.* 1997

Campbell, A (ed.). *Encomium Emmae Reginae.* 1949

Lapidge, M (ed.). *The Wiley-Blackwell Encyclopaedia of Anglo-Saxon England.* 2nd Edition 2013

Mason, E. *The House of Godwine.* 2004

Stenton, F. *Anglo-Saxon England.* 1949

10

Anscombe, A. 'The Pedigree of Godwine'. *Transactions of the Royal Historical Society.* 37 (1913): 129–50

Barlow, LW. 'The Antecedents of Earl Godwine of Wessex'. *New England Historical and Genealogical Register* lxi (1957)

Campbell, A (ed.). *Encomium Emmae Reginae.* 1949

Chefneux, H. 'Les fables dans la tapissserie de Bayeux'. *Romania* Vol. LX (1934): 1–35

Cowdrey, HEJ. 'Towards an Interpretation of the Bayeux Tapestry'. *Anglo-Norman Studies* X (1987) Proceedings of the Battle Conference

Douglas, DC. *William the Conqueror.* 1964

Barlow, F. *The Godwins: The Rise and Fall of a Noble Dynasty.* 2002

Barlow, F. *Edward the Confessor.* 1970

Campbell, J. *The Anglo-Saxons.* 1982

Thorpe, L. *The Bayeux Tapestry and the Norman Invasion.* 1973

Swanton, M. *The Anglo-Saxon Chronicles.* 1996

Howarth, D. *1066: The Year of the Conquest.* 1983

Mason, E. *House of Godwine: The History of Dynasty.* 2004

Walker, I. *Harold the Last Anglo-Saxon King.* 2000

Giles, JA. *William of Malmesbury's Chronicle of the Kings of England.* 1847

Forester, T (trans.) *The Ecclesiastical History of England and Normandy by Ordericus Vitalis.* Vol.1 1853

11 (and 6)

Bennet, M. 'Wace and Warfare' in Strickland, M (ed.). *Anglo-Norman Warfare.* 1992

Campbell, A (ed.) *Encomium Emmae Reginae.* 1949

Chibnall, M. 'Military Service in Normandy before 1066' in Strickland, M (ed.). *Anglo-Norman Warfare.* 1992

Crouch, D. *The Normans.* 2002

Douglas, D. *William the Conqueror.* 1964

Giles, JA. *William of Malmesbury's Chronicle of the Kings of England.* 1847

Gillingham, J. 'William the Bastard at War' in Strickland, M (ed.). *Anglo-Norman Warfare.* 1992

Howarth, D. *1066 The Year of Conquest.* 1977

Morris, M. *The Norman Conquest.* 2013

Neveux, F. *The Normans. Conquests that changed the Face of Europe.* 2008

Swanton, M (ed.).*The Anglo-Saxon Chronicles.* 1996

van Houts, EMC. 'The Ship List of William the Conqueror'. *Anglo-Norman Studies* X. Proceedings of the Battle Conference 1987: 159–183

—. (ed. and trans.). *The Normans in Europe.* 2000

12

Darlington, RR and McGurk, P (eds). *The Chronicle of John of Worcester.* Vol. II: The Annals from 450 to 1066. 1995

Dunlop, J. 'The Story of the Rye Road – Some Thoughts on Harold's Route.' *Battle & District Historical Society Transactions* 1962–1963

Jones, GA. *A History of the Vikings.*1968

Laporte J. 'Les opérations navales en Manche et Mer du Nord pendant l'année 1066'. *Annales de Normandie.* 17e année n°1 (1967)

Lemmon, C. H. *The Field of Hastings.* 4th edn. 1977

Monsen, E (trans.). *Sturluson, Snorri: From the Sagas of the Norse Kings.* 1973

Morris, M. *The Norman Conquest.* 2012

Short, I (ed. & trans.). *Gaimar, Geffrei: Estoire des Engleis* (History of the English). 2009

Swanton, M (ed.). *The Anglo-Saxon Chronicles.* 2000

Tyson, K. *Carmen de Triumpho Normannico.* 2014

13

Bates, D. *William the Conqueror* (2004)

Forester, T (ed. & trans.). *The Chronicle of Henry of Huntingdon – The History of England.* 1853

Freeman, AE. *The History of the Norman Conquest of England.* 1876

Lawson, MK. *The Battle of Hastings 1066.* 2002

Morillo, S. *The Battle of Hastings. Sources & Interpretations.* 1996

Morton, C and Muntz, H (eds.). *The Carmen de Hastingæ Prœlio.* 1972

Ramsay, JH. *The Foundations of England.* Vol. 2 1898

Stevenson, J (trans.). 'Chronicle of Chronicles', published as *Florence of Worcester: A History of the Kings of England from the Invasion of Julius Cæsar to the Accession of Henry II.* 1988

Swanton, M (ed. & trans.). *The Anglo-Saxon Chronicles.* 1996

Thorpe, LGM. *The Bayeux Tapestry and the Norman Invasion* (includes a translation of the Battle of Hastings portion of William of Poitiers' *Deeds of William, Duke of the Normans and King of the English*). 1973

Tyson, K. *Carmen de Triumpho Normannico,* 2014

Henry of Huntingdon, Greenway, D (ed.) *Henry, Archdeacon of Huntingdon: Historia Anglorum: The History of the English*. 1996
Guy, Bishop of Amiens. *Song of the Battle of Hastings*
Wace, (trans.) Burgess, GS. *The History of the Norman People [The Roman de Rou]* 2004
William of Jumièges. *Deeds of the Dukes of the Normans*
William of Poitiers. *Deeds of William, Duke of the Normans and King of the English*
Wilson, DM. *The Bayeux Tapestry*. 1985

14

Abels, R. 'English Logistics and military administration, 871–1066: The Impact of the Viking Wars', in Jorgensen AN and Clausen, BL (eds). *Military aspects of Scandinavian society in a European perspective, AD1–1300* (1997) Papers from an international research seminar at the Danish National Museum, Copenhagen, 2–4 May 1996
Chevallier, CT. 'Where was the Malfosse?' Lecture published in *BDHS Transactions* 1951–1952 and 1952–1953
Chevallier, CT. 'Where was the Malfosse?' *Sussex Archæological Collections*. vol. 101 (1963)
Clephane-Cameron, N and Lawrence, J. *1066 Malfosse Walk*. 2000
Freeman, AE. *The History of the Norman Conquest of England*. 1876
Gillingham, J. 'Richard I and the Science of War in the Middle Ages' in Strickland, M (ed.) *Anglo-Norman Warfare*. 1992
Gillingham, J. '"Up with Orthodoxy"– In Defence of Vegetian Warfare.' *Journal of Medieval Military History* 2 (2004): 149–58
Lawson, MK. *The Battle of Hastings 1066*. 2002
Mason, M. *The House of Godwine – The History of a Dynasty*. 2004
Moore, D. *The Welsh Wars of Independence*. 2007
Phillips, TR (ed.) and Clark, J (trans.). *Renatus, Flavius. The Military Institutions of the Romans (De Re Militari)*. 2011 – An on line translation of Vegetius' Book 1 can be found at http://www.digitalattic.org/home/war/vegetius/
Sharpe, J (trans.) and Giles, JA (ed.) *William of Malmesbury, Chronicle of the Kings of England*. 1904
Thorpe, LGM. *The Bayeux Tapestry and the Norman Invasion* (includes a translation of the Battle of Hastings portion of William of Poitiers' *Deeds of William, Duke of the Normans and King of the English*). 1973
Walker. 'Harold – *The Last Anglo-Saxon King*. 2000

15

Harmer, FE. *Anglo-Saxon Writs*. 1952
Hedges, JK. *A Short History of Wallingford*. 1893
Keats-Rohan, KSB and Roffe, D (eds.). 'The genesis of the Honour of Wallingford', *The Origins of the Borough of Wallingford*. 2009
Swanton, M (ed. & trans.). *The Anglo-Saxon Chronicles*. 1996

16

Austin, N. *Secrets of the Norman Invasion* (2012)
Barlow, F. *The Carmen de Hastingae Proelio of Guy, Bishop of Amiens* (1999)
Bates, D. *The Normans and Empire*. (2013)

Bradbury, J. *The Battle of Hastings.* 2010

Curry, A & Foard, G. 'Where are the dead of medieval battles? A preliminary survey'. *Journal of Conflict Archaeology*, 11:2–3, 61–77 (2016)

Dalché, PG. *Du Yorkshire à l'Inde: une 'géographie' urbaine et maritime de la fin du XIIe siècle (including the De Viis Maris attributed to Roger de Howden) (* 2005)

Douglas, DC and Greenaway DW (eds.) *English Historical Documents* Vol 2 (1996)

Foord, KD. 'Abbots of Battle Abbey' *Article A3.1 in http://battlehistory.btck.co.uk/ Collectanea-OurVirtualLibrary/ABlack (2017)*

Foord, KD. *Battle Abbey and Battle Churches since 1066.* (2011)

Foord, KD. 'Where did the monks of Marmoutier first try to build Battle Abbey?' *Article A3.2 in http://battlehistory.btck.co.uk/Collectanea-OurVirtualLibrary/ABlack (2017)*

Foreville, R (ed.). *William of Poitiers (Guillaume de Poitiers), Histoire de Guillaume le Conquérant.* (1952)

Grehan, J and Mace, M. *The Battle of Hastings 1066 – The Uncomfortable Truth.* (2012)

Hare, JN. *Battle Abbey: The Eastern Range and Excavations of 1978–1980.* (1985)

Hughes, P Roger of Howden's sailing directions for the English coast *in Historical Research Vol 85* (2012)

Kerr, B and Cromwell, T. Personal Communications: *unpublished English Heritage Battle Abbey Archaeology Reviews and Evaluations 1994-2000* (2018)

Knowles, DD, Brooke CNL and London, V (eds.) *The Heads of religious Houses England and Wales 940-1216* (1972)

Lemmon, CH. *The Field of Hastings.* (1977)

Morillo, S (ed.). *The Battle of Hastings: Sources and Interpretations.* (1996)

Morris, J (ed. & trans.). *Domesday Book.* vol. 2 Sussex. (1976)

Morris, M. http://www.marcmorris.org.uk/2013/12/time-team-battle-of-hastings.html

Morton, C and Muntz, H (eds.). *The Carmen de Hastingae Proelio of Guy Bishop of Amiens* (1972)

Order of St. Benedict. http://www.osb.org

Porter, R. '"On the very spot": In Defence of Battle'. *English Heritage Historical Review* Vol. 7 (2012)

Searle, E. *Lordship and Community: Battle Abbey and its Banlieu, 1066–1538* (1974)

Searle, E (ed.& trans.). *The Chronicle of Battle Abbey.* (1980)

Swann, A. Record of a talk given by Reuben Thorpe on *'Excavations at Battle Abbey'* to BDHS in February 1994 in *Transactions of Battle and District Historical Society No. 13* (1994)

Swanton, M (ed.&trans.) *The Anglo-Saxon Chronicles* (1996)

Tyson, K. *Carmen de Triumpho Normannico.* (2014)

Van Houts, EMC. *The Brevis Relatio de Guillelmo Nobilissimo comite Normannorum, written by a monk of Battle Abbey, edited with an historical commentary.* Camden Fifth Series, Vol.10 (1997)

Whitelock, D, Douglas DC, Lemmon, CH, and Barlow, F. *The Norman Conquest: Its Setting and Impact* (1966)

Willing, HCG. The Battle of Hastings – Mired in Controversy *Journal of Battle and District Historical Society No. 22* (2017)

INDEX

Because of multiple mentions in the text of some place names (e.g. Battle, Hastings, Sussex) and frequent repetition of the same personal names of many key individuals or groups (e.g. Anglo-Saxons, Edward the Confessor, William, Harold, Emma) these have limited entries in this index.